Psychological Portraits
of Children

Psychological Portraits of Children

An Integrated Developmental Approach to Psychological Test Data

Lillian Schwartz

Carol J. Eagle
Montefiore/Albert Einstein
College of Medicine

Lexington Books
D.C. Heath and Company/Lexington, Massachusetts/Toronto

Library of Congress Cataloging-in-Publication Data

Schwartz, Lillian.
    Psychological portraits of children.

    Bibliography: p.
    Includes index.
    1. Psychological tests for children. 2. Psychodiagnostics. I. Eagle, Carol J. II. Title.
RJ503.5.S38   1986   155.4′ 028′ 7   85-45076
ISBN 0-669-11199-6 (alk. paper)

Published simultaneously in Canada
Printed in the United States of America
Casebound International Standard Book Number: 0-669-11199-6
Library of Congress Catalog Card Number: 85-45076

The paper used in this publication meets the minimum requirements of American National Standard for Information Sciences—Permanence of Paper for Printed Library Materials, ANSI Z39.48-1984.

The last numbers on the right below indicate the number and date of printing.

10 9 8 7 6 5 4 3 2 1

95 94 93 92 91 90 89 88 87 86

*This book is dedicated to
the memory of our mothers,
Minnie Schwartz and Winifred M. Johnson,
and to all those who taught us.*

Contents

Introduction

The intent of this book is to provide clinical practitioners with demonstrations of the analyses of psychological test materials and their integration according to developmental expectations.

To provide the most complete and useful picture of a given child's functioning, the psychologist must understand the clinical interpretation of each psychological test performance in light of appropriate developmental expectations, and, finally, arrive at a comprehensive integration of the productions of the child. This way of evaluating children has evolved through our years of experience in testing thousands of children in school settings, in child guidance clinic settings, in psychiatric hospitals for children, in private practice, and in experimental programs for normal children. These children represent all ages from 3 years to 12 years, all socioeconomic levels from the welfare subsistence level to the wealthy, and most ethnic and religious groups within the United States.

The theoretical principles underlying our understanding of the child's developing coping strategies in relation to developmental needs derive from the ego psychological model of adaptation as conceptualized by Freud (1923); Hartmann, Kris, and Loewenstein (1946); and Rapaport (1951). In this view the ego is seen as the organizer of internal and external events in the organism's efforts at adaptation.

This conceptualization is that human neonates begin their existence with the capacities for the development of primary autonomy utilizing innate faculties of perception, motility, sensation, affect, language, thinking, and memory. These rudimentary ego functions, in interaction with a biological constitution and an "average expected environment" (Hartmann, 1958), lead to the development of the self. The ego represents the organizing process by which experiences are assimilated and through which emerges an individuated sense of self.

By the third year of life the basic structures for the development of the stabilized ego have begun. Therefore, from this time on specific ego functions can be evaluated. Beres (1956) has provided an outline of ego functions in seven areas: relation to reality, regulation and control of instinctual drives, object relations, thought processes, defense functions of the ego, autonomous functions of the ego, and synthetic functions of the ego. All of these functions in their evolvement determine the sense of self. Self is the totality of the ego structure (psyche), the body, and self representations, which are "the unconscious, preconscious and conscious endopsychic representations of the bodily and mental self in the system ego" (Jacobson, 1964).

The developmental conceptualizations of Erikson (1950), A. Freud (1934, 1965), Escalona (1948, 1950, 1961), Gesell and Amatruda (1947), Mahler (1952), Murphy (1962), and Piaget (1928, 1952, 1954) have guided our understanding of the maturation of ego function as the child grows.

We utilize the concepts of ego psychological theory because we find these concepts to be the most elaborated and detailed system in which we can account for normal as well as pathological development. These concepts also provide a psychological portrait of how the child experiences himself or herself in relation to the world. We summarize Beres's seven ego function areas into cognition, dynamics, defenses, and affect as the most efficient way of organizing all the data provided by a child's test battery.

A basic grounding in the fundamentals of administration of psychological tests, history taking, and report writing is helpful in understanding the principles underlying the level at which this book begins.

Standard texts on the administration and scoring of the intelligence tests in the battery are: Stanford–Binet, Form L–M (Terman & Merrill, 1973), Wechsler Intelligence Scale for Children (Wechsler, 1949), Wechsler Pre-School and Primary Scale of Intelligence (Wechsler, 1967), and Wechsler Intelligence Scale for Children (Revised) (Wechsler, 1974). Texts on the other tests include: Bender–Gestalt (Bender, 1938, 1946; Koppitz, 1963, 1975), figure drawing (Koppitz, 1968; Machover, 1949), Rorschach (Ames, 1974; Klopfer, Ainsworth, Klopfer & Holt, 1954; Rorschach, 1948), Children's Apperception Test (Bellak & Bellak, 1949), and Thematic Apperception Test (Murray, 1943).

Compilations of different tests with administration and scoring, examples of children's protocols, and descriptions of report writing are provided in books by Goldman, Stein, and Guerry (1983), Palmer (1970), and Slater and Thomas (1983). Halpern's (1953) clinical interpretation of children's Rorschachs remains a unique contribution.

Although norms for developmental levels have been provided for the intelligence tests and the Rorschach (Ames, Metraux, and Walker, 1952), the meaning of the child's response has not been integrated into the overall understanding of the child's ego functioning. This book begins at the point after the tests have been administered and scored. The psychodynamic interpretation of the child's productions within his age group makes obvious the need for appreciating each developmental level in understanding the significance of the child's responses. In integrating these interpretations in light of developmental expectation, diagnostic clarity as to the ego's strengths and weaknesses becomes evident as well as an understanding of the child's sense of self and the world.

Although each test protocol presented is produced by an actual child, all identification data and information suggestive of identification have been altered or removed to protect the child and his or her family. Batteries have been selected from our thirty years of testing experience with children that represent classic examples of normal to pathological adaptation. We chose batteries produced by children who were highly verbal and often intellectually gifted so that the nature of their ego functions is more clearly conveyed to the reader. Although children's interests and behavioral manifestations can change from time to time according to socioeconomic, ethnic, and cultural values, the essential nature of the development of the child's ego functions progresses on a consistent and predictable path. It is necessary to comprehend the integration of the ego functions for any given child in order to provide recommendations for the optimal intervention.

It is our hope that this method of interpretation and evaluation of each child's psychological portrait will be helpful to all professionals who work with children.

1
Diagnostic Categories

C hildren have patterns of coping and defenses that must remain flexible in order for them to meet each new developmental task adequately. It is not until late adolescence that the so-called fixed personality pattern emerges. It is therefore essential to understand the total developmental sequence of childhood to make valid interpretations of children's test data.

Since the advent of psychiatry, and more specifically child psychiatry, there has been no attempt to distinguish child diagnoses from adult nosology other than those in the manuals published by the Group for the Advancement of Psychiatry (GAP, 1966) and the American Psychiatric Association (DSM II, 1968). The most recent attempt, that of the DSM III manual (1980), has serious limitations. Although it makes a contribution in its detailed specification of symptoms, as well as its requirement for multiaxial evaluation, it in no way furthers our understanding of the various neurotic and psychotic disorders of childhood. The reason for the latter is because it lacks a developmental conceptualization. Adult psychiatric formulations have been immeasurably enhanced by the work done both theoretically and clinically in child development over the years. For example, Anna Freud's (1934) masterful conceptual exposition of the development of ego defenses has not produced any concomitant attempt to construct a child nosology, although this developmental idea has enriched adult nosological conceptualizations.

The neuroses and psychoses that have been specified over the years contain within them a concept of structure and stabilization appropriate to late adolescence and adulthood. This degree of structuralization is inappropriate to evaluating children diagnostically because their developmental level always must be taken into account. To give an example, the test battery of a 9-year-old child could present a classic obsessive–compulsive neurotic picture according to adult standards. For a 9-year-old this degree of integration and structure represents a very rigid and fixed picture, precluding the flexibility necessary for this child to move on to adolescence. Therefore, taking these developmental considerations into account, we would diagnose a 9-year-old child presenting such a pattern as a borderline picture. Unless the child is perceived as gradually evolving and developing to the point of a fixed personality structure, one totally loses sight of the normal disintegration and reorganizational requirement that adolescence presents. This is merely one example of the inherent difficulties in understanding child diagnostic batteries as though the child were a precise small edition of the adult.

Although in child psychology several unique identifiable childhood syndromes exist, there has been no consensus on the nosological labels for the syndromes. The severely disturbed child, for example, can be given the diagnosis of autism, symbiotic psychosis, ego deviant, atypical development, childhood schizophrenia, or childhood-onset pervasive developmental disorder. In addition, designations adopted from adult nosology increase the likelihood of confusion and inconsistency in so-called nosological groupings from place to place and person to person. Therefore, *real* progress in the child field is impossible because one has to insist on a detailed description of the child to understand what the given nosological designation implies.

These considerations notwithstanding, there is almost universal agreement on the following broad nosological categories to describe emotional status: psychotic, borderline, neurotic, and normal. In addition, there is general agreement on categories related to conditions considered to be engendered by physical factors: retardation, organicity, and learning disabilities. Consensus in the use of these broad labels enables us to employ them with a fair degree of confidence in communication. We are convinced, however, that they do not do justice to the uniqueness of the developing child. Although psychotic children resemble psychotic adults in their behavior and thinking, they are more malleable, flexible, and more manageable for adults because they are children. This means they can exhibit a more rapid return to normal life patterns when intervention is made to relieve their stress. Assisting the intervention is the impact of developmental forces encouraging growth, and therefore some childhood psychoses offer a more hopeful prognosis.

Children designated borderline differ from adults so designated in that they do not have an established defensive pattern to help maintain stable behavior. (With the borderline designation, confusion exists in both the child and adult fields in spite of the many papers published on the subject.) Children tend to be more labile, explosive, and impulsive than the adults and therefore can look more bizarre. What they have in common is a capacity for recovery to reality with structure and help.

The neurotic child differs from the neurotic adult primarily in that there is no fixed pattern of personality defenses, and the child must maintain his or her flexibility in order to develop through the various stages of growth. The neurotic child, like other children, is struggling with defenses that may or may not have yet been internalized and are not integrated or structured as are the different kinds of neuroses of the adult. Therefore, there is not a specific kind of childhood neurosis, but merely a description of a child that has neurotic characteristics. By neurotic characteristics we mean insufficiently internalized and easily penetrable defenses that are manifested as neurotic symptoms, creating difficulties for the child and for the family. Neurotic symptoms can be expressed in a wide array of behaviors, as, for example, in the shy, quiet child who experiences great conscious pain, or the demanding, infant-like whiner who more often than not elicits dislike from others.

Personality disorder in childhood is a borrowed diagnosis from adult nosology and used by some clinicians. We do not consider that the child has achieved a sufficiently stable or completed structure to warrant this diagnosis. We do recognize that enduring characteristics can persist from childhood into adulthood, and we refer to these as psychological traits.

The normal child is on the way to becoming a normal adult. To be normal in childhood means one must have a flexible array of, first, coping mechanisms, then, later, defenses that are flexible enough to permit the progression through a sequence of very difficult stages that may reflect normal periods of tension, unhappiness, and regression. However, the child must at all times be capable of accepting and expressing needs and drives appropriate to the age level. One's sense of self includes feelings of pride, respect, compassion, and security.

Other factors to be considered for any given child concern those nosologies generally considered to stem from physical factors, that is, retardation, organicity, and learning disabilities.

In assessing retardation in childhood, we find no essential difference between the retarded child and the retarded adult because the designation of retarded is based on the fact that there is a limitation to the potential for normal intellectual growth. The truly retarded child is one who functions at an overall lower level than expected for his or her age in social awareness, social competence, and intellectual and academic achievement, which is the same as for the adult. The child, however, is generally smaller in stature than the average and, therefore, is treated as younger than he or she is and does not have to live up to certain social expectations we begin to expect when an individual reaches adolescence.

Although the areas of interference in functioning for the child with an organic syndrome may be comparable to those for the adult with an organic disorder, the main difference is in the developmental potential of the child. This means that the child, in contrast to the adult, is more highly motivated to adapt and is not resigned to his or her deficits. The motivation to learn to adapt to the world is a primary hallmark of childhood that places the child with an organic disorder in good stead for intervention. In addition, concomitant emotional problems have become more entrenched by adulthood.

Unremediated or undiagnosed learning disabilities inevitably produce emotional disturbance in childhood or adulthood. It is obviously of greater concern for the adult because of the years of unsuccessful coping with the learning problems. When diagnosed early in childhood, the impact of learning difficulties on self-esteem is far more available for intervention, and, therefore, the entrenchment of feelings of inadequacy can be avoided.

After comparison of children to adults with these broad nosological groupings, we can now examine specific or unique child syndromes in greater detail. These are labels that over the years have impressed us with their validity in designating certain consistent syndromes. The DSM III (1980) diagnostic classification will also be included with a note of explanation or rationale for our agreement or disagreement, when appropriate.

The Psychoses

Infantile Autism (see GAP, "Psychoses of Infancy and Early Childhood," p. 253). Typically there is an aberrant developmental history for these children since birth. In infancy they tend to be slow in the development of most sensorimotor functions, but on occasion a single function will be markedly exaggerated. It is impossible to state which function will be underdeveloped or which will be exaggerated because the hallmark of these children's development is its idiosyncratic nature. The other most salient factor in their infant history is the lack of responsivity; that is, they appear to be "self-sufficient," "like in a shell," "happiest when left alone," "acting as if people weren't there" (Kanner, 1966). Speech is slow to develop and when developed is used primarily for some purpose other than communication. If use of language has not occurred by 5 years of age, there is evidence to suggest these children may not be able to improve by our current therapeutic techniques. These children have unpredictable panic responses to the world. One way this is seen is that a minor change in the environment can produce a panic reaction often expressed in excessive hyperactivity. The deficit most striking to all clinicians is the inability of these children to form a relationship of any but the most fleeting and intermittent nature. Equally striking is the sudden abrupt appearance of a cognitive function that is remarkably superior to any other functioning at that time. These children have a very poor prognosis. This diagnosis is clearly described in DSM III as 299.0X, "Infantile Autism" (p. 87).

Symbiotic Infantile Psychosis (see GAP, "Psychoses of Infancy and Early Childhood," p. 253). This diagnosis also relies on a specific history in which the infant seemingly developed along normal lines until 24 to 48 months of age. For no apparent reason the child suddenly becomes clinging to mother, unable to separate without panicking, and starts to lose habits such as toilet training that already had been established. Speech usually becomes infantile with autistic-like intrusions. When these children separate from the mother they become somewhat more independent in action than when in the mother's presence. Often they verbalize in an almost parrot-like, pseudomature fashion. There can be a peculiar relationship between mother and child in which the mother verbalizes her sense of the child's need, and the child immediately acts as if indeed it were a need. This behavior is so startling it is almost eerie. These children, too, cannot make normal relationships and also have a poor prognosis. This diagnosis is clearly described in DSM III as 299.9X, "Pervasive Developmental Disorder" (p. 90).

Childhood Schizophrenia (see GAP, "Psychoses of Later Childhood," p. 254). These children are usually undiagnosed until the age of 6. Somehow they seem to manage until faced with school, where the teacher recognizes the child as strange. These children generally present a stereotyped pattern of behavior; that is, they do not tend to be impulsive or explosive, despite the fact that there is an inner state of turmoil and disorganization. They speak in an expressionless manner, and their affect is always described as bland. They have difficulty relating and generally are isolated from their peer group. They can be seen as having peculiar ideation, sometimes can relate with a pseudoerotic quality (more typical of an adolescent), show poor social judgment, and some sporadically demonstrate sadistic behavior.

Schizophrenic children have the following characteristics: they have severe difficulty in interpersonal relationships; they suffer from a diffusion of ego boundaries; they demonstrate severe disturbances in affect; and, more often than not, they perform cognitively on a lower level than what appears to be their potential. They reflect such striking deviations in ego functions that with our current therapeutic techniques prognosis is guarded. Following the suggestion in DSM III, p. 35, the appropriate DSM III diagnosis is 295.0X, "Schizophrenic Disorder" (p. 181).

Psychosis (see GAP, "Psychoses of Later Childhood," p. 256). In order to differentiate this disorder from childhood schizophrenia we are borrowing the term *psychosis* for want of a better descriptor. These children, unlike childhood schizophrenics, have the capacity to interact with individuation and separateness, but they have not achieved a stabilized conformity and therefore tend to be more overtly agitated and openly aggressive.

The psychotic child generally develops normally to approximately latency with a healthy potential for relating to others. The history is generally that of a very difficult and/or traumatic home situation throughout life. This child's capacity for integrating and organizing an inner stability is generally unavailable because of the family situation. Such children are often flooded with gross sadistic fantasies, which may be either ego-syntonic or ego-alient. They can be impulsive, explosive, and destructive. One can see psychotic symptoms such as thought disorder, the substitution of fantasy for reality, labile emotionality, and shifting ego-identities. These children demonstrate a total inconsistency in cognitive functioning that is variable and unpredictable. Their response is as much to internal stimulation as to external real stimulation. They are prone to quick, severe, regressive behavior under stress. There is, however, a recognition of pain and distress, a hunger for relationships, which are at the same time perceived of as threatening. The prognosis is comparatively more positive than that for the childhood schizophrenic. This is particularly true if some intervention can be achieved in the environment. This diagnosis is best approximated in DSM III, under 298.90, "Atypical Psychosis" (p. 202).

Reactive Psychosis (not described in GAP). A child with a reactive psychosis is one with basically good ego strengths, but under the severe stress of trauma or crisis has responded with a clinically psychotic picture—that is, explosive behavior, thought disorder, fantasy overwhelming reality, and maybe even bizarre ideation. But this child is acutely uncomfortable and in great pain. Reactive psychosis has a sudden onset at the point of the trauma with a breakdown in functioning which, until that time, was normal. However, there is *no* gross regressive phenomenon, such as language disturbance, autism, or loss of toilet training, as seen in schizophrenic disturbances. Prognosis is excellent. Although this reactive period can last longer than two weeks, it is best described in DSM III as 298.80, "Brief Reactive Psychosis" (p. 200).

Borderline (GAP's "Other Personality Disorder," p. 251, is the most relevant of their nomenclature.)

The degree of pathology in the borderline child is very broad. One may see a child with many strengths who presents as fairly healthy, yet under severe stress can show either regressed behavior or looseness of associations in thinking. Or, one may see a child who is quickly and easily regressed and disorganized yet has one area of ego intactness and demonstrates some capacity to recover fairly quickly, either with or without help. Between these two extremes is a very wide range of possible combinations of degree of control and degree of pathology. Following the suggestion in DSM III, p. 35, the closest approximation is DSM III, 301.83, "Borderline Personality Disorder" (p. 321).

Another type of borderline child appears to be clinically normal with some occasional pseudomature responsiveness. Others can maintain this semblance of normal behavior only at the cost of inordinate expenditure of psychic energy, thus limiting their ability to perform cognitively. Therefore, they can appear slow or retarded. These children present with stereotyped conforming behavior with a reality orientation in their interactions due to their rigid, brittle defensive structures, but with little spontaneity and genuine affect. The nature of the rigid, brittle defenses makes predictable a psychotic break in adolescence under the stress of normal development. With intervention, prognosis is comparatively good. This form of borderline personality is found in our clinical experience and is not represented in the nosological systems of either GAP or DSM III.

Neurosis (see GAP, "Psychoneurotic Disorders," p. 229)

Neurotic children are related to others, reality-oriented, and demonstrate working defenses. They may or may not have been able to achieve repression of early conflicts, which should occur at the latest between 7 and 9 years of age. They have, however, managed to develop through the normal developmental phases to a greater or lesser degree. Their difficulty is that conflicts have not been resolved successfully, and symptom formation results which may or may not be experienced as painful. Symptoms can be expressed in any or a combination of the following: phobic reaction, frequent and excessive anxiety responses, a proneness to regressive behavior (for example, crying, temper tantrums, demandingness), inability to achieve at their potential, or inability to invest in anything but academic achievement. They may appear less spontaneous in expressing their feelings than normal children, and/or have difficulties in peer relationships. Most frequently, neurotic children present with a symptom picture of anxiety. This is designated in DSM III as 309.21, 313.21, and 313.00 under "Anxiety Disorders of Childhood and Adolescence" (pp. 50–57).

Another symptom picture presented by children is that of aggressivity, impulsivity, and lack of frustration tolerance. We call these children behavior and/or impulse disordered. This is described as "Neurotic Personality Disorder" in GAP (p. 249). Due to considerations specified in the Introduction, we do not join GAP in their conceptualization of personality disorders in childhood. Therefore, we view this category as the expression of the lack of repression of underlying neurotic conflicts where the family situation perpetuates the conflict with the child. Although these children have good ego strengths and the capacity to relate, they are quick to blame the environment for what they feel is denial of gratification. This is designated in DSM III as 314.01, 314.00, and 314.80 under "Attention Deficit Disorder" (pp. 41–45).

Retardation (see GAP, "Mental Retardation," p. 267)

It is important to detect indications of retardation as early as possible in order to introduce the appropriate training. Groupings are classified in DM III as 317.0, 318.0, 318.1, 318.2, and 319.0 under "Mental Retardation" (pp. 36–41).

Organicity (see GAP, "Brain Syndrome," pp. 263–267)

There are two major classifications of organic syndromes that will not be discussed here, the acute brain syndromes and the chronic brain syndromes (see DSM III, "Organic Mental Disorders," pp. 101–162). Gross central nervous system damage is most adequately evaluated by a pediatric neurologist.

Learning Disabilities (see GAP, "Developmental Deviations," p. 227)

Psychological testing can provide specific and detailed information as to a child's learning problems. Children with learning problems can show disturbance in perceptual and/or motor integration, unpredictability in the use of concrete and abstract thinking, failure in sequencing, lapses in either short- or long-term memory, problems in expressive and/or receptive language, and disruptions in spatial orientation. These problems can impinge upon the ability to learn via the usual teaching techniques. The earlier these difficulties are identified, the better the prognosis will be. DSM III specifies these disorders as 315.00, "Specific Developmental Disorders," (pp. 92–99).

Normal (see GAP, pp. 219–222)

The normal child progresses through each developmental level with relative ease. It is understood that development is not a smooth step-by-step evolvement from one stage to the next, but that there are unresolved conflicts that will persist into each new stage, and that there will be temporary regressions as well as sudden precocious jumps.

The mood and affect of normal children reflect their comfort, acceptance, and pride in the self when faced with age-appropriate tasks presented by cognitive demands, social expectations, and family pressures.

The hallmark of normal development is the ability of growing children to maintain flexibility in coping strategies to master each new stress as it is presented. They are aided in this immeasurably by some degree of self-awareness, which is accompanied by empathy for others.

In summary, by *normal* we mean children who have the capacity to relate to others, feel good about themselves, achieve normal landmarks at each level of development, and are free from undue pain or stress. Another aspect of normalcy is resiliency, whereby children faced with unfortunate circumstances creating stress and possible temporary regression can quickly return to age-appropriate functioning.

DSM III includes conditions "not attributable to a mental disorder" (p. 331) but that could bring a child for evaluation under V codes 62.82, 15.81, 62.89, 61.20, 61.80, and 62.81 (pp. 331–334.)

Summary

The major diagnostic categories described in this section are utilized in the evaluation of the test batteries presented in the text. Any one of these categories can be delineated further into specific descriptive groupings appropriate to the psychological portrait presented by the child.

2
The Classic Battery

The child is an evolving biological organism with concomitant cognitive and emotional landmarks. Achievements are reached at different stages, and needs have to be met, expressed, and experienced in order for there to be normal growth. Each test that will be discussed has within it the capacity to elicit the appropriate response for each age level. However, the norm for each age level varies considerably from each other age level.

The child's test responses offer a remarkably specific reflection of the point in development he or she has reached. If we judge the responses to be normal, it is because we are using established developmental norms based on the testing of many children rather than comparing the productions to standards established for adults. The purpose of testing is to determine where a given child is at a given moment in time with respect to age peers. Not to recognize this purpose will result in skewed or distorted interpretations not applicable to the specific age of the child. Inherent in this as well is determining the presence or absence of pathology in the child.

The classic battery is the one we feel provides us with the broadest base of data concerning the child as a whole. It has been adopted by child psychologists from what has been considered to be the classic adult battery. The battery consists of an intelligence test, the Bender–Gestalt (B–G), figure drawings (FD), the Rorschach, and the Thematic Apperception Test (TAT). In addition, when necessary, an academic achievement test, a test for language competence, and a test for perceptual ability should be used. Many other tests exist, but tend to be redundant to this particular battery once competence with the battery has been achieved. However, if one should prefer or have special competence with a different test, there is no reason it cannot be substituted or included providing it taps the same area of functioning.

Intelligence Tests

The intelligence tests selected for the battery include the Wechsler tests: Wechsler Pre-School and Primary Scale of Intelligence (WPPSI), Wechsler

Intelligence Scale for Children (WISC), Wechsler Intelligence Scale for Children (Revised) (WISC-R), and/or the Stanford–Binet (S–B), Form L–M, Form L, and Form M.

It is important to appreciate the basis for the establishment of norms against which any child's performance is to be compared in order to determine which test is most appropriate. The establishment of norms and standardization is based on the normal population distribution curve and derived from percentages at each three-month age span for the population of children and adolescents. Fifty percent of the population falls into the 90–110 scale of Intelligence Quotient (IQ). The distribution of scores achieved by the experimental populations was then applied to the normal distribution curve (bell curve), and these scores were weighted in terms of being above or below the mean producing scaled scores translatable into IQ scores.

The standardization procedure described applies to all the Wechsler tests and to the S–B, Form L–M. The latter was developed from the S–B, Forms L and M, because these two tests were originally standardized on a ratio of mental age to chronological age (MA/CA) and did not correlate directly with the Wechsler tests.

All of these tests, with the exception of the WPPSI (which covers an age range of only two and a half years) tend to skew at the lower and upper few years of their overall range. This is because the items are necessarily geared toward the middle of the range of years, therefore limiting the number of items a much younger child needs to achieve for a high score and expanding the number of items an older child needs to achieve for an average score.

The Wechsler tests differ from the S–B tests considerably. The S–B, Form L–M, is essentially a verbal test with a few performance items, whereas the Wechsler tests offer, in addition to the full-scale IQ, separate IQ scores for verbal and performance portions of the test. This means that a highly verbal child will tend to do better on the Binet than on the full scale of the Wechsler test, although the score on the Binet test should be comparable to the score on the Verbal IQ section of the Wechsler. Similarly, the child whose preferred mode is an action-oriented one should do better on the full scale of the Wechsler than on the Binet.

Another difference between these two tests is that the Binet is organized by age levels with each level incorporating several different aspects of cognitive functioning. The Wechslers are organized from easy to difficult items within single cognitive areas. Therefore, one can more readily appreciate particular areas of difficulty at a given age level on the Binet and more readily see inconsistencies within a particular cognitive area on the Wechsler.

In keeping with the basic theme that the test chosen should be suitable for the child's age, we would suggest the following choices: From 2 to 4 years, the S–B, Form L–M; from 4 to 6-7 years, the WPPSI (which appears to be sufficiently limited in range so that skewing does not become a major factor).

The WPPSI provides for both verbal and performance items, not the least of which is the geometric designs, which provide a standardization of visual–motor tasks at an age where the B–G is too difficult. From 6 to 12 years, we prefer the WISC-R.

It is important to note that often there are intrusions of cultural factors in the test items that may or may not be appropriate for some given group. This in no way allows one to deviate from the standardized procedures of administering and scoring the tests to obtain a valid score. However, it is necessary to be particularly aware of the possibility that these cultural factors may impinge upon and lower the score of a particular child and should be taken into consideration in the total evaluation of the child. Equally important, it should be remembered that these are tests standardized in English and therefore may present difficulties to the bilingual child, not only in language production, but also in the comprehension of directions.

Bender–Gestalt Test

The B–G is an additional test that generally, but not always, is sensitive to central nervous system disorders of a perceptual-motor nature. The Bender figures can be used starting at any age. Little validity can be ascribed to signs of organic brain syndromes before the age of 7 using Bender's norms (Bender, 1946, plate II). Koppitz (1963) does provide scoring for the lower age group.

Projective Tests

The projective tests include the Rorschach, TAT, the Children's Apperception Test (CAT), and FD. If interpreted against the age expectancy, these tests are all applicable and suitable for a child. Of the four, only the CAT is used exclusively for a limited age range.

Figure drawings from children provide useful information when used in addition to the test data, as with adults. Drawings from children, however, do not represent stable and consistent projections, as do drawings from adults, because the child is in the process of development and ever-increasing differentiation. The drawings may offer some gross information that is helpful in expanding the picture of the dynamic and cognitive functioning of the child. Administration is the same as with adults (see Goodenough, 1926, and Machover, 1949).

The Rorschach is sensitive, as are the others, to the developmental levels. Normal developmental expectations follow in predictable sequences as the child grows (Ames et al., 1974). Our method of administration is the same as is used with adults (cf. Klopfer et al., 1954). The inquiry is conducted immediately after the main performance for each card with children 8 years or under. For younger children (under 8 years of age) it is our experience that this immediate inquiry provides the opportunity for the child to describe his or her actual percept. The younger the child, the more likely it is that over time the image of the percept will fade. Analysis and scoring of the Rorschach are consistent with adult protocols, that is, responses, determinants, and so forth. Our scoring method follows the scoring system of Klopfer et al. (1954). Different scoring systems have been developed over the years, each system having its own strengths and weaknesses (Beck, 1949; Exner, 1974; Piotrowski, 1957; Rapaport, Gill, & Schafer, 1968). We limit ourselves to a simpler rendition of Klopfer, as his system was the original from which most of the others were developed. The resultant protocol must be interpreted and evaluated in terms of the expected developmental stage at which we find the particular child.

With many child psychologists it is common practice to use the CAT from 3 to 7 years of age. This use in our experience does not provide as much information as the TAT for interpretation of interpersonal interaction. Furthermore, our impression is that the older child (5 to 7 years of age) reacts to the "card pull" for regressive interaction, that is, interaction between animals. The "regressive pull" for this developmental level often seems to lead to an inhibition of imagination so the child limits the story to mere description. If the CAT is to be used at all, it is our preference to use it with the 3- or 4-year-old who has been tried on the TAT and cannot respond. One generally uses a few choice TAT cards, which can increase in number as the child grows older. The basic set should include at least the following cards: 1, 2, 3 BM, 5, 8 BM, 12 M, 16, and, for boys, 6 BM, 7 BM, and, in addition, for girls, 7 GF and 18 GF.

In general it should be remembered that one can add particular cards that may be reflective of the particular problem presented or cards that one has found through experience to be valuable. Cards do not have to be presented in order of their numbers. One might want to introduce particularly appropriate cards at a point where the child has begun to elaborate more fully.

Summary

All portions of the test battery reflect some aspect of the child. It is therefore essential that no single test or response be used as the primary focus for interpretation. All aspects of the test productions must be taken into consideration and integrated in order to provide a cohesive picture of the child.

In reading the following diagnostic studies, two points should be kept in mind. The first is that we are not writing a formal psychological report. Rather, as stated in the Introduction, we present a working model of the thinking that goes into the organization of the test data. The second point is that we do not presume that our summaries present an exhaustive use of the data. We are confident that our approach takes into account the salient material in the data leading to our conclusions. There is certainly more to be culled from the data, and a formal report would incorporate all. Ultimately, to the good clinician, the data will reflect the nature of the child.

3
The 3- to 5-Year Old

Developmental Expectations

Cognitive Functioning. Between 3 and 5 years of age there is a slowly developing sense of reality. This means that fantasy explanations can still be as valid as reality perceptions. For example, dreams and nightmares are experienced as real events without the capacity for distance from them. This is a period when children can have imaginary friends who really exist for them. At this time sex-typed play material and friendships are freely interchangeable. At the same time that fantasy determines much of their understanding, they are still developing an interest in and curiosity about language and number concepts and can take extreme delight in drawing the letter *A* or knowing that 1 plus 1 equals 2.

Children of this age have an enormous capacity for energy discharge. They love gross motor acts such as running, hopping, and jumping, but also can sit quietly absorbed and concentrate on tasks involving fine motor coordination. This capacity for attention and concentration gradually evolves over this period as their language and thought mature (cf. Piaget, 1967, pp. 22–29, 88–92).

Dynamic Picture. At 3 the child is a recent arrival into the real world. He has left dependent babyhood and can deal with personal care functions almost totally by himself. He is able now to begin meaningful interpersonal communication. He has recently left his omnipotent stage of "having a love affair with the world" (Fraiberg, 1959) and is beginning to experience the ability both to work and to play with others as well as to experience competitiveness, jealousy, and possessiveness.

The child has established himself as a separate, unique individual who can achieve gratification through autonomous acts and manipulations through coping mechanisms learned primarily in interactions with parents and/or siblings.

Mothering is extremely important to children at this age, as they are still dependent for most of their needs and care. For the boy, this takes on an added impetus via newly aroused oedipal wishes that bring him into conflict with the father. The girl, on the other hand, is experiencing oedipal wishes and fantasies directed toward the father. Therefore, she is brought more into conflict with the mother, who is still the most important caretaker in her experience. Children at this stage of development can express these feelings clearly by such announcements as, "I will marry Mommy (Daddy)," or, "Daddy (Mommy), go away."

Defenses. Coping mechanisms are the forerunners of defenses, and usually reflect the parents' characterological defensive style and unconscious wishes (Murphy and Associates, 1962). Typical coping techniques at this age are the precursors of denial, displacement, avoidance, and compulsivity. They elicit behaviors that either please or anger the parents and are generally related to manipulation of the situation in order to get gratification.

Affective Expression. The hallmark of this age is affective lability and affective intensity. This means the 3- to 5-year-old can move from screaming tantrums to great pleasure in a very short period of time. Modulation of affect gradually increases over time.

Normal Expectations on Tests

Intelligence Testing. Some normal 3- to 5-year-olds can show a great variety of levels of functioning in different areas. In the older child, one might suspect a variability in ego functioning, whereas at this age it can still be within the normal range. However, some children at this age will show consistency across all areas.

Bender–Gestalt. The WPPSI geometric-design subtest is the appropriate measure of visual-motor ability for the 3- to 5-year-old. Since it is standardized, it is a better choice than the Bender for this age.

Projectives. Figure drawings usually consist of a circle with some straight lines emanating from the circle and possibly some facial features and hair for the 3-year-old. This will develop gradually to having some shape representing a head as well as a body from which one can have either a single line or double lines for arms and legs. The arms can be placed randomly on the body, not necessarily at the shoulder. Facial features and hair are commonly included. There is rarely differentiation of sex differences before age 5.

In the Rorschach, generally one will get approximately five to seven responses, most of which will be *W*'s with an occasional popular detail, such as the animals on Card VIII. Also, the predominant determinant at this age is *F*. Perseveration, contamination, and fabulization are normal and can be accepted at this age. This tends to reflect the confusion of fantasy and reality, the remaining elements of omnipotence, and the lack of ability, as yet, to make finer differentiations and appropriate judgments of the environment. *M* does not appear, although *FM* is reported. Differentiated color and shading responses are not usually available, although pure color can be produced.

In the TAT, it is not unusual for a 3- to 5-year-old child to give a very limited story. One is likely to get a description of the person or people on the card, perhaps a description of what they appear to be doing, and/or identification of objects in the picture. As they get closer to the 5-year-old level, the story will take on more qualities of a formal story and/or elaborated fantasy.

Representative psychological test interpretations and psychological test batteries for children within this age range now follow. The raw test data from the psychological test battery follow the discussion of each child so that easy reference can be made to the examples selected for illustration of the interpretations. We include examples of children diagnosed as healthy, mildly disturbed, moderately disturbed, and severely disturbed in order to demonstrate how a psychological portrait is developed. Each child's tests are analyzed, interpreted, and concluded with an integrated summary.

As stated before, the summary is not a complete report, but represents the salient features leading to the diagnostic portrait.

Psychological Test Portrait

A: 2–11 Female

A is a girl aged 2–11 (2 years, 11 months), whom we observed in a normal nursery setting. She impressed us with her range of affect, her relatedness to others, her pleasure in her own play, and her comfortable relationship with her mother. She was tested as part of the nursery routine.

A is a very attractive, bright-eyed, bubbly child who entered the testing situation without her mother, eager to share her own experiences with the examiner (*E*). She was curious about the tests and seemed to anticipate that she was going to have a good time. She cooperated easily on all tasks. When the tasks became difficult, she turned the situation around to questioning *E*, or giving a wrong answer, only to laugh and say, "I'm teasing you." Throughout the testing she maintained her good spirits, relatedness, and motivation to achieve.

Cognitive Functioning

S–B, Form L–M: *A* was begun on the Picture Vocabulary, which determined beginning the S–B at IV. She achieved a mental age (MA) of 4 years 7 months, and because *E* did not push *A* to her maximal, a plus was added to her attained IQ of 147 (147 +). *A* was easy to test because of her motivation to achieve, but, because the testing did not go to a point of stress for her, we cannot evaluate how she would have dealt with a really demanding situation. Within her superior cognitive abilities her capacities for verbal and conceptual tasks are outstanding and on a somewhat higher level than her motor performance. All of this was obtained within the usual context of the 3-year-old's activity and movement about the room.

Testing of *A* was limited to one hour on each of two days. This time restriction led *E* to exclude three commissions (IV-6, 5), because it was possible that, if *A* opened the door, she would have to go on to look for her mother in the other room, expending extra time.

B–G: This test is not suitable at this age.

FD: *A* refused to draw a person or anything, even though she was encouraged (or asked) to do so at intervals throughout the testing.

Rorschach: *A* was able to produce at least one response per card, more often than not seeing a *W*. She had good form levels and in some instances was able to describe details. On Card II, for example, she was able to explain the parts of her *W* and finally produced a *P* with movement. Both are completely unexpected at this age. Her sense of humor was seen in the concept of "Mr. Potato Hat" on Card II, and, "Would you believe it's Snow White?" for the *S* in Card VII.

The repeated response of "beard" is an example of perseveration, not unusual at this age. What is unusual is her demonstrated recognition of these repetitions on Card VII.

The cognitive level achieved by *A* on the Rorschach is commensurate with the level of achievement on the S–B. She again demonstrated her superior perceptual-organizational, conceptual, and verbal capabilities. In addition, the response of "red tie" in Card III is remarkable in its integration of color and form.

CAT: The routine testing within the normal nursery required the use of the CAT rather than the TAT (see discussion in chapter 2). *A* performs in a typically age-appropriate way in listing and identifying figures in the CAT. In addition, however, she adds interpretations and develops rudimentary stories unusual for her age.

Summary Statement of Cognition: A demonstrates unusually superior cognitive abilities throughout all areas of functioning, as seen in her responses to different tests. In addition, for her developmental age she displays precocious organizational abilities as well as an unusually well-conceived sense of humor.

Dynamic Picture

S–B: In this task A is notably free from dynamic intrusions into her performance, which is task-oriented, concentrated, motivated, and to the point. The one suggestion of a dynamic is seen in her choice of teasing when faced with difficult items. She attempts to become the aggressor (that is, her perception of the aggressor), then to appease by turning it into a joke.

B–G: Not appropriate for a child of this age.

FD: It is speculated that this task was refused because of A's concern over not performing according to her own standard. She demonstrated difficulty in using a pencil in the S–B, item V, 1, and probably did not want to risk making an inferior product.

Rorschach: A's perseveration of beards became more understandable when E found out from mother that A's father had shaved off his beard the week before. A, therefore, in her preoccupation with faces, revealed her specific concern about the possibility of changes that can happen in familiar faces. It is felt that at the time of testing she had not yet gained mastery over a probably frightening event. In addition, the emphasis on faces (as well as the teasing) suggests a particular developing character style in response to social interactions, perhaps based on a fear of loss of the other.

Her budding ability for sexual differentiation is seen in percepts of male-like beards, boots, planes, and Mr. Potato Hat, in contrast to Snow White, butterflies, and pink Play-Doh.

CAT: Typically for her age, A expresses activities in the CAT of eating, petting, loving, and going to sleep. More personal dynamic concerns emerge in the mommy who is angry at the child who doesn't listen (Card 4) and in other aggressive actions, such as danger to phallic objects (Cards 3, 4, and 6). Although her denial of a baby in Card 5 and covering up of the bed with Play-Doh suggest an oedipal interest, the foregoing would seem to indicate a primary focus with phallic concerns. There is an emphasis on aggressive themes and the suggestion that this relates to the experience of being "forbidden" or inhibited by her mother in expressing her own aggressive impulses.

Summary Statement of Dynamics: A is free of dynamic intrusions in her superior cognitive abilities. Suggestions of dynamic concerns, manifested in the projectives, were seen in an already internalized interest in high achievement and a conflict over aggressive impulses. Otherwise, her concerns were appropriate to her developmental level.

Defenses

S–B: *A*'s coping strategies appeared only when she experienced difficulty in one item. She became a tease (IV-6, 4; V, 3) seemingly as a way of saving face. Otherwise, her performance was remarkably to the point (see S–B under *Dynamics*).

B–G: Not appropriate for a child of this age.

FD: Avoidance is seen in its pure 3-year-old form by *A*'s persistent refusal.

Rorschach: Generally, throughout this test *A* utilizes her intellect to achieve often remarkable percepts for her age. When faced with an unpleasant possibility, Card IV, she shows her first attempt to refuse the cards, but still responds to *E*'s request to go on after her usual teasing style. This sequence is particularly interesting, inasmuch as she denies the ordinary monster (in Card IV) after having seen a monster on Card III and denying this threat by putting a red bow tie on his face.

  Also, her perseveration of the beard response (Cards I, II, VI, and her response to Card VII as her mother enters the room) identifies her current area of fearfulness.

  A's sophisticated use of many different areas and determinants portends a developing compulsive style in response to perfectionistic demands.

CAT: In Card 10, *A* demonstrates undoing by changing "spanking" to "petting" and by seeing the small dog as sitting, not lying, on the big dog. After this, she avoids questioning by singing "Pop Goes the Weasel," an interesting choice. Card 5 elicits the most extreme defensive tactics in the CAT by *A*. She denies the possibility of the baby in the parents' room, and, in so doing, gets confused. She then avoids the issue of the bed by covering it over and regressing for the first and only time, into nonsense sounds. She avoids the whole task by seeking her mother and changing the subject.

Summary Statement of Defenses: As is appropriate for a 3-year-old, *A* utilizes avoidance, denial, and occasionally regression when faced with a need to defend against stressful stimuli. She shows a developing compulsive style in response to her own perfectionistic demands. In addition, her use of teasing as a way of avoidance shows a more mature level of interpersonal understanding—that is, a sensitive awareness of the interaction between herself and others.

Affective Expression

S–B: *A* enjoyed this test throughout, except on the occasions when her own judgment was that something was too hard.

B–G: Not appropriate for a child of this age.

FD: Persistent refusal (see comment under *Defenses*).

Rorschach: Generally, *A* responded positively to the cards and, at times, was playful. Although she was somewhat distressed (Cards IV, VII, and VIII), she still was able to respond to *E*'s encouragement and then become involved in her own developing idea.

Except for her precocious use of color on Card III, she was unable to integrate color beyond the 3-year-old level of naming colors applied to Play-Doh. She obviously enjoyed her response, as seen in her animating the Play-Doh to Card VIII.

CAT: In her CAT stories, *A* demonstrated a wide range of affective possibilities, such as loving, anger, happiness, and sadness.

Summary Statement of Affective Expression: *A* responded with a wide array of affective expressions throughout the testing. She shows a capacity for flexibility in her experienced affect. Therefore, the testing session was an enjoyable experience for both *A* and *E*.

Summary

A is an extremely intelligent and verbal 3-year-old. These abilities, combined with her generally happy and pleasant affect, result in a very appealing child. She is eager to attempt new challenges, able to cope with and master difficulties, and generally free to use her energies to try to investigate and understand the world.

It may be speculated that *A*'s preoccupation with interpersonal interaction may be related to her concerns with aggression. Her own experiences of anger are always prevented expression. This is handled sometimes through her sense of humor and at other times through changing the subject or engaging in appeasement tactics to forestall anticipated retaliation. In addition, she already has an internalized strong perfectionistic desire.

Diagnosis:

GAP: Healthy Responses

DSM III: Axis   I: V71.09 (No diagnosis)
            Axis II: V71.09 (No diagnosis)
            Axis III: None
            Axis IV: 1 (None)
            Axis V: 1 (Superior)

At 3 years of age it is appropriate for A to be responding to perceived parental preferences. If her discomfort with aggression and anger is in response to her parents' prohibition, it is anticipated that this could become a problem for her. Similarly, if her perfectionism is continually reinforced, this, too, could become a problem. If, however, her parents are able to accept these normal developmental responses, she should continue to grow in what appears to be her currently healthy state.

Psychological Test Data

A: 2–11 Female

Stanford–Binet, Form L–M

CA   2–11
MA   4–7
IQ   147+

Year IV

1. 15
2. 2
3. 4 a) girl; b) dark; c) girl; d) fast; e) night
4. 5
5. 8
6. 2 a) live in them; b) to color
Months credit at year IV = Basal

Year IV-6

1. 3
2. 4
3. 4
4. 1 a) —; b) —; c) paper
5. Omitted
6. 2 a) look; b) listen to things
A. 5
Months credit at year IV-6 = 5

Year V

1. 2
2. 0
3. 1 a) round; b) round, too; c) —
4. 0
5. 9
6. 0
A. 0

Months credit at year V = 2

[*Much playing with things, but is responsive and motivated to achieve. Will tease in and around difficult questions. Makes effort to conceptualize.*]

Rorschach

I.	1″	1. Beard
		2. Moustache
		3. Those are the eyes—a face—is he a angry one? [Q] Yeah.
II.	2″	1. Happy face
		2. Hat—two hats—Mr. Potato Hat.
		2a. Now they are ears.
		2b. This is a hat and these are ears [*upper red*] then [*center*] beard [*lower red*]
		3. [S] This is nose.
		4. A broken piece of hat.
		5. Bears playing—sitting—just standing.
III.	2″	1. A monster. [W] Whole face of the monsters.
		2. A tie. He has a bow tie on his face. [Q] A red one.
IV.	2″	1. A puppy face. [*tries to refuse*] I'm fooling you—ears and feet [*lower* D]. This puppy has eyes—he's eating grass [*lower center* D *is face—eyes are sides*] ears.
V.	2″	1. A butterfly in the air flying. [*points to wings*]
VI.	1″	1. A beard—the beard. [Q] The whole thing—[*points all around*] [Q] [*no response*]
VII.	[*Mother comes in at this point.*]	
	3″	1. A beard—I'm fooling you again. [*repeats*] No eyes—face [*points inside the S*] would you believe it's Snow White? [*She is standing beside me and looked at her mother.*]
VIII.	1″	1. A whole face [*very distractible*]
		2. Stockings [*lower* D]
		3. Pink Play-Doh animals [*side* D]—jumping—leaping.
		4. [*side* D] Boat. Sailing on water. [*water is the center color areas*]
IX.	1″	1. Sorta a airplane [*also playing with Play-Doh and making an airplane*]
		2. All Play-Doh—yellow Play-Doh.
X.	1″	1. Another butterfly. All over. [W]
		2. Spiders next to it [*blue side* D]
		3. A nose [*center blue*]
		4. Head—butterfly hat [*top center gray*]

CAT

1. Why, there are roosters over there. They're eating. [*What are they eating?*] Chocolate ice cream. Cock-a-doodle-doo, like roosters say.
10. A little dog and a big dog. The big dog is sitting, and the big dog is spanking [*denied spanking; called it petting*] the little dog sitting on the big dog. [*A sings "Pop Goes the Weasel." Questioned her about spanking.*] No, the big dog is *petting* the little dog. [*Says*

I misunderstood her. Questioned the petting.] Because the big dog loves the little dog, so he's petting it.

2. Baby bear and momma bear and poppa bear are trying to pull the rope. [*Why are they pulling the rope? Do it?*] Nope.

9. Bunny rabbit in a crib. He's getting ready to go to sleep. [*Want to?*] Yes.

8. Monkeys—baby monkey, momma monkey, papa and grandma monkey. But why is the mommy monkey angry? I don't know. [*Gives me some Play-Doh.*] Maybe it's because the baby monkey didn't listen to the mommy monkey. Yes, that's right. Daddy monkey is happy. Grandma monkey is happy, too.

7. Tigers—mushed up. [*Doing?*] There's a monkey. That monkey is a friend of that tiger's. [*Doing?*] Playing.

3. [Q] Why is that a sad lion? I don't know. Because maybe it's because he doesn't want to sit there. There's a hole and a mouse is coming out. [Q] The mouse is going to eat his pipe and the mouse is going to eat his pipe. That's why he's sad.

4. Two kangaroos—three kangaroos—a baby kangaroo walking. [*Going?*] One of them, that one—the baby—is riding a bicycle and that one is hopping. [Q] Going to New York where it's cold and sometimes it's not.

   Know why I didn't drive here? Mommy make a frankfurter [*referring to Play-Doh*].

5. A crib with nobody in it. No feet—only that in it—a bear. No feet—no baby. [*Indicates no feet because there isn't a lump where the feet should be. Shoves Play-Doh on the bed to cover it, and makes nonsense sounds, then goes to mother and talks about the Play-Doh.*]

6. A nose, and I'm shooting the nose. [*avoids this*]

Psychological Test Portrait

B: 4–4 Male

B is a boy aged 4–4 who participated in a normal nursery. He was observed to be an active participant and always followed a more aggressive boy he knew from outside the nursery. He seemed to enjoy himself thoroughly. At times the observers noted a blankness or a momentary *absence,* which occurred when he was engaged in a solitary craft activity.

B had a traumatic birth history. He was premature and had his first seizure at age 1 month. He was medicated with phenobarbital until 1½ years of age, when the parents took him off it. They did so because they felt it made him drowsy and passive, and they preferred to cope with his bouts of "hyperactivity" and their own fear of another seizure.

B is of average height, but looks taller because of his slimness. He is an unusually delicate-featured boy with striking contrast between his light green eyes and dark hair. He cooperated with the testing and worked hard.

Cognitive Functioning

S–B, Form L–M: B achieves an IQ of 111 with a wide spread from II-6 to VII. Upon examination, his errors below his chronological age (CA) are found to be in the memory areas. Indeed, he achieved a second basal at IV-6 at his CA. Above his CA, he demonstrates a superior capacity for abstract conceptualization and language usage. Failures above his CA are primarily in visual-motor tests.

B–G: Not appropriate for this age.

FD: *B*'s figure drawings are classic examples of the 3-year-old with the one exception of the hair being separated from the head. By 4–4, he should be able to achieve a body as well as complete the features and add fingers or hands. His difficulty may be related to the visual-motor problems evidenced on the S–B.

Rorschach: *B*'s Rorschach productions are a straightforward demonstration of perseveration and vagueness. Unfortunately, the Rorschach was stopped after Card VI and resumed on a later day at Card V. It is hard to know what *B*'s development might have been if the Rorschach had been completed (that is, the perseveration was broken with the clear structure of V, and a new response was introduced on VI). Although one might express some perseveration at this age, this amount is excessive. *B* is clearly dealing with a problem in the perceptual and/or conceptual areas.

TAT: *B* demonstrates age-appropriate perceptual accuracy in this test. However, he is not able to develop stories as expected at this age. The stories in response to 1 and 4 are the result of a great deal of inquiry on *E*'s part. Again, as on the Rorschach, there is an excessive amount of perseveration starting with Card 4. Therefore, we see constriction in his ability to conceptualize.

Summary Statement of Cognition: In spite of superior functioning in abstract conceptualization and language usage, *B* has considerable difficulty in the areas of short-term memory and perceptual motor coordination. He also demonstrates constriction in his ability to conceptualize when the stimulus requires him to develop his own internally generated ideas.

Dynamic Picture

S–B: *B* would seem to like the structure of the S–B and responds simply in terms of the question or direction. There is no evidence of dynamic concerns throughout this test.

B–G: Not appropriate for this age.

FD: The drawings emphasize the head, which implies a concern over control of body impulses. He has limited sensory equipment, relying only on the eyes and mouth, and does not offer an integrated concept. One might speculate that the hair separated from the head is part of a disassociative experience.

Rorschach: *B*'s preoccupation with fire and smoke bespeaks an inordinate inner tension that may reflect concerns over his own sense of damage and vulnerability and/or difficulties he experiences with others. Rather than seeing at least one furry animal, *B* perseverates birds. This suggests a child whose experiences with others are lacking in warmth. Due to the perseveration, *B* does not or cannot reveal other dynamic concerns.

TAT: *B*'s low self-esteem is seen in Card 1. He attributes achievement to his admired friend rather than to "a boy." Although his perseveration of "playing lotto" at least suggests some interaction between people, there is still no expression of feelings or communication. Similarly, as seen in the Rorschach, perseveration precludes the revealing of other dynamic issues.

Summary Statement of Dynamics: *B*'s ability to function in structured cognitive areas is free of dynamic intrusions. When required to produce on the projective tests, he shows an immature concept of his body, low self-esteem, feelings of damage and vulnerability, and constriction in his interaction with others.

Defenses

S–B: *B*'s compliance with the highly structured nature of this test reflects the coping mechanism he adopts with authority. Other than this, there is no observable coping tactic used.

B–G: Not appropriate for this age.

FD: *B* would seem to feel himself without adequate coping strategies to deal with body impulses and the external world. Instead, we can see his avoidance of the body and denial of ears, nose, and hands as a self-protective maneuver. Reliance on avoidance and the intellect is seen as his only mode of protection.

Rorschach: The excessive use of perseveration and vagueness by *B* in the Rorschach takes on defensive proportions. This tactic of repeating the same idea precludes our getting to understand *B*'s feelings and ideas. He even is able to avoid interaction with *E* (see *Limits, III*).

TAT: In the TAT, as in the Rorschach, *B* uses perseveration to imply compliance, but actually it serves avoidance. Negativism is expressed in a most passive fashion (Card 7 BM). Generally, he remains detached and unmoved even in the face of *E*'s attempts to involve him. The one suggestion of a meaningful story (Card 1) is projected onto his admired friend.

Summary Statement of Defenses: B has a limited repertoire of coping mechanisms. Primarily he uses avoidance, and his use of perserveration seems to imply his wish for compliance. However, he appears generally isolated from interaction with others.

Affective Expression

S–B: B proceeds throughout the S–B in a compliant and impassive manner. There is no suggestion of any positive or negative affect.

B–G: Not appropriate for this age.

FD: Similarly, impassivity would seem to be the affect expressed in the drawings. The straight-lined mouth does not permit any expression of feeling.

Rorschach: Affective expression seems to be fraught with danger for B (see Cards I–IV). The one positive note is in his stating, "I like red," in Card VIII. Also, in the Limits on Card VIII he responds with some indication of gratification. Otherwise, the Rorschach portrays a child with either great inner tension or detachment.

TAT: B's impassivity persists throughout the TAT. The one expression of feeling comes in his presumed anger when he rips the paper in Card 7 BM after being asked about feelings.

Summary Statement of Affective Expression: B presents himself in the testing sessions as well as in his responses to the test as an impassive, detached, but attempting-to-be-compliant participant. His degree of affective detachment is of considerable concern for his developmental level.

Summary

B's record is sparse and limited. He is a child of above-average intelligence with possibly superior potential in conceptualization and language usage. His response, however, to emotionally laden stimuli is one of constriction, avoidance, and withholding. Clear difficulties in memory and perceptual-motor coordination in conjunction with his early history point to the possibility of a developing learning disorder. With his intellectual potential, this in and of itself would not be of major concern. The difficulty, however, taken in conjunction with his feelings of vulnerability, low self-esteem, inhibition in responsivity, as well as the degree of inner tension, suggests a developing pathology of serious dimensions.

Diagnosis:

GAP:	Overly inhibited personality with Psychophysiologic Disorder (Nervous System Disorder)
DSM III:	Axis I: 313.22 (Schizoid Disorder)
	Axis II: 315.90 (Atypical Specific Developmental Disorder)
	Axis III: History of seizures
	Axis IV: 4 (Moderate)
	Axis V: 3 (Good)

Treatment is essential for this child and his family. Prognosis is guarded.

Psychological Test Data
B: 4–4 Male

Stanford–Binet, Form L–M

CA   4–4
MA   4–10
IQ   111

Year II

1. 1
2. 2
3. 7
4. +
5. 16
6. +

Months credit at year II = Basal

Year II-6

1. 3
2. 7
3. 5
4. 16
5. 2
6. 2

Months credit at year II-6 = 6

Year III

1. 4
2. 16
3. +
4. a) cow; b) big bird not other
5. +

6. +
A. 2

Months credit at year III = 5

Year III-6

1. +
2. +
3. + [*confused mouse and rabbit*]
4. − a) Sitting down and resting—a lady. [*Else?*] No.
       b) Going out—I think they're having a birthday.
       c) A dog! He's upside down.
5. +
6. a) get some water; b) to cook with

Months credit at year III-6 = 5

Year IV

1. + 16
2. a) dog; b) puppy dog; c) puppy dog
3. a) girl; b) dark; c) Mommy; d) hoppy hop; e) [*no response*]
4. +
5. +
6. a) to live in them; b) to read

Months credit at year IV = 5

Year IV-6

1. +
2. +
3. −
4. a) bricks; b) glass; c) pages
5. +
6. a) see with; b) [*puts finger in ear*] hear

Months credit at year IV-6 = 6

Year V

1. +
2. −
3. a) to bounce with; b) father wear it; c) to cook with
4. −
5. +
6. −

Months credit at year V = 3

Year VI

1. −
2. a) A bird flies, and a dog bites—he can't fly.
       b) A boot when it snows out get boots—a slipper in house.
       c) Piece of glass goes in window, and wood goes to build a house.
3. a) ear; b) nothing; c) handle gives; d) lace; e) wheel
4. −
5. a) glass; b) can't fly, go in water; c) to cut; d) a car

Months credit at year VI = 4

Year VII

1. a) It's raining, and he has a hat on. [*Silly?*] It is. b) He's cutting a piece of wood from here. c) —; d) no; e) nothing
2. a) They are the same—a piece of wood is coal; b) not the same; c) not the same; d) —
3. –
4. a) Take her home. b) Bring it to fixer shop. c) Come back home. d) Steering wheel. e) Hit him back and I won. f) I just say what.
5. a) forget; b) green; c) wings; d) —
6. –

Months credit at year VII = 0

Rorschach

  I. No, that's smoke. [*Q*] Over here. [*points to particular area—Coming from?*] From house—no, the house is burned up already. [*What makes?*] It looks like smoke.
  II. Fire. [*Q*] Over here [*lower red*] and this is black smoke. [*notices upper red*] Over here is more fire—smoke and fire.
  III. Fire. [*points to lower gray area*] Here—also it's two fires. [*center gray area*]
  IV. A lot of fire—a big jungle of fire.
  V. A bird. [*Q*] It's the whole thing—these are the wings. [*Other parts?*] No.
  VI. The sun. Over here. [*lower area*] Oh, here's a sun up here, too. [*What makes?*] Summer time it's sunny.
  VII. A bird. [*opens door, looks outside*] It's a bird. No one.
  VIII. A bird—the biggest bird. I like red—here's red.
  IX. A big bird. The whole thing is a bird.
  X. More birds—a lot a birds—no more.

TAT

  1. It's Tommy [*the more aggressive boy referred to in the description of B in the nursery*] playing with an airplane with wing. [*What happens?*] Nothing. [*encouragement*] He gets off the airplane in California—he sees his Grandma. [*End?*] He flies away.
  2. This is a horse—these two are girls. [*Doing?*] Nothing. [*What else in picture?*] Oh, yeah— he's riding on a horse. That's all.
  4. That's a lady and that's a man. [*Doing?*] They're playing something—lotto. [*Feel?*] They like lotto. [*Do they like each other?*] Yeah. [*What do after lotto?*] Nothing. I don't know. [*How know each other?*] I don't know.
  7 BM. That's a man and that's a lady (younger). [*Doing?*] Playing lotto. [*Anything else?*] They're cleaning up then they'll play lotto. [*Who'll win?*] The man. [*Feel?*] They're gonna get this paper. [*rips up paper*]
  8 BM. This man is sleeping. [*hears noise outside—goes to look*] The man is hot and he's playing lotto. Nothing else.
  13 MF. This man is tired and this man is tired. [*Why?*] I don't know. [*Do?*] They're going to sleep. [*And then?*] Nothing. That's all.
  6 BM. This man is playing lotto and this lady is cleaning up the house. [*Tell me story not playing lotto.*] They're both cleaning up the house, washing the windows. [*What else?*] Nothing. [*Do after cleaning?*] Play lotto again.

Figure Drawings

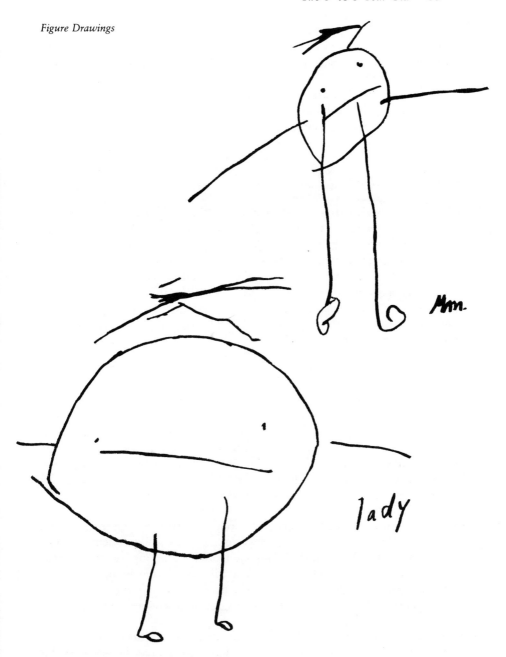

Mm.

lady

Psychological Test Portrait
C: 3–4 Male

C is a boy aged 3–4 who participated in a normal nursery setting. He is an only child and lives with his mother and father. He is average sized, fair-complected, and an appealing child. In the nursery he appeared dreamy and detached, although at times he did participate enthusiastically with others. Typically, he followed play initiated by other boys, but occasionally he would attempt to lead the others into his activity. He was never successful at this.

Entrance into the nursery was a very difficult transition for C. It took about three months for him to comfortably leave his mother and participate in the nursery activities. This was caused, in part, by his mother's reluctance to have him leave.

Cognitive Functioning

S–B, Form L–M: In spite of C's distractibility during testing, he is able to demonstrate his superior intellectual capacities. His first failures are at IV (2 and 6), which is already above his CA. His problem with memory seems to reflect an attentional problem rather than a memory problem. Also, his refusals and his complete failure on V seem related to his increasing hyperactivity. His capacity to tell stories on III-6, 4, rather than simply naming, is unusually precocious for this age. In other words, C's score appears to be a minimal statement of his intellectual potential because of motivational disturbances.

B–G: Not appropriate for this age.

FD: C did not make drawings.

Rorschach: The speculation that C's achievement in the S–B is minimal is borne out in the Rorschach. C produces at least a response per card, and maintains an excellent form level for his age. The array of percepts suggests a broad level of information. The use of *FM*'s and a large number of *D*'s for this age represents a level of conceptualization beyond his CA.

CAT: The CAT was used as part of the routine nursery testing requirement. C starts the CAT off with the same superior cognitive abilities demonstrated on previous tests. He organizes complete stories with temporal sequencing, interactions, and some details. It is not until Card 4 that he becomes confused. By Card 5 it is clear that he has been unable to sustain the concentrated effort required, and his stories become fragmented and free associative.

Summary Statement of Cognition: C demonstrates an unrealized potential for exceptionally high cognitive functioning. He is limited, however, by his inability to sustain attention and concentration on the tasks and often erupts into motor discharge. His responses to the projective tests reveal a remarkably superior cognitive potential.

Dynamic Picture

S–B: *C* initially attempts to control the situation. As the test becomes more difficult, he is not able to comply as easily as earlier. This leads to the speculation that *C* feels threatened by the loss of control through the possibility of failure, heightening his feeling of vulnerability.

B–G: Not appropriate for this age.

FD: *C* did not make drawings.

Rorschach: Due to the pseudomature content of *C*'s responses, there is little suggestion of the usual 3-year-old's concern. His focus is rather on achieving a level of maturity (II, III, VII) that he is unable to integrate at this age. This is also expressed in the *M:FM* ratio.

CAT: In spite of fearful associations, *C* is able to produce good stories in the first three cards. As the stimulus of the cards seems to get more frightening for *C*, he becomes obviously anxious with themes of disturbance in the area of sleeping and dangers implicit in interpersonal interactions. Also, as seen before, *C* has difficulty maintaining concentration when he feels pressured to perform. His CAT is striking inasmuch as there seems to be no expression of pleasure or gratification.

Summary Statement of Dynamics: *C*'s extreme sense of vulnerability is expressed through a heightened expression of the need to control. His vulnerability stems from dangers he perceives in performance, being alone, or in interpersonal interaction.

Defenses

S–B: *C*'s only way of handling his increasing sense of vulnerability (that is, loss of control) is to attempt to avoid the situation through distracting *E* and then becoming increasingly aggressively active. It is not clear whether his refusal to try (IV, 2 and 6; IV-6, 4) is in response to the difficulty of the item (that is, fear of failure) or negativism in response to the testing situation.

B–G: Not appropriate for this age.

FD: *C* did not make drawings.

Rorschach: *C*'s many responses to *S* bespeaks his negativism. Nascent obsessive-compulsive defenses are seen throughout the Rorschach in his use of *D*, distancing (use of the inanimate in I and II), and perception of facial features (III, VII, and IX).

CAT: As on the S–B, C's coping ability deteriorates into distractibility, avoidance, and negativism.

Summary Statement of Defenses: C's use of distractibility, avoidance, and negativism, although appropriate coping mechanisms for this age, are too exclusively limiting for him to achieve cognitively and socially.

Affective Expression

S–B: The one instance of pleasure evident in the protocol is C's story on III-6, 4b. Otherwise, C's affect seems to be largely unpleasant with hostility expressed toward E and the test.

B–G: Not appropriate for this age.

FD: C did not make drawings.

Rorschach: Although lacking any evidence of positive affect, the Rorschach is the one test that does not elicit unpleasant or hostile feelings from C.

CAT: The affect expressed throughout the CAT is either fear or anxiety. We can speculate that this amount of fear and anxiety must be a painful experience for C.

Summary Statement of Affective Expression: Affective expression throughout the testing experience was unpleasant or hostile; thus we infer that C must have experienced the testing as painful.

Summary

C clearly presents a dichotomous picture. He performs at either a precocious level or a regressed level. His nascent obsessive-compulsive defenses are brittle and collapse easily under minimal stimulation to fear. At that time, he cannot utilize his superior intellectual abilities and becomes diffusely active. He seems to be a very unhappy child who finds little opportunity for pleasure or gratification. Many of the positive attributes of the 3-year-old (humor, spontaneity, and joy) are not seen in C because of his preoccupation with issues of vulnerability.

Thus, we see a 3-year-old at risk. The test results evidence the early steps of a developing borderline personality. Of particular concern are the many indications of a paranoid interpretation of interpersonal experiences.

Diagnosis:

> *GAP:*   Overly dependent personality, severe
>
> *DSM III:*   Axis   I: 309.21 (Separation Anxiety Disorder)
>   Axis II: Borderline traits, Paranoid traits
>   Axis III: None
>   Axis IV: 4 (Moderate)
>   Axis V: 3 (Good)

Treatment, therefore, is an urgent need and must involve the parents. With such a treatment plan and because of C's age, we would offer a modestly hopeful prognosis.

Psychological Test Data

C: 3–4 Male

Stanford–Binet, Form L–M

CA   3–4

MA   4–3

IQ   127

I'll show you something. [*Puts car on desk next to yellow car—wants to show me something. Gets all—dropped one on floor.*]

Year III-6

1. 3
2. 1
3. 4
4. 2 a) The stove. b) She's ringing the bell. A guy has a present—see, it's a birthday—see candles. c) Dog—stealing the clothes. The mother is going to get mad. Chasing dog—hanging clothes.
5. +
6. 1 a) Drink some water; b) 'cause we have to

Months credit at year III-6 = 6 = Basal

Year IV

1. 15
2. 1
3. 3 a) girl; b) sunny; c) wife, lady; d) fast; e) —
4. 4
5. 8
6. a) need it—place to grow grass; b) [*won't answer*]

Months credit at year IV = 4

Year IV-6

1. 3
2. 3
3. 3
4. –
5. 3
6. 2 a) look; b) hear

Months credit at year IV-6 = 5

Year V

1. –
2. –
3. 1 a) a head; b) a head; c) for cooking
4. –
5. –
6. –

Months credit at year V = 0

Rorschach

I. 1. A dog. [*points to side* D] [Q] Here.
II. 1. A man [Q 1] a face. He's smiling [*points to*] eyes and nose. [*top red* D, *eyes; nose in middle*]
III. 1. Men pushing something. A ball. [Q] [*points to*] Head, body, and feet.
IV. 1. Tree [*points vaguely to* W]
V. 1. Bat
VI. 1. A fly [Q] a dragonfly [*top* D]
VII. 1. A neck chain
VIII. 1. Two bears climbing up a tree
IX. 1. Two bears climbing up a tree. [Q] [*doesn't see them*]
    2. It's a rainbow
X. 1. Flowers which you smell
    2. The pink things are the honey. Nothing else. [Q 1] [*blue* D]

CAT-H

1. Eating. A man is coming to look. He'll scare them. Boys ran outside to school, and they don't see him. He finds them at school.
2. They're pulling rope, shoes are off. They're at the beach. They pull and pull. The two boys win. He'll fall down and hurt his toe.
3. Man is sitting down. He has his pajamas on. The man is his daddy. He (little one) comes out and takes his cane.
4. Lady carrying a baby and boy riding bicycle and a balloon. [Q] Step on mushroon it'll die. [Q] Boy, he's nice. [*drops card*] All feel nice.
5. Babies sleeping in crib—a lamp falls. There are only lamps in picture. Fall asleep—nice—big bed doesn't feel nice. [*breaks plastic spoon*] [Q] Feels bad. Cause it has to feel bad—again. [*drops play dollar*] [*breaks Pick-Up-Stick*]
6. Falling asleep. He has eye open. [*playing with trucks, takes away money from truck; he's playing; roll back*] They'll get all dirty from bus. No like to get clean. Coming to clean up. Now it's a truck that cleans up everything. [*takes out truck—police truck—playing with pen*] He'll see what's happening in picture.
7. He wants to get that boy off. He took boy off—threw him out. Big one feels nice. He feels bad.

8. This guy on couch and lady wants the boy. He did something. She wants him to look at pictures that Daddy hung on wall. Don't get it again.
9. Baby lying down there. He's dreaming about truck. I have bad dream. [Q] That someone might walk in. That guy is taking board off. Guy fell. A happy dream.
10. This guy has to put him to sleep with big toes. He wants to stay there. He wants to go to sleep. Police come and take guy with big toes away. They'd like him and boy, too. Don't want him to throw him in there.

Psychological Test Portrait

D: 3–11 Male

D was brought for a routine physical examination at age 2–5, and the mother expressed her concern over his lack of language development. He was evaluated by a pediatrician and a pediatric neurologist, and a skull x-ray and electroencephalogram were obtained. All findings were within normal limits. Diagnoses were of developmental lag, primary aphasia, and the questions of mental retardation and hearing loss were raised. A speech and hearing evaluation found his hearing to be normal, but the psychologist's evaluation suggested autism or psychosis. At this point, he was referred to the child clinical psychologist.

D was a six-pound, twelve-ounce infant with a normal birth history (established by hospital records). Parents had no familial history of psychosis or retardation.

D was seen at 3–11 years. He is a handsome, average-sized boy. He was obviously unrelated and unresponsive to verbal communications. Formal testing, therefore, was not possible. Instead, the data discussed in the following section are based on an effort made with S–B items and the Leiter test administered by the speech and hearing psychologist when he was 3–9. We conducted two testing interviews with play material, not using any formal test, when he was 3–11.

Cognitive Functioning

The hallmark of *D* is that he responds to inner direction exclusively. Thus, requests as simple as to respond to his name—or, more complicatedly, to follow a direction—went unheeded. In evaluating what he did, it was clear that in some areas *D* demonstrated average to superior intelligence. He set himself the task of stacking eighteen blocks in a column. His attempts to stack in different ways in order to reach his goal of a stable tower showed excellent conceptual ability.

There was an almost uncanny memory for the original position of objects in the room. He returned each object to its place and, indeed, attempted to return *E* to her room before leaving. This suggests unusual spatial orientation (as does his knowledge of the time and channel for his television program), and his memory serves his need to maintain sameness.

His excellent fine and gross motor coordination was integrated with his visual perception when he wanted it to be.

For all intents and purposes *D* has no language. He is capable of making sounds such as grunting, screaming, or humming, but has not made any sound associated with precursors to language.

Summary Statement of Cognition: Despite the severity of *D*'s disturbance seen in his inability to interact and use language, he was still able to demonstrate average to superior skills in spatial orientation and memory, and excellent fine and gross motor coordination.

Dynamic Picture

D is driven by the need to do what he wants to do. We can tell what that is only by observing the course of his behavior. Thus, when he devotes a half hour to attempting to build his tower, we can say he wanted to build a tower. When he cries and attempts to get the screw and does not relent until he is given the screw, we can say he wanted the screw. Why he wanted these things is a total enigma.

For the same reason, his response to others seems totally to serve his current need. Thus, others are used as objects—that is, tools—to achieve his goal. He never seeks others (including his parents) for comfort or sharing, nor responds to the advances of peers or adults. Inconsistently, he will comply with his parents' requests, especially with the threat of their leaving.

Summary Statement of Dynamics: The only dynamic for *D* is a purely autistic one.

Defenses

If indeed defenses exist, *D* is total in his withdrawal and isolated from the world of people and feelings. He is totally protected from the external world by the shell he lives within, but he cannot defend himself against his own inner drives and needs.

Summary Statement of Defenses: *D* is totally withdrawn from interaction with the world of people and feelings. Therefore, we do not speculate as to his defenses.

Affective Expression

D is generally described as a somber child. He is capable of expressing joy, anger, and/or fear. The problem is that these feelings are expressed without any apparent relationship to a cause for joy or anger that we can perceive. Therefore, a sudden burst of joyous laughter will emerge without any stimulus that we can see, appearing to be related to his own internal experience.

Summary Statement of Affective Expression: While affect is expressed by D, it seems to be related only to his own internal experience.

Summary

D demonstrates a typical picture of an autistic child. Language is not used for communication, and D expresses himself only through sounds. Some autistic children at this age may be able to read letters, words, and/or state sentences, but even with language available do not use it for the purpose of communication. D demonstrates areas of average to superior intellectual skills, but, again, these skills are available only to inner direction. Some children may be able to master reading, writing, and arithmetic at a later age, but it is accomplished in a rote fashion and cannot be utilized for communication with the world.

Although affective expression is available, again it is not used in an interactional sense.

Thus, intellectually and affectively, these children are cut off from the interpersonal world. When they react to others, it is most often to use the other as an inanimate object to satisfy their own intention.

Diagnosis:

GAP:	Early Infantile Autism
DSM III:	Axis I: 299.00 (Infantile Autism)
	Axis II: V71.09 (No diagnosis)
	Axis III: None
	Axis IV: 3 (Mild)
	Axis V: 7 (Grossly Impaired)

D shows some potential for eventually learning and/or developing some language usage. This is most probable if he is placed in a school for autistic children. Since there is no identifiable etiology for this condition and no proved treatment method, prognosis for anything approaching normal development is dim (Hundley, 1971).

Psychological Test Data

D: Male

Test Data at 3–9

On the few S–B items in which he became interested enough to try to cooperate, he failed. For instance, he intently watched the hide-the-kitty game at the 2-year level on the Binet and searched eagerly for it, but could not remember its location consistently. In addition, he seemed to show fleeting interest in E's directions (give me the kitty, put the scissors in the box, and so forth), but seemed confused and finally put a block in the box. He could not be induced to mark with a pencil or chalk, or to cut with scissors, although he watched while E did it, and on several occasions directed her hand back to the pencil to make her draw some more.

D's gross motor coordination seems slightly immature, but he has normal finger dexterity. He would not cooperate in finger directions, with the exception of picking up pills with his thumb and first finger. He would not cooperate with tests for walking up stairs, hopping, jumping, or walking on toes, heels, etcetera. He refused to hold a pencil, but father reports that at home he will scribble. He reportedly takes off all of his clothes when he goes to the toilet, but will not put them back on. Also, he will not dress himself in the morning. Mother still spoonfeeds him.

Interview at 3–11

At age 3–11 he was interviewed again. D presented as a slender, neat, well-dressed, good-looking, serious little boy. During the first interview, he followed his parents docilely into the room, but would not respond to E calling his name, nor did he make eye contact with anyone. He went immediately to the doll house where, using E's hand as a tool, he moved the toys in and out of the house, without using them according to their function or placing them in any order. He did not respond to any command given. At one point during the interview, D found a screw and tried to put it in his mouth. E took the screw from him and put it in her pocket. D tried to get it back from her, but failing, began to cry. He finally threw himself down on his knees, first in front of E and then in front of his mother. His mother quickly picked him up, but D was not comforted until he had the screw. He was able to keep the screw out of his mouth at his mother's command.

On her lap, D examined his moving fingers attentively, as an infant might, holding them in front of him, and was observed to go off into a dream-like state where he seemed oblivious to his surroundings. At one point he laughed out loud for no apparent reason, then shook his head from side to side. Periodically he would make a little humming noise to himself. Later in the interview E left the room. D attempted unsuccessfully to open the door himself. But when E returned and tried to get D to go out with her, he refused and ran back to his mother. In her lap, in response to being turned around to face her, D was noted to flatten himself against her body, but with his head held straight, looking over her shoulder. The gesture lacked a sense of cuddling. Neither the arms nor the head were bent toward the mother. This was the only form of body contact, other than hand holding, D manifested during the session. Upon leaving, D stopped to look around the waiting room—then ran silently to his parents' hands.

The second interview with D had a different quality to it. E greeted D and his father in the waiting room, where D was sitting quietly with a magazine. Though D did not go to E in response to his name or take her hand, he did immediately make brief eye contact. He entered the room easily with his father and immediately went to some alphabet blocks that were set out on the table. Looking very serious and with great concentration and perseverance, D spent the next half hour trying to build all of the eighteen blocks into a single tower. This time no one else's hands were used as tools. It was noted that D was interested in the alphabet on the blocks, and E, sitting next to him, began naming the letters. He was soon handing her the blocks to name before he put them on the tower, making occasional eye contact. Over the course of the interview, D tried various methods to make the tower stand. First he tried stacking the blocks with the letters up, then holding three in each hand and steadying the tower while he placed the last few blocks on top. Then he tried standing on the chair to get the last few blocks on, and, finally, he tried to stack them with the smooth side up. At home he apparently will stack them against a wall in an attempt to make them stand. Whenever the blocks fell, D would frown and start again. As time passed and nothing worked, D became more excited at the falling itself. Once the blocks started to fall, he would swing at them, jump up and down, wave his arms, and squeal to himself. At the end of the hour, D expressed his pleasure in the blocks with squealing and a smile. Before leaving, he arranged the blocks exactly as he had found them when first entering the room.

During the interview, D was taken to the nursery. He left his blocks easily as long as he was accompanied by his father. He would not go out with E alone. Upon entering the nursery, he made straight for a set of blocks on the table, completely ignoring the existence of the other children. D was greeted by the nursery-school children and approached by one child. At no time did D acknowledge their presence. He concentrated totally on the blocks, putting them in and out of their position without hesitation and trying to build them into a tower. Despite the tremendous racket in the room, D never once placed his hands in his ears or even appeared to notice it. D left the blocks reluctantly, but without fuss, when his father moved to lead him away. At the end of the interview, E attempted to walk D and his father to the outside door. D quietly but firmly took her hands, led her back to the office, and closed the door. He then left with his father, without a backward glance.

4
The 5- to 7-Year-Old

Developmental Expectations

Cognitive Functioning. Concomitant with the completion of neurological development, the child is ready to begin to develop the precursors of logical thinking. Precursors available at this age are the abilities to begin the mastery of reading, writing, and arithmetic. The process of ever-increasing distinction between reality and fantasy heightens the child's curiosity and leads to questioning of all aspects of personal experience and of the world.

The need to be as able (big, strong, smart) as the adult cognitively leads the child at this period to self-satisfied solutions and answers. This is not to say that simultaneously the child is not eager to learn as much as is offered about the true or real solutions and answers.

Dynamic Picture. This age range represents a major growth spurt. Reality experience becomes stabilized, which is not to say that fantasy is not readily available for play. There evolves, however, a capacity for a clear differentiation between the experiences of reality and fantasy.

This is the period of resolving the Oedipal conflict, through which the child achieves an identification with the parent of the same sex. This leads to the development of boundaries for the ego structure of a self-concept. This lays the groundwork for the evolving concept of sexual identification. Because of the difficulties inherent in the resolution of the Oedipal conflict, regressive behavior can be typical for this age group. In this setting of maturing behavior there will be moments of earlier forms of actions and feelings.

Children in this age group can be extremely competitive with the parent of the same sex as well as wanting to achieve adult behavior. They carry into this period an unreal sense of their own omnipotence and assume, at times, that they can do almost any adult act. At the same time, they can also attribute this same omnipotence to the adult.

Defenses. The two major defenses at this point are denial and avoidance, which are clearly related to the process involved in the resolution of the oedipal conflict. These two defenses seem to be intricately related to the development of successful repression. Denial is seen in the proclivity to lying at this age as well as the forthright denial of an event that everyone has observed. Punishment or discipline is responded to with an "I don't care" statement in spite of the obvious fact that the child does care. Avoidance is seen in the total disregard for verbal instructions to the point where the adult can be concerned about the child's hearing. Another example is the need for a night light to avoid fear of the dark, which is common at this age.

At this stage, compulsive behavior is clearly seen for the first time. Great energy is invested in the acts of ordering, counting, and repetitive behaviors. These acts seem to be done with a great sense of pride and pleasure, unlike the adult's experience of boredom or even irritation. In the same way that these compulsive behaviors aid the child in achieving a sense of mastery, obsessiveness begins to be seen at this time in the mental processes of ruminating over the qualities of reality experiences. The latter can be observed in the child's limitless and repetitive questioning of why, how, when, where, and so forth.

Affective Expression. Although not labile, there is a wide discrepancy in affect during this period. These children can go from paroxysms of giggling to periods of intense, inconsolable weeping. The adult is often mystified as to the seemingly benign cause producing such an intense response.

Overall Picture. The easy access to regressive levels of this age group means that the content of their humor is often scatological in nature, and the content of their pain is concerned with feelings of humiliation over the issue of adequacy.

Development up to this point leads 5-year-olds to the beginning steps of independence. They go off into the world of kindergarten on their own to meet the new social and cognitive demands so different from those they have known in the home. This is accompanied, hopefully, for the child, with a feeling of pride as well as pleasure and excitement in what each day holds.

Their relationships with peers are earmarked at this point with the emergence of cooperative efforts and the beginning of organized play that requires rules and a format. The investment in play at this time is so extreme it may indeed be the origin of the statement that the play of the child is his work.

Fantasy, during this period, is typically shared through the medium of play with others. Two of the most common themes are playing house and playing doctor. In the former, one can see an exaggeration of parental roles enacted, both realistically and in terms of wish fulfillment. In the latter, there is the opportunity for expressions of sexual curiosity that can be very stimulating. Later during this period girls play school, and boys tend to engage in large motor activities such as running and climbing, and in games such as cowboys and Indians. There is also a resurgence of frightening content to fantasy experience, so that this age group can show a great deal of different transient phobic reactions as well as nightmares. Nightmares, however, at this point can be distinguished by the child as dreams, although they are certainly still experienced as being frightening.

Normal Expectations on Tests

Intelligence Testing. For the aforementioned developmental aspects—that is, physiological and psychological—one expects a far greater degree of stability and consistency in cognitive functions than previously. Therefore, on intelligence tests a greater similarity in subtest scores is expected, and wide discrepancies gradually decrease with age.

Bender–Gestalt. The geometric designs on the WPPSI are the best meaures up to the age of 6½. By 7, there is a clearer capacity to produce the B–G design in recognizable form, but one should have a great deal of experience with the productions of this age group before making judgments as to the existence of neurological deficit.

Projectives. Figure drawings during this period show a significant growth in the drawing of the figure from a simple defined body at age 5 to a clearly delineated male or female clothed figure with two-dimensional limbs by age 7.

On the Rorschach one can expect more responses than previously. A greater use is made of *D, M* starts to appear with *FM* larger than *M*, a larger amount of *CF* than *C*, and a preponderance of *A* responses. Generally speaking, there is a broader range of determinants. *FC* may start to put in an appearance during this time, since the child is in the process of establishing repression. Inanimate movement (*m*) and three-dimensional vista responses (*FK*) are usually not present. Shading and texture (*c*) can appear occasionally, although it is considered to be a very sophisticated response at this age.

The child's stories on the TAT will be unelaborated productions at this stage. There will be more details and sometimes a fanciful theme. There can be great variability in how this age group approaches the TAT task. Some children give short summary statements, some rely on compulsive accounting of everything in the picture, some become obsessive with a certain theme, and some ignore the important aspects of the picture or deny their existence.

Representative psychological test interpretations and psychological test batteries for children within this age range now follow. The raw test data from the psychological test batteries follow the discussion of each child so that easy reference can be made to the examples selected for illustration of the interpretations. We include examples of children diagnosed as healthy, mildly disturbed, moderately disturbed, and severely disturbed in order to demonstrate how a psychological portrait is developed. Each child's tests are analyzed, interpreted, and concluded with an integrated summary.

As stated before, the summary is not a complete report, but represents the salient features leading to the diagnostic portrait.

Psychological Test Portrait

F: 6–6 Male

F was referred because he was not learning in first grade. He has poor motor coordination, difficulty in reading, and shows some disruptive behavior in the classroom.

F is a 6–6 boy who is sturdy and handsome. He lives with his parents, 2-year-old brother, and 6-month-old sister.

He is left-handed, and in the testing situation clumsiness in right-left coordination was obvious. Hyperactivity was not seen in the testing session, as he was obviously reassured when he was told he would not have to write, spell, or perform any school work. He concentrated on each task, but there were moments of distraction, as if he were expressing a shift in his level of consciousness.

Difficulties in motor control were noticed throughout the testing. His wrist tonus was often lacking, and his hands would hang limply. When he became excited—which happened often in the Rorschach, where he was terribly stimulated by what he saw—his hands would fly up and out in athetoid-like gestures accompanying his verbal expressions of excitement. Similarly, he would start to stammer, and at times his language would become garbled, which seemed to reflect poor enunciation rather than garbled thinking.

The TAT was not given because of time constraints. The parents could not bring him back for another testing session, and E believed she had sufficient data for interpretation.

Cognitive Functioning

WPPSI: F was given the WPPSI and achieved a Full-Scale IQ of 117 with a Verbal Scale of 115 and a Performance Scale of 116, with scaled scores ranging from 5 to 17. His extremely high scaled scores were 17 on Vocabulary, 15 on Similarities, and 15 on Block Design—tests associated with language abilities, abstract reasoning, and analytic cognitive ability. These scores would seem to indicate, in numerical terms, an unusually gifted child intellectually, if severe problems in perceptual-motor coordination did not interfere.

He attained a scaled score of 5 on Animal House. He began with ease, but became confused at the point where he attempted to use both hands instead of continuing with his left hand alone. It would seem that the resulting confusion in right-left orientation disrupted the sign-symbol nature of the task.

B–G: In reproducing the figures, *F* showed enormous effort and attempts to compensate (by rotating the paper), which reflect his high intellectual capacity. Although young for the test, his reproductions reflect a great deal of difficulty in controlling his pencil; for example, circles and dots become dashes. He is unable to make the alpha curve on 6, and difficulty is evident in poor sequential organization of the figures.

FD: His *FD*s are easily identifiable by sex and body parts. The difficulty is seen in the rigid stylistic tube-like bodies with the legs as extensions of the body sides. We would speculate that this is the only human body he could produce because of dynamic considerations (see *Dynamic Picture*).

Rorschach: *F*'s performance on the Rorschach supports the WPPSI indications of superior intellectual potential. He produces unusually precise and imaginative percepts, displaying a remarkable fund of knowledge for a 6-year-old. This is in spite of evidence of word-finding probems (I, 4; II, 1 and 3; III, 5) and memory lapses (see WPPSI). His pleasure with a well-delineated structure is seen in his response to Card V, where notably his language shows no confusion or distortion in concept or enunciation.

Summary Statement of Cognitive Functioning: *F* portrays the complicated picture of a child who demonstrates very superior intellectual abilities, yet is handicapped by a perceptual-motor problem and suggestions of word-finding difficulties and memory lapses. There is limited evidence that he is, at this time, making efforts to compensate for his inherent weaknesses.

Dynamic Picture

WPPSI: There are a few instances in the WPPSI where *F* demonstrates certain overriding dynamic problems. Humiliation is clearly reflected in his enormous difficulty in responding to questions 6 and 8 in Comprehension. Both of these problems appear to be more poignantly expressed in his response in the Vocabulary section to *nuisance*—"Somebody doesn't want you." Vocabulary testing also elicits a response to *knife* that is unique in this child's record for its primitive aggressivity.

B–G: The Bender does not reveal any particular dynamic problem.

FD: *F*'s drawings suggest problems in body concept that may be reactive to his perceptual-motor difficulties.

Rorschach: The sense of vulnerability noted in the WPPSI becomes clearer in *F*'s Rorschach responses. In Card I, upon much questioning from *E*, he struggles to achieve a complete percept, but offers only body parts. In Card III we again see his difficulty in formulating a whole percept, and it becomes clear only upon *E*'s repeated questioning. In Cards VI and VII he reports the process of construction after identifying his percepts. From this we infer a sense of vulnerability as to his feelings about himself, that he lacks a sense of his own body integrity. In Card IX his association to his percept sounds as if he were reassuring himself that there will be compensation in case of damage. In Card III his response to the stress of miscommunication between *E* and himself suggests the feelings of inferiority associated with his sense of damage —that is (Card III, 1,2,3), "I wouldn't say it's the goodest person . . . "

F's sense of a lack of body integrity is the main dynamic revealed in our interpretation of the symbolic content of the Rorschach. He portrays a solid masculine identification in Cards III and IV.

Summary Statement of Dynamic Picture: *F* would seem to be reacting to his experience of difficulty in learning areas by feeling a lack in body integrity. That is, he experiences himself as damaged and vulnerable, which leads to feelings of inferiority and humiliation. The dynamic conflict for *F* is between recognition of where his deficits lie and his strengths can be utilized.

Defenses

WPPSI: When not absolutely sure, *F* attempts to avoid the question or deny his competence with an "I don't know," or "I forgot" response. As can be seen in the protocol, the reassurance and persistence of *E* elicited the correct (and often excellent) response.

B–G: The Bender demonstrates excellent attempts to compensate for his perceptual-motor difficulties in contrast to other tests.

FD: Only in the drawing of the male figure do we see the suggestion of the use of intellectualization as a defense by *F* in the discrepant size of the head to the body.

Rorschach: The use of avoidance is seen again in Card III when difficulty in lack of communication between *E* and *F* leads him to feel pressured, resulting in his saying, "I don't know" (Card III, Inquiry 1,2,3).

The primary defensive pattern seen throughout the Rorschach is the gaining of distance from his percepts and associations through intellectual content. This is seen in Cards I, II, and V. It is also noteworthy that *F* rarely reports the more common percepts for a 6-year-old such as the bat or butterfly on Card I, bear in Cards II and VIII, giant or monster on Card IV, rabbits or girl on Card VII, and crabs or bugs on Card X. This suggests a more pervasive need to distance himself from simple reality and a more overdetermined effort at intellectualization.

Summary Statement of Defenses: Intellectualization is *F*'s primary defense and is used well to gain distance from the dynamic implications of his percepts. Denial and avoidance are used indiscriminately in response to most questions, as his insecurity leads to fear of failure and need to avoid humiliation. Reassurance, however, from *E* permitted him to try and frequently succeed.

Affective Expression

WPPSI: As expressed throughout the WPPSI, *F*'s affects ranged from shame and fear (of being wrong) to anxiety expressed motorically in restless fidgeting. Similarly, anxiety was felt to be experienced in his stammering and garbled enunciation.

When he was absolutely sure of his response, he expressed comfortable ease in his demeanor.

B–G: The primary affect throughout the B–G was suffering with the enormous output of energy required by him for the task.

FD: No affective expression on *F*'s part was recorded by *E* in his execution of the drawings. However, the mien of both faces is happy, and when asked how they felt, he responded that they were happy.

Rorschach: Intermittently throughout the Rorschach are expressions of distress when *F* felt unsure of his responses. However, the predominant affect throughout was one of excitement, pleasure, and—when he was absolutely sure, as on Cards V and VIII—pure joy.

Summary Statement of Affective Expression: If *F* were not struggling with the effects of his perceptual-motor problem or his feelings about himself, he could be a happy child.

Summary

F is an emotionally healthy and well-adjusted 6-year-old boy. His emotional stability is all the more remarkable in light of the severe and extraordinary learning disability with which he is burdened. He suffers right-left confusion, word-finding problems, and memory lapses. In spite of his handicaps, he is able to perform in a superior fashion when he must reason, think logically, or abstract and display his knowledge of the meaning of words and the world about him. He is most inept when he has to produce a sign-symbol test motorically, in arithmetic, and in copying geometric designs.

Diagnosis:

GAP:	Developmental Deviations, Specific Dimensions of Development	
DSM III:	Axis I:	V71.09 (No diagnosis)
	Axis II:	315.50 (Mixed Specific Developmental Disorder)
	Axis III:	Question of Neurological Stability
	Axis IV:	3 (Mild)
	Axis V:	5 (Poor)

This evaluation is not complete without a complete neurological workup including hearing and visual tests. It is predictable that without remedial help F is going to become more and more functionally retarded, as he will continue to suffer blows to his already shaky self-esteem.

Psychological Test Data

F: 6–6 Male

WPPSI

		Scaled Score
Verbal Tests		
Information		11
Vocabulary		17
Arithmetic		8 (9)
Similarities		15
Comprehension		11
(Sentences)		(13)
	Total	62 (63)

Performance Tests		
Animal House		8
Picture Completion		14
Mazes		13
Geometric Design		12
Block Design		15
(Animal House Retest)		(5)
	Total	62

	Scaled Score	IQ
Verbal Scale	62	115
Performance Scale	62	116
Full Scale	124	117

Information

		Score
1.	Points	1
2.	Two	1
3.	Your thumb	1
4.	Soda	1
5.	Lots of animals, fish, octopuses, squids, and whales, sharks and barracudas and frogs and millions of fish	1
6.	Green	1
7.	Two kinds? Kangaroo, gorilla, and baby elephant	1
8.	Cow	1
9.	Moon	1
10.	1, 2, 3, 4	1
11.	A stamp	1
12.	Nails or glue	1
13.	A ball, orange	1
14.	You have to—you have to put hot water; you have to get hot water from the sink—comes from reservoir. [Boil?] Put it on stove.	1
15.	The grocery store	1
16.	Don't remember	0
17.	Leather and stuff like that of both of yours—sneakers made out of rubber	1
18.	I don't know. [guess] Seven?	1
19.	Dough, [LP] powder, [Q] and I don't know	0
20.	All kinds of them—turkey day, summer, Halloween, firecracker	0
21.	All kinds of colors like pink, yellow, blue, mostly white	0
22.	[counting to self] Don't know [guess] 101	0
23.	It comes up—the morning [Set?] don't know	0
	Total	17

Vocabulary

		Score
1.	Something you put your feet on	2
2.	Something you kill someone with	1
3.	I don't know. [yes you do] You ride on it.	1
4.	Something you put on your head	2
5.	Something to keep the rain off you	2
6.	Something to hammer in wood	2
7.	What a letter? Something that is somebody's name like A	1
8.	Something you put in car to make car run	2
9.	Animal—like a horse	2

10. I don't know—oh, yeah, it's a plaything—
    you swing on it. [*describes a swing*] 1
11. I don't know—a castle is a fort 2
12. I don't know—you'd snap your fingers 2(?)
13. Warm—for animals like wolves, dogs,
    and bears 2
14. You're nice [?] I don't know; you have
    good manners. 2
15. I don't know what it is—it's a bug—like
    an ant, but it's a flying bug 2
16. Join something like a club and stuff like that 1
17. I think I know—it's like a winner 1
18. A diamond is like a shiny thing 1
19. Something like a knife, but it isn't 1(?)
20. Somebody don't want you [*etcetera*] 2(?)
21. I don't know—I can't say. [*hear*] Don't know
    see, [DK] [*Use?*] see little things like bugs 1
22. Gambling? I don't know—they like spin
    the wheel, and you get money if you
    pick the right number 2

Total 35

Arithmetic

	Score
1–8.	8
9.	0 (1)
10.	1
11.	1
12.	0
13.	0
14.	1
15.	0
16.	0
17.	1
18.	0
19.	0
20.	0
Total	12(13)

Similarities

		Score
1.	Boat	1
2.	Socks	1
3.	Bat	1
4.	Cup	1
5.	Eat	1
6.	Feet [*Feet?*] I don't know; I don't know, arms	1
7.	Pen	1
8.	Women's	1
9.	Drink	1
10.	Huh [?] Break—one breaks, other don't. [*R?*] I don't know.	0
11.	[*no response until E repeats question*] Both keep you warm.	1
12.	I don't know. [*yes you do*] Both musical instruments	2

13.	I don't know—oh, both fruits		2
14.	Both money		2
15.	Both drinks		1
16.	Both animals		2
		Total	19

Comprehension

			Score
1.	'Um, a fire could go on [*he Rs*] could get on fire. [*takes off sweater*]		2
2.	To keep you clean		2
3.	Cut up your whole finger? Just a little bit? [*?*] I don't know, maybe put a Band-Aid on it		2
4.	To tell the time it is		2
5.	Get him a new one		2
6.	What? [*Q*] 'cause if you have to go to bathroom, yuh, you don't have to . . . I don't know, I don't know why. [*He says he forgot the words. He looks at E pleadingly, then squints and opens eyes*] Huh, oh, I can't think. I just can't think of anything else. [*fidgeting*]		0
7.	To look out of		1
8.	I don't know. [F *smiles and is whispering to himself*] I don't know. [*?*] It's too hard.		0
9.	To get money		1
10.	Might burn. [*What?*] The candles might get on fire		1
11.	Huh? [*didn't hear?*] No. 'Cause they . . . they shouldn't go to *gool* if they was sick, and he might get the same thing—not—he might—uh, get the same—uh, thing he had		2
12.	Go to another store		2
13.	Push him down		0
14.	They're *bofe* good—I don't know why		0
15.	They're bad. [*?*] They steal things— without people giving it. They steal one's, peoples, money		0
		Total	17

Picture Completion

		Score
1.	Thing	1
2.	Wheel	1
3.	Arm	1
4.	The stem	1
5.	The mouth	1
6.	The ear	1
7.	The chair's leg	1
8.	His friend—nobody could be up alone	1
9.	The finger	1
10.	The whiskers	1
11.	The half size	1
12.	Clothing	1

13.	The big hand of the watch	1
14.	Lady's old heel	1
15.	Person, oh no, this light	1
16.	Little wood piece	1
17.	Oh, I know! Knob	1
18.	Doorway	1
19.	The little dot	0
20.	Should be more of these	1
21.	[OK points]	1
22.	Don't know	0
23.	Don't know	0
	Total	**20**

Block Design

	Score
1.	2
2.	2
3.	2
4.	2
5.	1
6.	2
7.	2
8.	2
9.	2
10.	2
Total	**19**

Geometric Design

	Score
1.	2
2.	2
3.	1
4.	0
5.	2
6.	2
7.	1
8.	2
9.	3
10.	3
Total	**18**

Mazes

	Time	Score
1A.		1
1B.		1
2.	9"	2
3.	10"	2
4.	7"	2
5.	10"	2
6.	10"	2
7.	20"	3
8.	25"	2
9.	40"	3
10.	45"	3
	Total	**23**

Animal House

	Time	Score
Time	1′ 40″	
Errors	0	
Omissions	0	
Errors and omissions		0
	Total	46

Animal House Retest

	Time	Score
Time	1′ 0″	
Errors	0	
Omissions	0	
	Total	46

Bender–Gestalt

Figure Drawings

Rorschach

I. 1. A design . . . I don't know. I know how you do those. You put black paint on it and shut it up like [*illustrating*] and out comes this same design as the aller. [*sic!*] Um, um, we did—I did one of these. We had black paper, and we put on some white and one came—and out came a design. [*Else?*] There's two things—the same. This, the same. That line is not the same 'cause this is one thing. [*Something looks like something?*] These two look like the same . . . [*etcetera*] [*R?*] This. [*points to bottom D*] [*whispering to self*]
2. [*See before?*] Could be a beak—
3. or a tooth—a tooth of a whale [*side D*] I don't know anything else it could be.
4. Hey! Could be a piece of a tail. [*Of what?*] Uh, desert. [*?*] A lizard or something like that.

II. 1. Oh! [*smiles*] These two things right here [*bottom projection*] just like points—I know what they could be—they could be a *veil* . . . [*?*] Whale—long noses [*indicates*] they're almost extinct—like whales with big point at end. [*Extinct?*] I mean a century ago—their nose is an ivory thing—like a whale—I have a book about fish—like the polar bear—and they show all kinds of whales—the white whale.
2. [*Else?*] And these two things [*top reds*] look like a thing. [*?*] These two. [*?*] I don't know. [*Remind you of?*] Might be of—reminds me of seals. [*?*] I don't know—just reminds me, up here looks like their heads, and there—that looks like their feet down there.
3. This thing right here reminds me of elephants. [*points out nose and eyes of* P] Could be right over there, and that could be, oh, right there—their ear. [*Doing?*] I think they're—could *clock*—think they're clapping—just two elephants. [*?*] Oh, there's the trunks—oh, there's their teeth—the little ivory things over there.

III. [*Makes clicking sound with tongue as staring at card*]
1. This looks like feet over here [*center projection*]
2. This looks like a hand
3. This looks like he's holding a suitcase. Looks like . . . [*turns away from card*]
4. And this, [*turns back to card*] what could this be? That could be a butterfly. [*enunciated very clearly*]
5. This could be a *line* if it turn over—head, tail, leg, and leg.
1,2,3. [*1 and 2, head and feet of?*] The color? [*Mean?*] I don't know— what you said again—I don't know—just the design—head, neck— that could be a little suitcase. He's holding a suitcase. [*Therefore 1, 2, and 3 are all one percept.*] I don't know—it just looks like a person—yeah, kind of—I wouldn't say it's the goodest person in the world. It would have to be—it just looks like a person—right— just put a little imagination to your mind, and you see what it looks like.
5. [*Establish line is lion*] Running—have to be because look at the feet.
4. [*Butterfly?*] Flying, I'd say.
3. [*Suitcases?*] Suitcases—*bowelding* [*bowling*] suitcases.

IV. [*Suddenly uses spastic-like gestures*]
1. This could be a person too—his feet, arms, his head, and that could be a chair. I don't say it would be. I don't say—the *aller* person's better than this one. A person sitting on a chair—that's all— the *aller* one. Just a design—put your imagination on it—right?

V. 1. Oh aaahh! This looks like a *bat*! [*very excited*] Look! Wings—two wings—two legs—head—ears. [*?*] He does have wings—that's all. [*Make it look like a bat?*] Head and besides, a person wouldn't have wings and legs like this—a bat has long ears. Big arms like that. [*Mean?*] Big arm—look how fat they'd be. Besides, wouldn't have a point up like that. Bats do have

			arms—little ones like that. We saw a real one [*like lecturing. Tells a long story about finding a dead bat in a dresser, and falls off chair as he says it was scary. Says they put it in a freezer, and it turned into an ice cube, and it was all very funny.*]
VI.	V	1.	Hmmm, oh, I know what this could be—you, you, you know the Indians have totem poles. This could be a totem pole. They're—like just building it—they're going to carve something—just building it—OK? Just building it—now they need—they just put it in and two Indians here.
VII.	V	1.	Naah—it could, yeah, it could be a chair—right? Pretend they're just making it, right? Pretend they're just putting it together, right? Pretend they're just putting the springs in, right? [*puts card away*] [*When shown card to locate, he points out white as "soft part" and illustrates with his arms the arms of the chair.*]
VIII.	V	1.	Ahhh-eeee, it is—it is an animal. It can be—see right here—head, feet, uh—and tail. That's all I can think of. [*Animal?*] It can be a lizard—I think it can. OK. [*Doing?*] Climbing, walking.
IX.	V	1.	A hammer—this side—right here, right side, down go bar—that's all I can think of. [*using pink*] [*Kind of hammer?*] Not one that has nail puller off—if this breaks has other side to use.
X.		1.	[*LP*] Scissors! [*very excited*] It isn't the goodest scissors. [*green*] Clips. [*leans back in chair holding card*] They get . . . [*What?*] They get hard.
		2.	This can be a telescope—don't say the goodest—all not the goodest, right? Just have to put some imagination in it. Boy, on a few of these—you do a lot of writing. [*Now F is walking around the room as he is asked which card he liked the best. He says, "the bat," then picks out V.*] 'Cause it really looks like it—it really looks like a bat. [*Didn't like*] I like all of them—I don't know which one I don't like. I like all of them. [*takes out VII, VI, and I*] Can't think of *anyone*. [*as puts cards back, says*] Oh, I left something out—it could be mirrors—and have only one thing.

Psychological Test Portrait

G: 6–11 Male

G was referred because of "uncooperative and defiant behavior in school." He cried easily when reprimanded, had poor achievement, and was reported to have verbally threatened suicide. There is a history of suicide in the family.

G is a tall, handsome child, with excellent motor coordination. He lives with his mother and a 9-year-old brother. His parents were divorced a year earlier.

During testing he was in continual motion, although he never left his seat. When he felt threatened or challenged, he became verbally aggressive and provocative. However, he recovered easily when there was no response to the provocation and worked diligently. Except for provocative behavior and restlessness, he worked with concentration and effort, and related in a good appropriate manner.

Cognitive Functioning

S–B, Form L–M: G achieved a MA of 11–4. His IQ was 168 with basal at IX and maximal AA. Obviously, with a basal at IX and an IQ of 168, G is an intellectually gifted child. His range on the Binet is consistent with extraordinary ability. He demonstrates particular giftedness in the functions of reasoning and memory.

B–G: The reproductions of the B–G figures are extremely well executed for a 6–11 child. G's perceptual motor coordination is excellent, and consonant with his performance in the S–B. In drawing the figures he was thoughtful and attempted a plan of organization.

FD: G's drawings are well defined, sex difference is obvious, the body is differentiated, and all parts (fingers, facial features) are present and in two dimensions. Therefore, G for this age expresses a high level of cognitive ability, again consonant with his S–B performance.

Rorschach: G uses form in a well-structured and delineated way. He can integrate various aspects of the blot well. However, the overall record is not commensurate with what one would expect from his achievement level on the S–B. One would have expected more original and creative responses, utilizing the greater organizing and synthesizing abilities he demonstrated in the S–B. Therefore, we conclude there is constriction and depression in the freedom to use the environment when faced with ambiguous stimuli.

TAT: G's stories show, as in the Rorschach, well-delineated and reality-oriented use of the picture with appropriate stories. The stories are reasonably well developed with use of organized sequencing. However, again, there is constriction in the elaboration of his themes and even an unwillingness to use the examiner's questions as encouragement for further development. In two instances (Cards 12 and 6 BM) following a strong affective discharge, his cognitive functioning is interfered with by a momentary slip. And in one instance (Card 5) there is a temporary loss of distance.

Summary Statement of Cognition: G is an obviously intellectually gifted boy with extraordinary talent in reasoning and memory. The only limitation in his precocious functioning is seen in his more constricted responses to ambiguous stimuli.

Dynamic Picture

S–B: G's responses are appropriate to the stimuli, relevant, and free from preoccupations.

B–G: The B–G does not reveal any particular dynamic problem.

FD: G drew a girl first in contrast to the more usual choice of representing one's own sex first. This suggests a heightened concern with the female. Although we would expect 5- to 7-year-olds to be concerned with phallic themes, G's preoccupation is excessive in both drawings—as, for example, in the long extended arms, fingers, and neck.

Rorschach: G expresses in the content of the Rorschach his conflict between aggressivity ("wolf," I, 1; "black-widow spider," IV) and passivity ("butterflies," II, 1; V, 1; VII, 2; VIII, 2 and 4; and X, 1 inquiry) which seems to be a core problem for him. Preoccupation with phallic themes is seen in exaggerated projections ("squirrels with long hats," III, 3; "a bug, his eighteen-foot-long head," X, 1 inquiry) or its opposite ("little head," II, 2; "little men," III, 4; "little head," X, 3 inquiry), and the specifying of missing parts ("little men with no feet," III, 4; "mouse, except no tail," VIII, 1).

TAT: We see more clearly in the TAT stories the Oedipal conflict with which G is struggling. Although a normal concern for his age, G expresses it as dangerous, potentially inviting of castration, and—in the instance of Card 5— total destruction. Castration anxiety is particularly evident in Cards 5, 8 BM, and 12M. There is a great deal of aggression expressed in his stories, but the poor victim has no one to help him. In 6 BM there is evidence of a regression to orality from the oedipal dangers as he associates through a parapraxis the "chimney" to the mouth that is missing.

Summary Statement of Dynamics: Obviously, G's cognitive functioning is free from dynamic concerns. In the projectives he displays a preoccupation with phallic themes and a conflict between aggressivity and passivity. He is still struggling with Oedipal concerns, which intensifies his fears of castration.

Defenses

S–B: G's very high level of functioning in this test is without any particular suggestion of defensive operation.

B–G: On figures 1, 2, 3, and 5, G counted all the dots on the card and recounted them several times (except for figure 5) as he drew. There is a suggestion of compulsivity seen in the achievement of complete accuracy in the number of dots on figures 1 and 2, and the near accuracy on figures 3 and 5.

Figures A through 4 show the use of an intellectual approach in the planning and the organization of a sequential order for each figure moving up the page. This plan does not work, however, because of the limits of the paper. Thus, figure 4 is limited by the edge of the paper, and this seems to induce the failure in planning seen in the collision of figure 5 with figure 3. For a 6-year-old, this adherence to a specific sequence is usual, but in G's case he provides a spatial arrangement more typical of an older child in the figures from A to 3. Therefore, the cut-off of figure 4 at the edge of the page and the collision of figures 5 and 3 appears to be more of a break in an otherwise well-executed Bender.

FD: G's compulsivity is seen in the clear delineation of features and in the careful details of five-fingered hands. His ability for organization is seen in the well-proportioned figures. The use of shading, although clearly related to G's anxiety and tension, indicates the effort to which he will go to deny impulses—that is, to cover up the body.

Rorschach: In comparison to other 6-year-olds, G makes greater use of constriction—seen in the use of tiny areas (I, 2 and 3), little head (II, 2), and limiting his responses to only a D (Card IX)—and compulsivity, seen in his great use of detailing in most of his responses. A strange flavor is added to some responses through his use of projection, "a wolf with four eyes and four ears" (I, 1), "if you put a red spot in the middle" (IV), "eighteen-foot-long head" (X, 1 inquiry), "tail going up and eighteen feet" (X, 3 inquiry), and "I don't know who put them there, but somebody did" (X, 3 inquiry). As mentioned under *Cognitive Functioning*, a certain detachment is present at other times through the use of cheap responses (for example, butterflies), which could imply the use of denial.

TAT: In this different task G makes use of different defensive techniques. There is little use of constriction and compulsivity with only one example of the latter ("windows") seen in the attention given to a missing detail on Card 8 BM. Projection is seen in its extreme form in Card 5, where the associative fantasies become more and more imbued with dangerous ideas and with accompanying panic. Projection is again seen in Card 8 BM, where he elicited castration anxiety in the report of the nightmare fantasy of the monster, and on Card 12 M, where he imposes murderous intent onto the man. Denial is used more extensively in this test than in the Rorschach—for example, when he says in Card 1, "I don't know what it is"; in Card 8 BM when he states, "nothing frightens me"; and in Card 12 M when he finally states that the murderer cannot murder him; and in Card 6 BM when he states they have no mouths so they cannot talk.

Rationalization is seen in Card 3 BM as an explanation for why the boy got hit, in Card 8 BM rationalization is used to support denial of any fear of his nightmares, and in Card 12 M rationalization is used to justify that the boy is not alone because the murderer is there.

G's uses of avoidance in this test are literally demonstrated. Avoidance is seen in Card 5 through avoiding the conflict implied in his story followed by ignoring both E and the card through shifting his attention to his drawing on the blackboard. When E tries to bring his attention back to the card, he maintains his avoidance through his insistence on the fantasy associated with his own drawing. In Card 8 BM he initially attempts to avoid the whole stimulus, but finally concedes. Then he successsfully engages E in his avoidance techniques so that both of them leave the card.

Summary Statement of Defenses: G employs a wide array of defensive strategies. He uses denial, avoidance, constriction, compulsivity, projection, and rationalization. He is successful in the use of these tactics except on the rare occasion when an association to danger interferes.

Affective Expression

S–B: This test, by its very nature, was the most enjoyable for G. He was obviously pleased with his achievement and E's positive response. He is comfortable even when presented with questions at the adult level that he could not answer. Occasionally he would try to answer, but was easily able to accept that he did not know.

B–G: G's affect was appropriate to the nature of the task. At the outset there was a suggestion of negativism in his interaction with the examiner over the positioning of the cards or the paper.

FD: In G's behavior his affective expression was cooperative and appropriate. Conflict in his affective experience is seen in the drawings in extreme tension (represented in excessive shading) along with a happy-go-lucky smile.

Rorschach: Generally G's overall affective reaction to the Rorschach was one of comfort and appropriate task-related behavior. Examining the content shows overcontrol in his affective expression to the degree that there is no spontaneous expression or free use of color. Colored areas are used only in a limited and carefully controlled way.

For a child of this age the lack of CF represents an unusual constriction in affective expression and spontaneity.

TAT: Throughout the testing (as indicated previously) and on the first two cards of the TAT, G maintains appropriate affective expression to the various demands made upon him. However, at the point of the third card administered (Card 5) there is a sudden intrusion of an extreme affective response. As pointed out under *Defenses,* G begins an avoidance to the card by drawing a house on the board; he then effects complete avoidance to the card stimulus by an angry response to *E*'s questions. He becomes increasingly agitated as he describes a new story relating to his drawing. The story is filled with danger and features a character yelling for help. The agitation mounts to the point of a mild loss of distance, indicating a feeling of being overwhelmed. The frightening nature of the next card, 8 BM, although he initially responds to the content, again elicits a frightening association of danger. He uses denial (see *Defenses*) to aid in recovery. The next card, 12 M, produces a more depressive reaction to another frightening story. By the final card presented (7 BM), he attains the easy affective control that has characterized the major part of his testing behavior.

Summary Statement of Affective Expression: Although G was generally comfortable in the testing situation and his affect was appropriate, test responses show an unusual constriction in affective expression and spontaneity.

Summary

G's protocol is an excellent example of the value of utilizing many different tests to achieve an understanding of a child. If one were limited to just the S–B or the Rorschach, one would not have a clear understanding as to the underlying reason for his presenting symptoms. In this particular child's case, the TAT provides critical information to corroborate what were only suggestions found in the Rorschach.

G is an intellectually gifted child whose defenses are prohibiting the use of his talents in more unstructured situations, particularly affectively laden situations. His core conflict, as expressed in the Rorschach and TAT, is between aggressive impulses and a need to be passively dependent. While typical for his age, evidence of castration anxiety and Oedipal strivings are overdetermined. His major defenses are denial, avoidance, and projection.

His propensity to be overwhelmed by anxiety in response to situations eliciting castration fears requires mobilization of these defenses. The energy required in these efforts at maintaining avoidance of fear is such that there is little free cathexes left over to invest in more neutral material, such as academic subjects. On the other hand, it is possible that his projection makes the nature of the learning-teaching process threatening, in that he must be forced into a more passive, dependent role, which triggers a defensive counteraction expressed either in "uncooperative and defiant behavior" or in "crying when reprimanded."

Diagnosis:

GAP:	Psychoneurotic Disorder, Anxiety Type
DSM III:	Axis I: 313.00 (Overanxious Disorder)

Axis II: None
Axis III: None
Axis IV: 4 (Moderate)
Axis V: 4 (Fair)

From this diagnostic picture of neurosis, psychotherapy is recommended to help G with his feelings of distress and his fears. Only through achieving more inner comfort or stability will G be able to realize his unusual intellectual gifts.

Psychological Test Data

G: 6–11 Male

Stanford–Binet, Form L

CA   6–11
MA   11–4
IQ   168

Vocabulary

1. A fruit
2. Something you put letters in to mail
3. You drink from it
4. A hole with water
5. [*Demonstrates on table*]
6. Something that goes under your dress—in the night
7. Something a lion—that's how the lion talks
8. [*Points to brow then to lash*]
9. A planet
10. He twirls balls on his head
11. I don't know
12. I don't know
13. When you can do something very well
14. No
16. I don't know
17. No
18. No

Year IX

1. +
2. a) Put trousers over head—wouldn't fit—can't go through one of legs.
   b) He didn't tell him the name—and said they'll find name—they won't know what letter it is.
   c) Smoked cigar and then put out fire—should put out fire first.
   d) I don't know anything.
   e) Snow can't be melted by water—by heat it can.
4. a) red; b) three; c) bear
5. a) 6¢; b) 4¢; c) 21¢

6. a) 6-5-2-8; b) 7-9-3-4; c) 9-2-6-3

Months credit at year IX = Basal

Year X

1. +
2. 6, 9, 6, 5, 5, 18, 5
3. a) don't know; b) curious—want to see something; c) I don't know; d) when something unusual, and it's new
4. a) They won't be able to hear the teacher's instructions, and they won't be able to hear the teacher.
   b) Car doesn't—you don't have to turn pedals and—two reasons? [*yes*] a car goes faster.
5. Dog, at, socks, shoes, dresser, telephone, book, house, clothes, feet, head, chair, paid, desk, air conditioner, shade
6. a) 4-7-3-8-5-9

Months credit at year X = 10

Year XI

1. +
2. a) I don't know.
   b) It only killed one person.
3. a) Like two wires. [?] No.
   b) I don't know.
   c) I don't know.
   d) You want somebody to behave.
   e) No
4. +
5. He didn't get a pet
6. a) all animals
   b) all plants
   c) all fabrics

Months credit at year XI = 6

Year XII

1. +
2. –
3. Man doesn't have his other hand
4. a) 9-7-3-8; b) 2-8-5-9-6
5. –
6. +

Months credit at year XII = 4

Year XIII

1. +
2. –
3. a) –
   b) –
4. a) spider; b) I don't know; c) bicycle
5. a) For the started home country—I can't figure it out—they're all mixed up
   b) My teacher correct my paper I asked—can't do it [*laughs*]
6. +

Months credit at year XIII = 4

Year XIV

1. –
2. a) 1; b) 2; c) 3; d) 6; e) 12; f) 24
3. At five or ten minutes to five. [*Why?*] I don't know—the father left, and brother left earlier than five.
4. a) Take five-pint can, fill it, and pour into three-pint can, and empty three-pint can, and have two pints left.
   b) Fills up nine pints, then fills up five pints and pours one pint out.
   d) Fill three-pint can, pour two pints out, and don't fill eight pints and have one pint left.
5. a) N; b) S; c) E
6. a) both seasons
   b) don't know
   c) don't know
   d) I don't know
   e) don't know

Months credit at year XIV = 4

Average Adult

1. –
2. –
3. a) I don't know.
4. a) almost a year; b) 20; c) don't know
5. a) I don't know what a proverb is.
6. a) E; b) N
7. Don't know—they're both things to do.
8. a) don't know
   b) When you can, like our cat is independent—he hits Nugget, our dog, in the nose.
   c) no
   d) no
   e) no

Months credit at year AA = 0

Bender–Gestalt

A. [*Holds pencil in all fingers against thumb—well done.*]
1. [*Counts all dots first, then connects them as he does them on sheet.*]
2. [*This time counts and does as goes along for first three, then counts all and does them; recounts; both on example and own.*]
3. [*Tries to rotate card; when E puts back, says*] Can't see it. [*then proceeds; counts aloud; rotates as does it.*]
4. [*Again attempts rotate; can't see it; not enough room at top of sheet; goes up from center of sheet.*]
5. [*To right on top of page: Counts and dots without looking at sheet—right over everything; says as he looks*] I can't help it—not much room.
6. [*Makes "gyup" sounds at each curve he has to do; turns sheet 180 degrees clockwise to do down curve, then underlines each of them.*]
7. [*Paper at ninety degrees; correct postion for card and paper.*]
8. [*Does diamond first, then surrounds it.*]

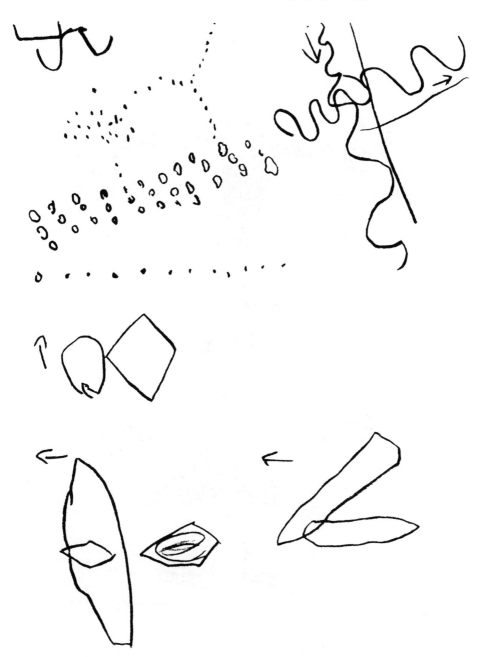

Figure Drawings

Rorschach

Inquiry

I.	4″	1. A wolf with four eyes and four ears	I.	1. Just the face
		2. Nose		
		3. Two feelers		

II. 14″V 1. A butterfly; eyes
            —antenna,
            mouth—feet
            with wings—
            white spot [W]
        2. A little head

III.   3″   1. Two men play-   III.
            ing football
            going to throw
            two balls
        2. Bow tie   2. Circle in middle
                                                and fins
        3. Two squirrels
            with long hats
      V   4. Two men, little   4. Don't know
            men with necks   where feet are.
            and no feet   There's hand and
                                                 mouth. Mouth
                                                 open.

IV.   8″V 1. Spider—two
            legs—heads, an-
            tenna, eyes, a
            black-widow
            spider—because
            black and it
            looks like it, if
            you put a red
            spot in the
            middle.

V.   4″   1. A butterfly—an-
            tenna—head
            and mouth—feet
            and wings—
            flying

VI.   4″   1. Tiger—whiskers,
            eyes in tiny
            dots; body—
            neck, head, and
            whiskers

VII. 7″   1. Two heads—
            rabbits—ears,
            feet, turning
            their heads
            back, ears and
            head makes
            look like a
            rabbit
        2. Butterly be-
            cause of wings—
            that's all

VIII. 8″   1. A mouse and   VIII.   1. Four legs—
            another mouse   mouth like it
                                              and ears and
                                              body looks like
                                              mouse, except
                                              no tail.

			2. Butterfly		2.	Wings—they didn't put head in—colorful, too.
			3. Wolf head		3.	Gray and has eyes with little dots—looks like a wolf and scares me [*joking as if*].
			4. Butterfly		4.	Same reason as other [2].
IX.	8"– 21"					
		V	1. Buffalo head— those pink part fat—can't see eyes—no pig head			
X.	6"		1. A bug	X.	1.	That gray has eighteen-foot-long head and two-wing butterfly wings.
			2. Spiders		2.	Four feet and head and has body like a spider.
			3. Rabbit head with two sea-horses on it		3.	The rabbit head has a nose, no eyes and ears. [*Seahorses?*] Little head and tail going up and eighteen feet and ears attached to the rabbit head. I don't know who put 'em there, but somebody did.
			4. Crabs		4.	Those are crabs because feet, tail, and round body.

TAT

1. A boy's watching something, and I don't know what it is. He looks sad—doing this [*why sad?*] probably because this won't work. [*Do?*] Fix it [*Then?*] feels happy.

3 BM. A boy lying down crying probably because probably somebody hit him—probably he hit them first. [*Happens?*] He starts to cry. [*What happens?*] I don't know. [*Anybody come help him?*] No, nobody.

5. Mother peeking in door—she's going to stay there—wants to see who yelled—and she didn't find anybody yelling. [*Who did yell?*] Her child, and she can't find him—he's hiding. [*Why?*] Because he yelled, and I told you that a million times. [*drawing house on board with smoke*] Look at all the smoke; who's burning? who's burning up? [*Happens?*] He just gets burned, that's all. Someone's up there [*the drawing of house*

on top] yelling "help." Can't you see someone up there yelling "help?" Part of house already burned up—house burning, chimney burning, man just burned—burning the ladder from fire engine—burning—help—got burned more—help fire engine come police car—he just got burned—all burned. . . .

[*She ever find boy?*] No, because house is already burning—too late, house all burned. Floor just burned up, fire coming toward us, [*moves from his drawing on board to picture*] blowing up—all the smoke is all over, blowing—bit gone—another bit—all gone. . . .

8 BM.   I don't want to do this. I just see a doctor with a knife, going to stick in the man—and windows, that's all I see. Boy found man outside when no one was there, and he can't find anybody to help. He just found a doctor—don't you know. [*Man?*] He got a bullet in his house, got a bullet in him that's what's wrong—who's that? [*draws on board*] [*What?*] A ghost—I have to write what he's saying. [*Do you have nightmares?*] Yes—ggrroow, monsters, nutty monsters—they fall apart—head comes off, arms come off—everything comes off. [*Is that what makes it scary?*] No, nothing frightened me—everything falls off—not off me, so what to frighten me?

12 M.   All I see is a man and a boy—man putting hand over boy's face. [*Why?*] Probably wants to kill him [*Why?*] I don't know why wants to kill him, but he must. [*Does he kill him?*] No, or I'll staple him. [*playing with stapler*] He just wants to kill him—thinks he can kill him with his hands. [*Who helps boy?*] Nobody [*He's pretty much alone?*] in the night especially—how is he alone with that man there? [*No help?*] No. [*Frightening?*] No, because he thinks he can kill him, and he can't.

6 BM.   A woman and man next to a window, nothing else. [*Doing?*] I don't know. [*Know each other?*] She's the grandma, and he's just born twenty years ago—just looking around —not talking. [*Why?*] Don't have any chimney to talk with; they don't have any mouth at least how gonna talk.

7 BM.   Boy and man talking about theirselves or somebody else. [*Know each other?*] Yes, grandfather and grandson. [*Like each other?*] Yes, of course they do. [*You have a grandfather?*] Yes, [*?*] about going places—we went to Disneyland two years ago.

Psychological Test Portrait

H: 5–10 Female

H is a 5–10 girl who was brought to the clinic by her parents because of a "burning ambition to grow up to be a boy, heightened sexual interests, and self-disparaging attitude."

H and her two younger brothers live with their parents, who are totally ineffective in providing discipline, control, and structure.

She is a youngster of average size with pretty features who initially gives, with sleepy eyes and a slack mouth, the impression of dullness and little animation or spontaneity. Stimulation from either inner excitement or *E* and the tests led her to reactions of inappropriate giggling, nonsense sounds, exaggerated gestures, anger, and hyperactive movements, including crawling. Reassurance and support from *E* could elicit more age-appropriate behavior and functioning for limited periods of time.

Cognitive Functioning

S–B, Form L–M: *H* achieved an IQ of 158, which places her in the "very superior" range. The age span was very broad, extending from a basal at VI to a maximal at XII. She is a gifted child with excellent capabilities in all areas of cognitive functioning. She has unusual capacities for conceptual and practical reasoning, abstract thinking, attention, concentration, and retention. Her failure to copy the diamond at year VII is not considered significant for a child aged 5–10.

Her achievement is even more striking when one considers the amount of intrusive fantasy of gory, sadistic themes, which resulted in motoric discharge due to her discomfort. Her discomfort was in part caused by her inability to maintain reality boundaries to her fantasies so that she repeatedly had to question whether they were true or not.

H's ability to function cognitively on a superior level is intact. This is maintained in spite of a constant ongoing struggle with her problem in distinguishing reality from fantasy.

B–G: The B–G, although not suitable for this age, can be helpful in understanding a complicated diagnostic picture. This is particularly true for *H* because her only failure in years VI, VII, and VIII of the S–B was in copying a drawing. In the B–G, however, she again demonstrates unusual ability in her perceptual-motor coordination for a 5-year-old, ruling out the possibility of perceptual-motor immaturity.

FD: Again, as in the B–G, *H* demonstrates excellent perceptual-motor coordination in her execution of clearly differentiated figures as well as body parts for each figure. Her realistic distinctions between the girl and the boy are denied in her verbalizations to *E* when she states with each, "I will make it partly boy, partly girl."

Rorschach: *H* was able to make use of each of the ten blots and offer more than sixteen responses, many of which made good use of the structure. This is a high number of responses for her age and reflects the high level of potential seen in the S–B.

H's responses can unpredictably become overrun with idiosyncratic associations, which result in a breakdown in her reality communication.

TAT: *H* again demonstrated her unusual cognitive ability in that her stories are elaborated and, often, well formulated far above the expectation for an average 5-year-old. Her language usage is superior. This is in spite of the obvious difficulties with the same intrusions of idiosyncratic associations seen in the other tests.

Summary Statement of Cognitive Functioning: In spite of the persistent intrusion of idiosyncratic associations, *H* is able to demonstrate a very superior cognitive ability across all areas of functioning. Her primary problem is in maintaining the distinction between fantasy and reality.

Dynamic Picture

S–B, Form L–M: *H*'s intellectual capacity and functioning are free from expression of dynamic conflict until she reaches Verbal Absurdities on Year IX. She responds to the cumulative stimulus of the dangerous content of the questions here with an associative story reflecting primitive oral concerns of death by ingestion.

B–G: *H*'s test performance does not contribute to our understanding of her dynamic picture.

FD: From her verbalization, *H* is obviously preoccupied with a sexual identification conflict, and, because of the intense scribbling within the body outlines, there is the suggestion that there may be a more primitive concern over body integrity.

Rorschach: Card II of the Rorschach elicits from *H* an initial response that suggests a preoccupation with the result of aggressive impulses associated with inner tension. She is triggered to associate blood with the color red, and later associates *dead* to bugs seen on Cards VII and X. Her association to Card VIII of colored ice-cream cone stimulates regression to a more primitive level in speech and motor behavior. This bespeaks an obviously unresolved oral dependency conflict.

TAT: The same dynamic conflicts are expressed in *H*'s TAT stories. She expresses her concern over aggression in the form of killing in Cards 1 and 16 and her concern over oral incorporation in Card 9GF. Also, oral dependency themes are portrayed in stories to Card 7 GF and Card 5.

Summary Statement of Dynamic Picture: *H* demonstrates considerable concern over aggression, which is quickly associated to oral dependency conflicts. There is such a degree of confusion in sexual identity that it would seem to stem from a more primitive concern over body integrity.

Defenses

S–B, Form L–M: In the S–B, when distressed, *H* attempts to avoid the provoking stimulus by silliness and giggling, but can recover when her need to achieve intellectually is challenged.

B–G: *H* begins the task by negativistic avoidance, but again is able to recover when challenged to achieve.

FD: *H*'s drawings are unusually large, and she limits herself only by the size of the paper. This suggests an effort on her part to defend against feelings of inferiority through her expansive rendition of figures.

Rorschach: *H*'s defenses hold up in the Rorschach to the degree that she is able to use the structure of the card adequately and, in some instances, appropriately. Her use of projection is seen in her second response to Card II and in her final responses to Cards III, VII, and X. Her major difficulty is in the failure of her defenses when faced with intrusions of primary process. This is seen in the contradiction expressed in her first response to Card I and the anthropomorphic percept expressed in her second response. Failure of defense is also seen in the regression in behavior and speech in response to Card VIII, where seemingly this regression is triggered by the oral content. However, *H* is able to recover very well on Card IX, probably because of help in restructuring through *E*'s exerting control over the regression.

TAT: In Card I of the TAT expansiveness is again reflected in *H*'s story where the master is both the creator and destroyer. This same defense against probable feelings of vulnerability is expressed in the story to Card 9GF, where the orally incorporated girl is alive and well the next day. *H* makes ineffective attempts at denial in her protestations that she "amen't" in the card (5 and 3) when queried about feelings.

Summary Statement of Defenses: Despite negativism used in service of avoidance and easy regression in both speech and motor behavior, *H* is capable of recovering when faced with a challenge to achieve intellectually. She is also able to use projection and expansiveness when dealing with feelings of inferiority and can utilize *E*'s help in controlling and restructuring.

Affective Expression

S–B, Form L–M: Before the S–B was begun, that is, when *H* entered the testing session, she immediately conveyed a sense of "dullness" to *E*. In other words, she did not appear to have the appropriate affect one would expect of a 5-year-old.

In the S–B, although she became somewhat anxious and sometimes clowned, she generally maintained her attention and persistently worked to achieve.

B–G: *H*'s anger, expressed through negativism, was most pronounced in the B–G. Motivated as she was to achieve, she reluctantly complied to drawing each new design.

FD: Both drawings are accompanied by unpleasant affect expressed through *H*'s self-deprecating remarks.

Rorschach: It is obvious that the introduction of color on Card II elicits another type of affective response from *H* than the achromatic cards. She expressed anxiety through a time delay on II and III as well as in her spontaneous vocalizations.

This same kind of anxiety is elicited again by Card VIII, and this time *H* gets carried away by her clowning with a quick regression to silly behavior.

Affectively, she recovers to Card IX, but again on X (similar to her behavior in the B–G and S–B), when anxiety is elicited, she is first angry, then produces an association with frightening content.

TAT: *H* attempts through avoidance to defend against anxiety aroused by several of the TAT cards. In addition, anger is expressed more often indirectly through squeezing a sponge, crumbling chalk, and so forth. Card 5, for some reason, elicits a similar type of affective response in spontaneous vocalization as seen to Card II in the Rorschach plus an association with frightening content.

Summary Statement of Affective Expression: *H* has great difficulty in dealing with her response to affectively laden material. She ranges from flatness of affect, to easily aroused anger, to regression, to more silly behavior.

Summary

H is an exceptionally gifted girl aged 5–10 who responds most appropriately and at the highest level when challenged by structured, intellectual, non-affectively-laden stimuli. She is quick to regress to infantile modes when anxiety is aroused by affect. The degree and extent of her regression is sufficient to lead to the intrusion of primary-process thinking, overwhelming her reality-testing and coping mechanisms. At the same time, if given support and structure, she has an excellent capacity to recover and again perform appropriately. Her affective range is limited and curtailed by intensely unresolved conflicts at the oral dependency level of development. Thus, she appears affectively flat or uncomfortable, tense, anxious, or distressed.

Diagnosis:

GAP:	Psychoneurotic disorder, anxiety type. (We would modify this with "severe.")
DSM III:	Axis I: 309.21 (Separation Anxiety Disorder)
	Axis II: Borderline traits

Axis III: None
Axis IV: 4 (Moderate)
Axis V: 5 (Poor)

It is because of the variability and unreliability in the various spheres of ego functioning that *H* is diagnosed as preborderline. She is at risk for developing into a borderline child and, given her pathological family interaction, she is at risk for developing psychosis. Treatment is urgently needed with both individual therapy for *H* and family therapy (or marital therapy for the parents).

Psychological Test Data

H: 5–10 Female

Stanford–Binet, Form L–M

CA   5–10
MA   8–10
IQ   158

Year VI

1. +
2. a) A dog can't fly, and bird can, and has long ears, and bird doesn't [*etcetera*].
    b) Slipper you don't go out in, and boot you do.
    c) Glass you could cut yourself, and wood you could get splinters.
3. a) one wheel; b) one ear; c) one shoelace; d) a handle; e) one finger
4. a)   +; b) +; c) +; d) +
5. a) glass; b) swims; c) sharp
6. a)   +; b) +

Months credit at year VI = Basal

Year VII

1. a) He doesn't have the umbrella on his head—'cause no room for it. [*referring to sheet top*]
    b) He's using the saw upside down—how did he ever get started?
    c) Dog's face looks like it's not goin' to chase rabbit, and his track going this way, and rabbit's going the other way.
    d) They're sitting outside in rain—also, chair isn't right. Two legs not on ground and leaving door open, too.
    e) Cat isn't chasing the mice.
2. a) Wood could start a fire and so can coal.
    b) Both round
    c) Both move
3. [*Failure on all three trials at copying diamond*]
4. a) Bring him to police
    b) Replace it
    c) Run
    d) The wind on the sail
    e) Just talk to them and tell them not to do it
    f) I don't know—ask the police

5. a) short; b) black; c) feathers; d) rough
6. a) 3-1-8-5-9

Months credit at year VII = 10

Year VIII

1. +
2. a) Wet Fall; b) I don't remember; c) in a farm; d) father; e) Boy fell down and got covered with mud from foot to head.
3. a) He got killed, so how could he get alive again?
   b) How could he . . . lose both arms and hands are on his arms.
   c) A hill can't go down all the way and go down into ground.
   d) If went half way round and half way to go back, why didn't he go all the way around because the same amount?
4. a) Baseball you play with, and orange you eat, and baseball and orange are both round.
   b) Airplane takes you places and could have people on, and kite doesn't, and kite and airplane could both fly.
   c) Both have water, and ocean has waves, but river has much smaller waves.
   d) Penny and quarter are both money, and a penny has less money than a quarter.
5. (See VII, 4)
6. Wednesday; Friday; Saturday

Months credit at year VIII = 12 basal

Year IX

1. a) −; b) −
2. a) No head hole in trousers
   b) Man should go look in mailbox
   c) Fire be all gone by time finished cigar—if burned to fire—why smoke and waste time—people all be dead. [H *tells a "spooky story" told to her about mountains with ants and bees in the millions who ate a boy up.*] I got scared with that. He said it's only fake—unless it might come true. I'm scared, but we don't have mountains here.
   d) I wasn't even born then. [R] I don't know.
   e) I don't know.
3. a) +
4. a) red; b) [*no answer*]; c) bear; d) rose
5. a) 10¢; b) 30¢
6. a) 6-8-5, I don't know; b) 7-4-9-3-7; c) 9-3-2-6

Months credit at year IX = 4

Year X

1. −
2. +
3. a) I don't know; b) [*shrugs*]; c) [*shrugs*]
   d) Something that people don't know what it is till they open it.
4. a) Because higher grades can't work and also because can't listen to teacher
   b) Auto could go faster, and also you can't go all kinds of places with a bike and can with auto.
5. [*Starts to say alphabet, then*] I can't do; [*keeps talking*] don't know what to say; I don't know what to say.
6. a) 4-7-3-8-5-9

Months credit at year X = 6

Year XI

1. [*Cannot do designs*]

2. a) What does hanged mean? I don't know
    b) I don't know
3. a) Something that could get hooked onto something else, like a train, and comes into long train
    b) I don't know
    c) Never heard of that
    d) Never heard of that
    e) Nope
4. a) +
5. That sounds silly, especially about burning his clothes—all his clothes? Burn him?
6. a) All alive
    b) Both things
    c) Wool and cotton and leather are all soft
    d) Don't know
    e) Don't know

Months credit at year XI = 2

Year XII

Months credit at year XII = Maximum

Bender–Gestalt

1. [*Jabs pencil onto paper; no pencil control or deliberate dot making.*]
2. Have to do all those circles? Ay yi yi!
3. [*Now began to count—very tired—lazyish—getting tired. Counts back on groups—repeats count—until finally gets it set.*] I got six to do more—one now—I only got five . . . [*etcetera*]
4. [*Curve drawn first.*]
5. Hard. [*Ask her please to do accurately after three, and she does try on the remainder.*]
6. Hard.
7. This looks hard, hard. [*works at it*] I did this wrong—what do now?
8. I'm going to school today—today is a school day.

Figure Drawings

[*Female*] I know what I'm going to do—make this partly boy and partly girl—gonna be a ballerina girl. [*shows me the skirt*] This is stupid! Look at those long legs—finished with the giant.

[*Male*] Ugh, look at that stupid hair—looks more like a girl's. Look, the nose is up too high—yach, terrible. [*as looks at face*] I do terrible drawings—I draw better in school. [*returns to female to put on arms had omitted at point where putting arms on male*] Boy's got on long pants and long legs. [*extends legs down from bottom*]

Rorschach

I. 2" 1. A bull with no nose
          and sharp
          teensly, weensly
          nose
       2. A bridge with a chin
          and fat cheeks. [*Are
          chin and cheek part
          of bridge?*] Yes.

II. 10" 1. Eeyaaa—don't see
           anything except
           blood dripping
           down the bell, a
           bell.
        2. Top part of blood
           too—piggy blood.
           [*See pig?*] No.
           [*What makes it look
           like blood?*] It's red,
           so blood.

III. 43" 1. A nose and a smiling
            face, ear, eye [smile
            denied]
         2. With water in the
            middle here

IV. 2" 1. A pig [*points to
           lower center
           projection*]
           grunt, grunt
        2. A lion—looks
           like whiskers

             IV. 1. Just the head
                    of the pig and
                    whiskers of him

                     2. Lines in it

V. 2" 1. A bat

             V. 1. Wings—little feet
                    or legs—anten-
                    nas—wings out
                    there flying

VI. 26" That's hard.
         1. A lion, and here's
            the big head, and
            here's an eye, here's
            another eye, the
            whole thing is a
            lion.
         2. Bone, bone [?] little
            things sticking out
            [*side* D]

VII. 38" Never saw a picture look-
           ing like that.
         1. A big black bug,
            and it's killed in the
            middle. It's killed
            dead because if
            weren't dead would
            have part of it still
            here in here, [*in-
            dicates* S] and it
            doesn't.

VIII.   4″   1. This looks like a colored ice-cream cone. [*makes believe licking it—giggles*] Mmm, that's good. [*puts card on E's head*] That's all I see—a colored ice-cream cone. [*goes off about room—to go into things*] [*Very quick regression in overt behavior— crawling—speech is play on baby talk—etcetera.*]

IX.   3″   1. Another ice cream cone—three different flavors. No, I mean it's Jello—mixed Jello. [*What about it makes it look like jello?*] Very kind of light and all different colors mixed—mi-ixed.

X.   3″   1. A dead bug—so many different kind of bugs are dead here and there, and here and there, [*vague staccato-like jabs at the card*] that's all.
Here's a spider—here's a—all spiders—different kind of spiders. I was in the country where my big brother is, and we saw a big spider, and it was alive. One side had no legs, and other did, and it had polka dots and was walking.

TAT

1. What is this thing? It looks like a monster. He was working on this monster, and now it is done—no more. [*Before?*] [*She spoke very quietly.*] Before he started about a minute ago, now he is done, wow! That was quick—here is the monster [*picks up sponge*] he was working on—I have to squish him. [*wrings sponge*] [*Later?*] The monster will go out and kill—now that the monster killed everybody in what city? New York—the master of the monster will now kill him.

7 GF. Before I didn't have a baby, now I will have a baby—here she is. Now here she is, what do you want to do with her? [*Later?*] Later, she will have lunch, and then she will go and have a nap, and I will take her out to play then come home. Today we will meet daddy and then go home and have supper. Then I will have to put baby down, and father and me will talk. You know in my school we don't even have homework. [*Feel about baby?*] Baby is very soft and nice. We shall use her to—use her for—we will use her to—uh—I don't know. [*What?*] I don't know—ice cream, she will eat ice cream wherever we go. Yaa-oh-pheu.

5. Now mommy will open the door to let me in to my room for now baby is up—my little brother baby. [*Why do you go to room?*] Because I want to get a book for baby for me to read to baby.
Will this clay [*holding old hardened mass*] get soft—if this building falls on it? [*goes to window*] Aye yikes, aye yikes, is this floor ten? Ummm, ah—it's higher than that building—that building is very old and dirty.
[*Mother puts her in room?*] To get a book for sister to read to baby [*How does sister feel about baby?*] Baby is soft and nice. [*Feel?*] I don't know because I amen't on there—I am not on the picture.

16. What are you showing me? This is nothing—I don't see anything but paper.
Once up time a little boy and little girl who lived in the jungle, they went out one day to kill the gorillas, and that's what I'm going to do, kill the paper. What's it for? How make up story with plain paper?

3 GF. Nothing. [*Doing?*] Putting hand over face to think. [*About?*] What she's going to do when she goes out. She's going to watch TV, and that's all. [*Feel?—happy?*] No, unhappy—I don't know why. [*What would make her unhappy?*] The children are jumpy and wild and everything. [*Do?*] She goes out in the living room and she—shimm shesu, and she watches TV. [*Children feel?*] They're outside jumping and getting wild, and she told them not to. [*they feel*] I don't know because I amen't one of the children. They don't know she's watching TV—are outside.

9 GF. They're going to the beach, and I don't want to see any more of these cards. Their little girl will go into water [*Happen?*] and she will play into—in the water. [*crumbling chalk all over place*] She goes out very deep, and she will get lost in the water. She got eaten by a whale. [*Feel?*] Sad. [*They do?*] Go home and next day come back looking for her—she is still alive—the whale didn't eat her up—she just got caught in his mouth. [*Girl feel?*] OK—lying on beach. [*When whale got her?*] She felt warm, you know, warm—but because whale's water that he had in mouth was there a long time, and she was floating in it, and she got hot. [*continued crumbling chalk and asking how much longer*]

8 GF. She is thinking what she will do with her children and her husband tomorrow. They will go on to the beach. [*And?*] I don't know [*asking how much longer*].

2. The farmer is going onto the farm. He has a big tractor. He's taking the horse on. Now he got the horse in the tractor. He will go fetching some more horses. He has millions of them. [*Other people?*] The people [*women*] will stay right where they are and wait for them to come around, then people will get in—had to get horses first. It's all right if he left people because had no room. They could have ran behind, but they didn't want to—that would be a silly idea, wouldn't it? And each stayed where they were. [*Feel?*] felt all right because he wanted to stay behind. No more cards!

Psychological Test Portrait

J: 5–5 Male

J is a boy aged 5–5 who has no friends, is impulsive, will hit or bite on occasion, has speech difficulties, a sing-song voice, is obsessively preoccupied with boats, and is selective in food. At school he has poor impulse control, is unable to concentrate, is aggressive, has low frustration tolerance, and has poor reality testing.

He is an angelic-looking blond child whose behavior in the testing sessions replicated the referral problems. Additionally, there seemed to be some wish to gain acceptance from *E*, which *E* was able to utilize in eliciting cooperation.

Cognitive Functioning

WPPSI: During the intelligence test he was extraordinarily hyperactive, negativistic, destructive, and uncooperative. Testing required constant reiteration of limit setting and making bargains. He was able to cooperate better on the performance items where personal interaction was at a minimum. In spite of this kind of behavior, *J* was still able to achieve an average IQ, suggesting a much higher potential. Another indication of a higher potential is the higher level he at times can achieve within subtests. A sudden correct response, after many failures, demonstrates the importance of including all test items of any subtest when dealing with an unusual child.

J's language varied from nonsense sounds to well-articulated sounds, and from meaningless content to well-formulated content.

Obviously from the protocol, J's cognitive functioning is interfered with by extraneous material, making his above-average achievement on Arithmetic, Picture Completion, and Block Design all the more remarkable. Due to the inconsistencies in performance and intrusion into cognitive functioning, one cannot predict when or where he will achieve.

B–G: The B–G is not suitable for this age, but, with this type of child, one wants to try different areas of functioning. J, however, responded to this task with effort, but negativism and impulsivity interfered with accuracy of production.

FD: He refused to draw a person.

Rorschach: J is able to use structure in a far more mature fashion than one would expect from a 5-year-old. He is able to integrate and organize more complex percepts than the average. This ability, again, supports the indication in the WPPSI of a far superior intellectual potential than his average achieved IQ.

In contrast to this unusual ability is also the equally unusual intrusions of idiosyncratic images and/or language.

TAT: J was unable to respond to the TAT pictures with any comprehensible language production and became extremely hyperactive, throwing the cards around the room, trying to tear them, and so forth. Therefore, the CAT was attempted.

CAT: In spite of the overwhelming idiosyncratic associations to the cards, J is still able to communicate that he perceives the cards realistically.

Summary Statement of Cognitive Functioning: In spite of the continual intrusion and expression of J's idiosyncratic world, he still was able to demonstrate average abilities in cognitive functioning. Although there are indications of superior potential, to all intents and purposes his unpredictability and erratic responsiveness make his average achievements all the more remarkable. His erratic responsivity was also seen in his use of language.

Dynamic Picture

WPPSI: Rather than any clear-cut dynamic concern emerging in the content of the WPPSI, there are only slight hints of fear of bodily harm and concern with aggressive impulses. The important issue in the WPPSI is seen in the discrepancy between his behavior in response to the Verbal tests, where he fooled, joked, threw things, and was negativistic, and his behavior on the Performance items, where he proceeded without these distractions for the most part. The exception on the Verbal test was in the Arithmetic which held his interest and did not elicit an affective response. It is evident that, where the interaction is with inanimate objects, J is able to concentrate with greater focus than where there is a need for personal interaction. Therefore, it can be hypothesized that there is a threat posed by interpersonal interaction to his need for control, a sense that he can feel some security only with impersonal objects.

B–G: The most striking quality of his B–G production is their largeness. A separate page had to be used for the majority of figures. This suggests the possibility of expansiveness or grandiosity.

FD: He refused to draw a person.

Rorschach: The salient dynamic theme in the Rorschach responses is the failure of differentiation of self from others. For example, on Card I is the difficulty in one versus two people; on Card VII there is a personalized intrusion with two Indians becoming one Indian, and then himself; then on Card VIII, after achieving a well-integrated original percept of a boat, J goes on to become anxious, seemingly in response to his association of "no river." This suggests that the preoccupation with boats for J is a total identification of self with boat so that the missing water becomes as threatening as the loss of a life force.

   Although the lack of fixed sexual identity is not unusual for this age, his is represented in a totally fluid fashion on Card I.

   The suggestion of grandiosity seen in the B–G is again hinted at in the Rorschach content of the percepts of "growing a big head" (Card I), "King Kong" (Card IV), and the "Zarn, it goes oom, oom, and it breaks the people up, everybody" (Card VI).

CAT: J's identity is very confused throughout the stories. When identification is clear, it is usually with the victim. Therefore, often within the story content he appears to be in the position of experiencing fear from feelings of vulnerability. It is speculative to infer, as we do, that J's identity is still considerably fused with his mother, intensifying feelings of vulnerability. This is suggested in Card 8, where he can express only the feelings she wants of him. At 5 years of age, he still has experiences from various psychosexual developmental levels. Some, particularly his Oedipal wishes, result in exaggerated expressions and retributions (see Cards 2 and 4). Similarly, Card 5 elicits sexual implications with the use of denial expressed in "hiding," followed by his own attempts to "hide" the card.

Of dynamic significance is the total lack of any reference on Card 1 to any oral dependent issues, even to the point of not identifying the chicks as "babies" or the chicken as "mommy."

Summary Statement of Dynamic Picture: The most salient feature of J's very disturbed dynamic picture is the lack of individuation of the self from the world around him. He has not developed to the level where conflict exists and all psychosexual levels of development are represented in a hodgepodge of exaggerated expression and discharge.

Defenses

WPPSI: Summarizing what has already been described under *Cognitive Functioning* and *Dynamic Picture,* J handled the WPPSI in a highly defensive manner. When faced with the demand for interpersonal interaction, he became negativistic, evasive, or avoiding. He avoided the demand of the task by hyperactivity, somewhat destructive behaviors, and foolishness.

B–G: Again, negativism is seen in J's response to the demands of the B–G situation. He performs erratically and avoids any prolonged contact with the task.

FD: He refused to draw a person.

Rorschach: The main defensive tactic taken in the Rorschach is regression. His language moves from comprehensible language to unintelligible sounds and words. In most of his performance he accomplishes good percepts followed by regression. Regression is seen in noisy, hyperactive, acting-out behavior and in his verbalizations. Initially in response to E's questioning and later spontaneously, as he describes his percept, regressive behavior continues. Cards VI and IX elicit total nonsense words as a response followed by grossly destructive content. It is striking that J's option in handling those often-rejected cards is not to refuse to respond, but rather to give those regressed responses in conjunction with uncontrolled, aimless, motoric discharge. With each new card he is able to mobilize again through the use of his cognitive abilities to come up with a decent response, no matter how extreme the regression has been. Also, it is noteworthy that his first attempt to handle the red on Card III is his typical regression into the use of nonsense words (III, 2), followed by a good response to the next red area, followed again by a regressive response (III, 4), "zoands."

CAT: The regression so prominent in the Rorschach is strikingly absent in *J*'s CAT productions. His verbal productions are well organized and clear, with the only difficulty in pronunciation rather than a regression into nonsense words. There are two instances of denial. It is unclear in the first example (Card 3) why he must deny the mice, but in the second example (Card 7), he states clearly the reason for the denial, "because he's a very big tiger."

Summary Statement of Defenses: *J*'s use of defenses is as unpredictble and erratic as the rest of his functioning. When faced with the need for interpersonal interaction, he becomes negativistic, evasive, and avoiding, or regresses into motoric discharge with unintelligible language. At best, he can mobilize his intellectual potential to provide some coherent productions.

Affective Expression

WPPSI: The affective expression in the WPPSI was inappropriate, inconsistent, and unpredictable. *J* was at times excited, depressed, furious, or happy, and would contradict his angry expression at times by laughing and giggling as he verbalized or acted out the anger. The only relationship between the task and the affect was when, at those times that he could cooperate, he seemed happy (for example, in Comprehension and after the Block Design when he was able to respond to a request to put the blocks away).

B–G: *J* was consistent in his affective expression throughout the B–G, being angry, annoyed, irritated, and in a state of tension and impatience.

FD: He refused to draw a person.

Rorschach: *J* gradually loses distance in the Rorschach, becoming increasingly agitated vocally and physically as the stimulus seems to evoke idiosyncratic associations. Therefore, we can observe him exhibiting only increasing agitation and distress.

CAT: *J* is most at ease with his feelings in this task, seen before only in Comprehension in the WPPSI and the first two cards in the Rorschach. His affect is most appropriate to the task as well as to the content, and, therefore, his relatedness is at a maximum in this test. To the last card (Card 8) he unexpectedly produces a story that seems to explain the inappropriate smiling that accompanies his negativism and anger—that is, "he pretends he's happy."

Summary Statement of Affective Expression: *J*'s affective expression is extraordinarily labile and inappropriate. He was able to express appropriate affects in only one test.

Summary

J is a boy aged 5–5 who presents with many problems. He has no friends, is impulsive, will hit or bite on occasion, has speech difficulties, a sing-song voice, and is obsessively preoccupied with boats. At school he has poor impulse control, is unable to concentrate, and becomes aggressive because of low frustration tolerance and poor reality testing.

The testing confirms the suggestion in the referring problem that J is a very disturbed child. His central problem is the most basic one of ego identity. There is evidence that J has not negotiated the earliest separation and individuation phases, so there is very little sense of self. Therefore, he is at the mercy of any environmental stimuli as well as internal impulses.

The problem is seen in all of the tests in his erratic and unpredictable behavior and language, varying inconsistently from uncontrolled impulse-driven behavior and unintelligible language to very superior achievement for a 5-year-old.

J demonstrates a typical profile on psychological testing of schizophrenia. Consistent with his erratic performance is the emergence of exaggerated psychosexual drives and wishes. At the same time he is seemingly unable to express more ordinary concerns of the 5-year-old in dependency versus autonomy issues. Therefore, in contrast to a more neurotic picture is the lack of conflict and expression of anxiety. Rather, we see behavior that we can only infer is the product of fear, sometimes bordering on panic, at the level of intensity of one who could be totally annihilated.

Diagnosis:

GAP:	Psychoses of Infancy and Early Childhood, Early Infantile Autism	
DSM III:	Axis I:	299.00 (Infantile Autism, full syndrome present)
	Axis II:	V71.09 (No diagnosis)
	Axis III:	None
	Axis IV:	3 (Mild)
	Axis V:	7 (Grossly impaired)

Despite the poor prognosis for this diagnosis, J demonstrates evidence of several areas of adaptability. He is able to use denial at times to reduce the perceived threat. He, at times, demonstrates the ability to recover from gross regression, and, most important, at times he was able to take pleasure in performing a task for E, indicating an ability for relatedness at those moments. A residential treatment center specializing in schizophrenic children is recommended.

Psychological Test Data
J: 5–5 Male

WPPSI

		Scaled Score
Verbal Tests		
Information		13
Vocabulary		(Omitted)
Arithmetic		11
Similarities		9
Comprehension		10
Sentences		(7)
	Total	50

Performance Tests		
Animal House		10
Picture Completion		12
Mazes		8
Geometric Design		9
Block Design		11
	Total	50

	Scaled Score	IQ
Verbal Scale	50	100
Performance Scale	50	100
Full Scale	100	100

Information

		Score
1.	Points	1
2.	One there, one there two	1
3.	This little piggy went to market	0
4.	A grin [*laugh*] blinds—pencils—soda— funny people [*Q*] [*Funny?*] jumps and yells. That's what really comes in bottles—funny people.	1
5.	Helicopters—fishes—and sink in water	1
6.	Green and blue	1
7.	Zebra, cocktron—I said—want to know what it does? Zee-ba cock cow—it eats everything it sees [*fooling*]	0
8.	I want to play—goat farm	1
9.	Sun that's what comes in the night, day —moon [*joking—laughing*]	1
10.	He lawks like a man—two legs. [Q] He'll have gins on his head.	1
11.	Cock-house-meeows	0
12.	[*Takes two "houses," holds with hands*] I'll show you. [*piles of two matching blocks*]	0

13. Cause—rooms mice [*rep. Q*] two
    rounds—we will send the cards by—voo
    —buy gas [*throwing things over the*
    floor around the room]   0
14. Cook it   1
15. Soven kinds [*very hyperactive all over—*
    grabbing things]   0
16. Five   1
17. I don't know   0
18. Very hard   0
19. Very hard   0
20. [*No response*]   0
21. Brown   0
22. 2 + 2   0
                                                    ____
                              Total   10

Animal House   10

Vocabulary (*Omitted because of lack of cooperation.*]

Picture Completion
1. Don't know like that   1
2. A wheel   1
3. Arm   1
4. A sun [*indicates correctly*]   1
5. Girl's mouth   1
6. One of his ears   1
7. One of those   1
8. One boy   1
9. A nail   1
10. These there   1
11. That—missing there   0
12. One of those   1
13. A number   0
14. One of these   1
15. Number   0
16. I don't know [*points correctly*]   1
17. One of those   1
18. Door   1
19. One buttons   0
20. What's missing there?   0
21. One of those   0
22. That—some of that   0
23. One of those   (1)
                                                    ____
                              Total   15 (16)

Arithmetic
[*Excellent cooperation to 15, then begins fooling*] Total 12

Mazes
1A.   0
1B.   1
2A.   2

2B.	0
3A.	1
3B.	0
4.	0
5.	2
6.	0
7.	0
8.	0
9.	0
10.	0
Total	6

Geometric Design

1.	1
2.	1
3.	1
4.	2
5.	0
6.	0
7.	1
8.	0
9.	0
10.	0
Total	6

Similarities

1.	Car	1
2.	Dresses	1
3.	Guns	1
4.	Plate (*Repeat?*] cup	1
5.	Not eat	1
6.	Guns—ball, [*demonstrates by throwing things across room*] and nobody takes ball	1
7.	Pen	1
8.	Women	1
9.	Dink	1
10.	Both	0
11.	A gun and a nightgown you wear	0
12.	I don't know	0
13.	I don't know	0
14.	Money	2
15.	Cause they look the same	0
16.	Cause they—so they could get mice	0
	Total	9 (11)

Block Design

1.		2
2.		2
3.		2
4.		2
5.		2
6.	35″	1

7.		2
8.		0
9.		0
10.	[singing "I know where they belong" as returns to box]	0
	Total	13

Comprehension

1.	'Cause they may make a fire	2
2.	'Cause then everybody'll say you are dirty; wash your hands and face	0
3.	You have to go to the hospital	1
4.	To see what time it is	2
5.	You have to—say Daddy says you can buy another	2
6.	'Cause then you go to the potty	0
7.	Then the body would see—see out	2
8.	Then everybody will like zee	0
9.	Then they would get sick—then they wouldn't have any money	1
10.	'Cause the candle will make a fire	1
11.	Then they'll get even more sicker	1
12.	You just have to go to another store	2
13.	You have to call the mommy	1
14.	Bricks don't hurt you. Bricks don't make you bleed.	0
15.	'Cause they do bad things.	0
	Total	15

Sentences

A.		1
B.		1
C.		2
1.		2
2.		2
3.	Found three houses in the bird house	0
4.	And a brown teddy bear [no longer listening]	0
5.		0
6.	Peter could like a cowboy	0
7.	Can give you a stomachache	0
8–10.		0
	Total	8

Bender–Gestalt

A.
1. [*Holds pencil up in fist.*]
2. [*Holds pencil in fist and stabs at the paper.*]
3. [*All over*] That's a hard one [*back and forth, left—right—left.*]
4. [*Rotates—says no room for curve, then produces strange bit—resistive.*]
5. [*Rotates but closes circle and makes line.*]
6. [*Makes dots and then scribbles.*]
7. [*Ask him to try—more attempt. Quickly and with need to be done.*]

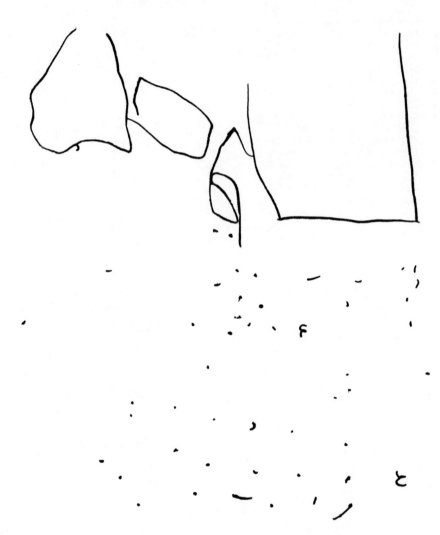

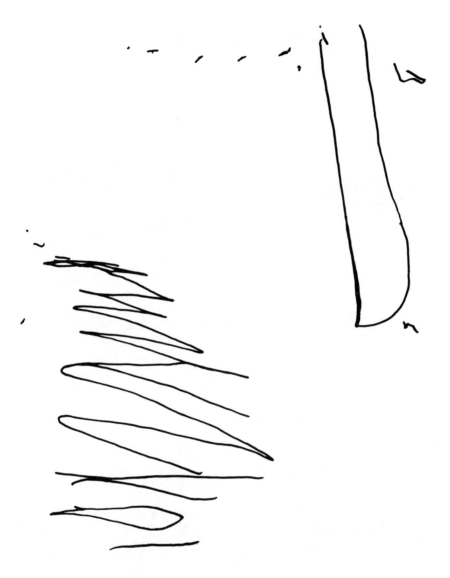

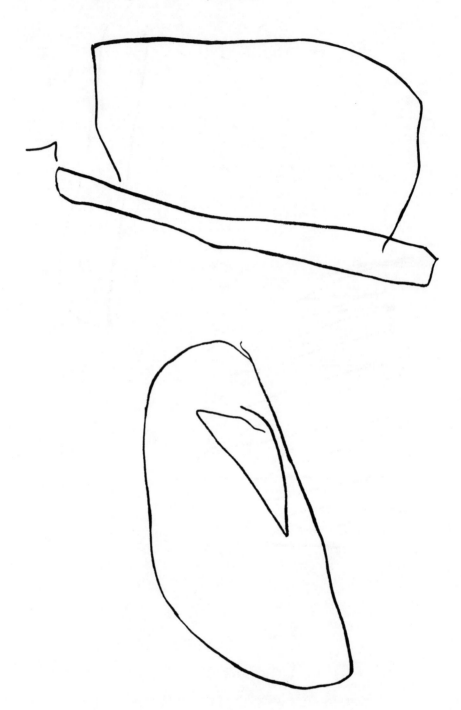

Rorschach

I. People, and they are both the same people. [*Q*] They are men—women and are growing great big head. [*side* D]

II. 1. Dogs with sodda say—I see them saying woof, woof.
2. Windows. [*S*] 'Cause windows don't have anything.
3. Flag. [*bottom red*] I see it float, 'cause I see float.

III. 1. 'Cause two people and—standing like that [*leg up to demonstrate*]
2. Frisses [*sic!*] [*top* D *red*]
3. Ribbons [*center* D] A ghost ribbons because ghosts live in the city. It's a ghost city, where ghosts live. [*Are ghosts frightening?*] Yes, they go whooo [*loudly*] whooo, like that [*noisy, hyperactive, acting out verbalizations*].
4. Zoands [*?*] fishes
5. Rain [*center bottom light gray areas*]

IV. That a mm—tintong cartoon. [*King Kong?*] Yes, he goes, aah [*jumps, pounds fist*] ooo—like that.

V. A bat—aah—oo, bat amboo there's teeth and looking at Pintom. [*King Kong*] He's going to fight King Kong. Show him King Kong. [*card IV set aside before presenting V*]

VI. A zarm. [*Zombie?*] It goes oom, oom, [*dashes about*] and it breaks the people up—everybody.

VII. 1. Two Indians injuns, which are the same indarns, [*How are they the same?*] because I see malark [*Rep?*] 'cause I am. They are saying sss, sss [*Why?*] 'cause they are.

VIII. 1. A sailing boat—there's no river. I don't see the river—sails. [*upper two thirds*] Where's the river? Every rit is on the sailboat. [*steps on E's foot—holds the pen hand so E cannot write. When E persists, he pinches tighter and tighter.*]

IX. A zom—a set [*What is it?*] it's a breaking away. It breaks away from a road [*?*] [*running about—sounds—ignores E*].

X. Fondues [*Funnel?*] yes; pink—paint; yes, funnel [*top* D *gray*], and all of that is the paint—pictures of paint [*Looks like paint?*] 'cause it's gars [*?*] [*no response, hanging out window*].

CAT

9. A baby—she looks like a rabbit. She is thinking when her mommy will come. She was seeming. [*Screaming?*] No. [*Sleeping?*] No—she doesn't know when her mommy will come. [*Is she frightened?*] Yes [*Why?*] 'cause she is.

3. Yes, a lion. He—he's pretending he's a king, and a mice is here. He doesn't know where the mice is. [*poked finger with pencil point through a piece of thin cardboard—wanting to stab lion. E asks him not to do it, he then suddenly stabs finger with pencil.*]

4. A mommy got a bad dog, and she's going to fuck him. [*mean?*] It means you are dead. [*He repeats sentence with "fuck" three times as I repeat question—what?*] She's going to fuck him. [*with a smile*]

2. A bear—about a bear, about a daddy getting his mommy, and that little boy is crying [*Why?*] because that mommy is going to fall down. [*Happens to her?*] She's going to die—that's the end of the story.

1. That's—all the beds—and one bird is singing about her—singing about that [*shadowed figure*] about a sick—her [*A chicken?*] yes—nothing—she's just saying—now you just sit there.

5. That bear is lying the wrong way. [*sees only one in crib*] [*How come?*] Bears don't know how to sleep. Mommy is on top of bed, and Daddy is on top of bed. [*Doing?*] Hiding. [*From?*] I don't know—doing nothing else—that's the end of the story [*pushes it away—tries to hide it*].

7. Tigers biting that monkey—he doesn't because he's a very *big* tiger, and he's standing on a stone and saying "ahahah"—like that, does that seem anurving? [*Is it?*] Yes. [*Happens to monkey?*] Noffing, he's getting novay. Something happens to tiger. Monkey is saying "no, no," and climbing up the tree.

8. That monkey is saying, "now play with your toys like I told you to," and he doesn't like that. [*Do?*] He does what see [*she*] says. [*Do?*] He pretends he's happy. [*Feel happy?*] Yes [*Why pretend?*] because she wouldn't be loving. [*What would she be?*] Shooting, like this, bang, bang, bang!

5
The 7- to 9-Year-Old

Developmental Expectations

Cognitive Functioning. The child is now well into the concrete operational stage of cognitive development. This means that he now takes an interest in and is able to classify data, is able to understand more complicated causal relationships, and is entering into a new moral developmental phase. During this period reading, writing, and arithmetic become reliable tools in his ability to communicate with the world. Reality has been firmly differentiated from fantasy, and fantasy is known to be exclusively within his inner experiences.

During this time, riddles and puns put in an appearance as the child explores the use of language and his mastery over it.

At this time the child accepts his stature and his role, which makes him available to learning and being taught.

Concomitant with the neurological maturation for coordination, the child is able to begin to learn and master more complex motor activities.

Dynamic Picture. By now there is clear sex role identification and sufficient resolution of the Oedipal conflict for the child to move into wider experiences with his peers. This becomes an ever increasingly major concern for both the child and his parents. At 7, this leads to an inner tension in the child over issues of separation and rejection. By 9, felt competency in peer relationships reduces this tension, and the child enjoys a broader experience outside the home.

With the distinction between reality and fantasy finalized comes the sense of self and a reduction in the potential for regression.

Not enough work has been done with the dynamics of this period to allow us to be more explicit. Therefore, we are in the position of treating this time as if it were truly a "latent" period of development. The tremendous investment in intellectual and physical mastery beginning in this period masks continual dynamic unfolding, which we see in our clinical practice.

Defenses. The whole repertoire of defenses is available to the child during this period. Coming into it with avoidance and denial, the child begins to give them up in face of the demands of reality. The compulsive and obsessive defenses are now more productive in the learning process and are commensurate with the concrete operational cognitive stage.

The beginning of the internalization process starts here, and it is in this way that we begin to see the first inklings of the potential character formation. The beginning of internalization also means that there is less need to enact the conflicts and defensive struggles with others, so that the child can execute sharing and compromise easily in spite of the highly competitive nature of this period.

Affective Expression. Between 7 and 9, there is a change from the tension of the 7-year-old negotiating separation to the equanimity of the 9-year-old established in his or her world away from home. The push for mastery during this period brings great joy and pleasure with achievement. Similarly, as the child begins to feel greater security in peer relationships, he feels a great sense of well-being.

Pain, despair, and depression are the feelings of the child who, unfortunately, for physical or emotional reasons, cannot meet the demands of social and motor requisites for this period.

The great investment in repeating riddles exemplifies the humor at this age. Great pleasure is taken in stumping not only the adult, in particular, but also peers. Obviously, this is related to the sense of mastery, and, in this instance, feelings of superiority over the other. This is an acceptable way of expressing the intense competitive strivings of this age. To lose during this period, whether at a card game or at a significant Little League game, is tantamount to devastation expressed in inconsolable misery.

Enacting adult social roles plays the major part in 7-year-old fantasy. By 9, children are more involved with heroes and idols in their fantasies and take great pleasure in "dreams of glory."

Normal Expectation on Tests

Due to the developmental issues described previously, the testing experience itself is a source of great pleasure at this age.

Intelligence Testing. Consistency in both *intratest* and *intertest* functioning should be established at this point. There is one exception to note, which is the child who demonstrates very superior verbal skills (Verbal IQ over 130), who may not be able to match that level on the Performance section.

Bender–Gestalt. Although children of this age are increasingly capable of copying the B–G design, it is still risky to make diagnostic judgments on the basis of their productions. Observing the process of their approach, however, can be helpful in understanding how they cope in facing a difficult perceptual-motor challenge.

Projectives. The child is capable of producing clearer representations of the human form in his figure drawings at this time. He can elaborate more specific details, such as fingers instead of lines and shoes instead of feet. Some children can now express the human form in action or in dimensionality.

Determinants of the Rorschach established during this period show an increase in number of responses (there should be twelve to fifteen responses available): at least two to three *M*'s, although *FM* should still be higher; although there may be shading or three-dimensional responses, it is still not expected; *FC* should be represented by now, but *CF* can equal or exceed the number; *C* is no longer expected; and there is still a preponderance of *A* responses, although *H* should put in an appearance. With the increase in kinds of determinants, there is a gradual decrease in the high *F* percentage, although it still represents the highest percentage in the determinants.

At the lower age of this period—that is, 7 years—there may be *m* responses, reflecting the inner tension associated with this age. This should disappear by 9. By 9, *c* is expected in relationship to the increasing developmental ability to be socially aware.

TAT stories can now begin to contain real story elements (plots), a beginning and an end, complex themes, and motives and feelings attributed to the characters. The task of storytelling can be so absorbing at this age that the children may sometimes request that their stories be read back to them, even in mid-telling.

Representative psychological test interpretations and psychological test batteries for children within this age range now follow. The raw test data from the psychological test battery follow the discussion of each child so that easy reference can be made to the examples selected for illustration of the interpretations. We include examples of children diagnosed as having a reactive disorder, being mildly disturbed, moderately disturbed, and severely disturbed in order to demonstrate how a psychological portrait is developed. Each child's tests are analyzed, interpreted, and concluded with an integrated summary.

As stated before, the summary is not a complete report, but represents the salient features leading to the diagnostic portrait.

Psychological Test Portrait

K: 8–11 Male

K is a boy aged 8–11 who has an increasing tendency to withdraw from people, is overprotective of mother and younger brother, and is unable to express feelings, particularly anger. He has fears of open windows, death, separation, and new situations. His schoolwork is poor, and he has difficulty controlling his impulses. His parents have been separated for three-and-a-half years, and he rarely sees his father.

K was restless in the testing session, exhibited coy mannerisms, and showed his resistance when requested to perform by yawning and repeatedly stating how tired he was. He worked slowly, but carefully and with perseverance, after self-derogatory remarks at the beginning of each new task. When he did not feel challenged, he related well, in an open and friendly way.

Cognitive Functioning

WISC: *K* achieved a superior Verbal IQ score and an average Performance IQ score with a difference of nineteen points. His scaled scores showed wide variability in both areas, in Verbal, 9 to 19, and in Performance, 9 to 14. His Verbal achievement demonstrates a superior fund of knowledge (see the Information, Similarities, and Vocabulary sections), excellent language usage, superior conceptualizations, and an occasional display of humor. There is an indication in the Verbal tasks of the difficulties seen more clearly in the Performance items. He is able to achieve a superior number of digits forward, but can perform at only an average level backwards. He is able to do the Arithmetic items only so long as he feels certain, and then refuses to try. This is striking, as it is the only test that he "hates" and will not make an effort to try.

On the Performance items, a confusion in left-right sequencing was clear on both Picture Arrangement and Block Design. This confusion may have been the reason for his slowed time on the Coding and the last two items in Block Design. Also, this slow performance may be related to more defensive tactics. In the same way his Picture Completion may be only average due to a defensive stance.

B–G: The Bender provides striking confirmation of the right-left reversals seen in the Performance items in the WISC. The demand to start B–G figure 8 from the right is so strong he goes to the extreme of rotating the page ninety degrees in order to complete the design. Obviously, this invaluable information would not be possible if one relied only on the end product and did not have a record of how the designs were executed.

In spite of the fact that *K* does not order the designs in sequence, his overall perceptual-motor achievement is excellent for an 8½-year-old.

FD: *K* demonstrates difficulties in either the right side (see male drawing) or the left side (see female) and states his own awareness of his need to compensate for his difficulties in each. It is not known whether the male stance reflects disequilibrium or an action stance without information from *K*.

The drawings have a superior quality to them without much elaboration. This is due to the way he communicates clear sexual differences, adequate proportions, good body integrity, and in inviting openness in expression of both the face and body.

Similarly to the perceptual problem seen in *PC* in the WISC, *K* does not pay attention to sensory organs in the drawings, disregarding hands in the male, and ears and eyelashes on both figures.

Rorschach: Again, *K* displays a fund of knowledge and imaginative ideas in his percepts. He produces a large number of well-delineated percepts commensurate with his Verbal IQ of 125. He pushes to achieve an integration of all aspects of the blot, sometimes assigning arbitrary relationships while maintaining good form level. This bespeaks a great availability of intellectual energy, which he has consistently manifested in all of the tests.

TAT: *K* repeats the type of performance he gave in the Rorschach. He utilizes the reality of the pictures, but cannot always maintain consistency in his theme, changing from one plot to another, shifting the identities of the characters, and on occasion becoming confused. In spite of his avowed dislike for the test, he still perseveres and demonstrates his unusual intellectual energy.

Summary Statement of Cognitive Functioning: *K* demonstrates throughout the tests a superior intellectual capacity. His problems in left-right sequencing and spatial organization are manifest, but his capacity to compensate results in minimal interference in his functioning. In spite of this problem and dynamic concerns, he consistently shows an investment in intellectual mastery.

Dynamic Picture

WISC: *K*'s concern about aggression is expressed most clearly in his responses to Comprehension items, his definition of *hero* (Vocabulary, 1), and his reversal on *FISHER* (Picture Arrangement, 6). This concern seems related to conflicts about authority. His peculiar handling of *FISHER* suggests a reaction to the story theme in which he uses an oppositional approach to solving the task. Similarly, in Arithmetic, he opposes the demands of the task by becoming vague and guessing in a flip manner. All of this is in striking contrast to his usual precise and clear style.

K is obviously motivated to achieve (Block Design, 6, 7), but experiences difficulties when his aggressive impulses are evoked or he feels he is being controlled. We can speculate at this point that K is also concerned about body integrity or damage (through the way he handled the Comprehension items, the face on Object Assembly, and the Picture Completion), but we need further information from projective material to confirm this.

B–G: His handling of this test does not reveal any dynamic information.

FD: Again, there is confirmation of K's concern with his body inasmuch as he expresses dissatisfaction with how he executes the proportions and says he is more comfortable making the female figure. His problems with control are expressed in his unrealistic statement that the heads are too big. In fact, he draws large bodies, suggesting the attraction body impulses have for him. Also, the effort he puts into coloring in the male body reflects his anxiety. Part of his own body concern may stem from his perception of the woman as "strong-armed" and powerful.

Rorschach: K's problems with aggression are expressed repetitively in the Rorschach. He has an explosion on Card II, a rocket blasting off on Card IX, and fire on Card VIII. In addition, he elaborates an ordinary fur rug on IV to tell the gory details of how it became a rug. Also, his fear of aggression from outside is expressed in the many monster percepts and description of aggressive acts in Cards IV, VI, VII, and VIII.

TAT: Aggression is the predominant theme in all of K's TAT stories. One new note appears in 7 *BM* where the father kills his own son for money. For the first time there is a suggestion of an oedipal concern on K's part, which may be the explanation for the persistent and repetitive preoccupation with dangerous and monstrous actions of others.

Summary Statement of Dynamic Picture: Oedipal concerns appear to be the major focus of K's anxiety. He expresses conflict between being the aggressor and being the victim of aggression. In response to his own fears concerning body integrity, he produces unrealistic portrayals of men. In spite of this, he has achieved a comfortable masculine identity.

Defenses

WISC: When K is under stress (for example, Arithmetic), he becomes physically restless, flip, and off-hand in his responses, producing an oppositional stance. In Comprehension, where he was made anxious by aggressive associations, he began to mumble and had to be questioned in order to be understood. This negativism is enacted in his handling of Picture Arrangement in reversing orders, and perhaps explains his trouble with the Digit Span Backwards. This is quite in contrast to his almost compulsive and persistent efforts in tasks like Block Design and Similarities, where he does not experience demands being made on him. Indeed, the nineteen-point difference between Verbal IQ and Performance IQ may reflect the slowing down on the timed Performance items as another expression of his negativism. Another tactic used in structured tasks was to become coy, as if to placate *E*.

B–G: *K*'s perfectionistic drives produce an excessively compulsive approach accompanied with self-demeaning, critical comments and projections of blame onto *E* and the test. This is because he does not feel his productions are precise and accurate. On B–G figure 8, he again demonstrates his oppositionalism.

FD: *K* behaves similarly here as he did on the B–G, although he was more relaxed on this test. This time he introduced spontaneous conversation about himself. He still, however, is extraordinarily critical of his productions and uses flippancy as his way of denying his concern over his lack of perfection.

There is a projection on the female of great power and strength (cf., her hands versus the lack of hands on the man).

Rorschach: In light of the push of aggressive content, it is remarkable how well *K* is able to hold on to realistic and well-formed percepts. His negativism disappears on this task because he seems to enjoy the lack of structure and the opportunity to allow his own fantasies free play without feeling that the task or *E* is imposing a demand for perfection.

On a deeper level, since he says, "I just thought up most of these," he seems to reinforce the denial that the aggressive percepts could be real.

His other defensive tactics to handle the aggressive context are seen in his distancing (I, II, III, IV, VI, and X), attempts to deny (II and III), and use of a W approach to gain control. He also attempts to undo the aggressive threat of the card by preceding the aggressive percept with a benign percept (VII and IX).

TAT: In contrast to the Rorschach, *K* refuses to continue by stating, "Get a happier one—I don't like to do all killings." Therefore, although he is able to stay with the reality of the cards, his associations are very frightening. His defensive tactics seen in the Rorschach do not work as well here to contain the fear of aggression, since these are portrayals of human interactions. The least he can do is produce happy endings, often in an arbitrary fashion.

Summary Statement of Defenses: K defends against anxiety-arousing situations by becoming negativistic or, on occasion, seductive. His compulsive defenses serve him in good stead for achieving his own internally driven demands for achievement. His use of creative imagination seems to be permitted through his ability to gain and maintain distance from content that could be frightening.

Affective Expression

WISC: K's mood varied from delight to anger, depending on the task and his perceived ability to achieve. He felt his best on Similarities and Block Design (note his singing) and was angry at having to do the Arithmetic. At times, although he was annoyed at E's making him repeat the response when he mumbled, he still worked hard at attempting to achieve.

B–G: The Bender seems to have been a struggle for K. He complained throughout, yet never ceased working at the task.

FD: Although K again complains about his product, this task seemed to make him feel comfortable and spontaneous. He related warmly to the examiner during his performance. In addition, his figures convey a feeling of pleasantness and comfort in the world.

Rorschach: K enjoyed this task, responding easily with no problem in communication. In contrast to this behavior, he was seemingly unable to deal with color in his percepts, producing only explosions and fire. This bespeaks of his problem in handling his own feelings as well as the feelings produced in interpersonal relationships.

TAT: The difficulty referred to in the Rorschach in terms of interpersonal feelings is expressed vividly in this task. K does not enjoy the nature of the task, is somewhat angry at having to do it, and initially makes attempts at avoidance. Although he complies and formulates stories, he still ends by expressing his distress with this task.

Summary Statement of Affective Expression: Throughout the testing K demonstrated a wide range of affect. When he experiences himself as being controlled, he reacts with anger, particularly when he anticipates failure. His discomfort with his affective experience is most apparent when he is faced with interpersonal interactions.

Summary

It is clear throughout the testing that K is experiencing great difficulty in accepting his aggressive and sexual impulses. The content reveals how threatening these ideas are to him. The symptom picture represents the different ways he is attempting to deal with these unrelenting impulses that plague him at school, at home, and in his interpersonal relations.

It is a testimony to K's ego strength that, in spite of the preoccupation with such frightening fantasies, he consistently maintains a reality orientation, and his defenses remain intact and workable. Moreover, he always maintains good relatedness to E. It is only when he perceives himself to be in conflict with authority that his negativism interferes with his good functioning.

Mainly, K's problems stem from Oedipal concerns where aggressive and sexual meanings are fused so that he is unable to discriminate whether one is friend or foe. His preoccupation with these issues leads him to perform poorly in school and withdraw from others. With the loss of his father, K feels he has to assume the protective paternal role toward his mother and brother. This burdensome feeling at such an early age is expressed through his problem in controlling impulses.

Diagnosis:

GAP:	Reactive disorder	
DSM III:	Axis I:	309.90 (Adjustment Disorder with atypical features)
	Axis II:	316.90 (Atypical Specific Developmental Disorder)
	Axis III:	None
	Axis IV:	5 (Severe)
	Axis V:	4 (Fair)

In K's case, the widespread symptomatology seems like "a cry for help." His experienced inner discomfort in association with his good ability to relate makes for an excellent prognosis in psychotherapy.

Psychological Test Data

K: 8–11 Male

WISC

	Scaled Score
Verbal Tests	
Information	12
Comprehension	13
Arithmetic	9
Similarities	19
Vocabulary	17
(Digit Span)	(14)
Total	70

Performance Tests

Picture Completion	10
Picture Arrangement	9
Block Design	14
Ob ect Assembly	12
Coding	9
Total	54

	Scaled Score	IQ
Verbal Scale	70	125
Performance Scale	54	106
Full Scale	124	117

[*Tires quickly, yet can work if given time. Tendency to swallow words or mumble. Distractible. Frequent requests by* E *to repeat. Resists by yawning and claiming he's tired.*]

Information

		Score
1.	Two	1
2.	Thumb	1
3.	Four	1
4.	Cow or goat	1
5.	Put it on stove	1
6.	Grocery	1
7.	Five	1
8.	Seven	1
9.	Columbus	1
10.	Twelve	1
11.	Spring, summer, fall, winter	1
12.	Green. If green, that's my birthday thing.	0
13.	West	1
14.	Well, it holds food.	0
15.	I don't know.	0
16.	I don't know Caesar.	0
17.	Something like our flag.	0
18.	Don't know	0
19.	Five feet, ten inches	1
20.	Mexico	0
21.	100	0
22.	Don't know	0
23.	Don't know	0
	Total	12 (13)

Comprehension

		Score
1.	Go to hospital, no—go to medicine cabinet, wash it, and put Band-Aid on.	2
2.	Buy him another one.	2

3.	Go to another store.	2
4.	Just walk away.	2
5.	Well, I would go [*waves hands*] I'd put a block—fire on track so it will stop.	0
6.	Can't catch on fire and get a splinter on wood [*laugh*] could chop down a wooden house	1
7.	For stealing, murdering—for being bad—going against law	1
8.	Because it's kinder. I don't know why children; maybe because grown-ups rather save their child than selves.	1
9.	Because not nice to fool around with money—can't just fill out a check, if find one or steal it unless it's filled out already	0
10.	Because they're working to help something. Beggar don't.	1
11.	Because could be a bad guy, a robber, and steal all the things.	0
12.	What's fiber?	0
13.	I don't know what a senator does.	0
14.	Not nice to break a promise	1
	Total	13

[*Some mumbling—have to ask him to speak up.*]

Arithmetic

		Score
[*Aside:* "I hate arithmetic."]		
1.		1
2.		1
3.		1
4.	2—You could cut it into a thousand pieces	1
5.	6	1
6.	13, no 14	1
7.	7	1
8.	About 50¢	0
9.	Can't—[OT]	0
10.	Can't do	0
11.	Can't do	0
	Total	7

[*Can't sit still too well. Restless.*]

Similarities

		Score
1-4.		4
5.	They're fruit.	2
6.	Animals	2

7.	A drink—a drunk drink	2
8.	Instrument—musical	2
9.	Coal. Can write on paper	0
10.	Like measuring	2
11.	They're metal.	2
12.	Make the world beautiful. Both made by nature.	2
13.	I don't know. Too close. Salt doesn't go in water.	0
14.	They're like, uh, both right! For the law, like.	1
15.	Both opposites	0
16.	Both numbers	0
	Total	19

Digit Span

F 7 + B 4   Total Score   11

Vocabulary

		Score
1.	Two wheels. You ride it.	2
2.	Something with a sharp blade and cut or carve with it.	2
3.	Something you wear on your head.	2
4.	You sent a letter to someone for a thank you or for a happy birthday.	2
5.	When raining something to cover your head or keep the sun off.	2
6.	Something you use to lay on— comfortable	2
7.	Fingernail	2
8.	Like a horse—bigger ears.	2
9.	Something soft. Hair from animal.	2
10.	A jewel—like a rock—looks like glass and shines	2
11.	Get together	2
12.	Like on a card	2
13.	Like a long knife—usually fight with it or hang for souvenir	2
14.	Someone who's a pest or bothers you	2
15.	Strong—courage	2
16.	Nothing—like no sense	2
17.	Someone who's usually cowardly. A hero—always scared. Who wins something.	0
18.	Play cards for money	2
19.	Kind of formula—chemical	2
20.	Something to look through to see germs	2
21.	A coin from England	2

22.	Something that—a story that's not true	2
23.	No	0
24.	Like a—something like fighting organization	0
25.	Never heard of it	0
26.	Never heard of it	0
27.	Spangled flag	0
28.	No	0
29.	No	0
30.	No	0
31.	Ballet teacher	0
32.	No	0
33.	No	0
34.	No	0
	Total	42

Picture Completion

		Score
1.	Two teeth	1
2.	One leg	1
3.	One ear	1
4.	Mouth	1
5.	Nothing—neck?	0
6.	A latch and hinge. [indicates hinge]	1
7.	Fingernail	1
8.	One more spade	1
9.	Something to hold together	1
10.	Holes for buttons	1
11.	Flapper from other side	0
12.	One of these missing?	0
13.	Nothing	0
14.	Little flappy things that go out	0
15.	Other eye	0
16.	Nothing	0
17.	Something looks wrong, but I can't figure—another ear?	0
18.	Nothing here	0
19.	Leg	0
20.	Grass	0
	Total	9

Picture Arrangement

	Time	Order	Score	
ABCD			8	
1.	9″	FIRE	6	
2.	12″	HTUG	0	
3.	7″	QRST	6	
4.	25″	FEGH	0	
5.	27″	EPRCY	0	
6.	59″	SFIHER	0	
7.	OT	MASTER	0	(4)
		Total	20	(24)

Block Design

		Time	Score
A–C.			6
1.		20″	4
2.		73″	4
3.		43″	4
4.	[*Sings as he works*]	16″	5
5.		110″	4
6.	[*Gets stripe idea immediately, but not directional shift. Tends to give up. Yawning, tired. All correct at 5′ 10″.*]	150″	0 (4)
7.	[*Doesn't hold to a square, but does do design in pieces of two or three blocks together. Then can put it together as a whole.*]	150″	0 (4)
		Total	27 (35)

[*Seems restless; has difficulty concentrating, yet holds to it and works intently.*]

Object Assembly

	Time		Score
M	17″		5
H	58″		6
F	180″	[*At time has hair pieces correct, eye in eye piece, chin, mouth, nose on, but can't put eyepiece on.*] It looks like a girl, a whole face.	4
A	49″		6
		Total	21

Coding B   Total Score   25

Bender–Gestalt

A. That's very easy. [*He does the square first.*]
1. [*Counts visually*] They're not spread apart that much.
2. [*Counts and recounts at 4 then at 7*] That's all I see.
3. [*Counts each grouping*] I did that a little out of order. [*Maintains sheet in proper position. Perseverates last group, although he counts aloud.*]
4. [*Does open square first with uneven lines, then corrects. Curve done in single stroke.*]
5. [*Does/first*] Hard to count the dots.
6. [*Right to left*]
7. [*Does each figure in one sweep.*]
8. [*Right to left again. Turns sheet ninety degrees to get parallel sides.*]

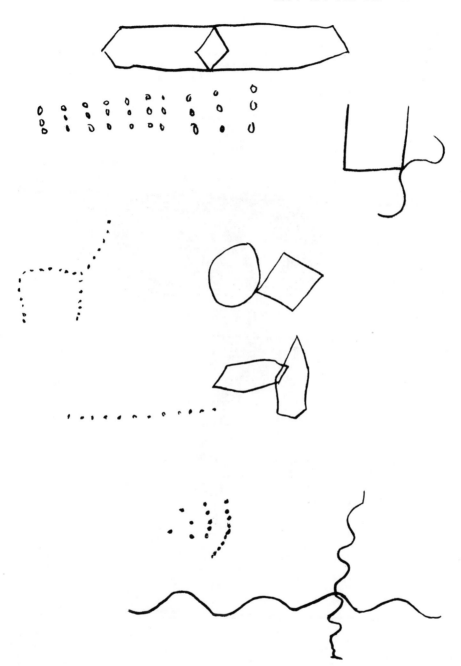

Figure Drawings

I did this before. [*trouble with head*] I keep on making big heads. [*fills in features*] [*On the male, trouble with right underarm so colors in, then colors in the shirt.*] I better color it in because I made a mistake. [*Very conversational as he draws. Related—reality oriented. Just started at a new school*]

Lady now? I'm better at those; better making long hair. [*Again has head, but can't handle body, then goes at it.*] I don't like starting at the shoulder. I'll make a little neck. [*Arms come large. He laughs.*] Strong-armed.

Rorschach

I.	9″	1.	Some kind of moon lizard.
		2.	Fox—two eyes—bump on head and ears.
		3.	Island
II.	14″	1.	A big palace—step up—walls that were broken up, and someone just discovered it, and there's a palace way up there, and here's an explosion—dynamite blowing up walls to get through.
III.	3″	1.	Two Africans or any people—men—picking up pots out of a fire or stones out of a fire.
		2.	Head of a monster—two big eyes— nose [*covers side* D] People not here.
		3.	A butterfly.
IV.	6″	1.	Looks like a big monster who just came from outer space, just broke down a tree, and there's a stump of tree behind him. His arms are over here—shoulders, and head, feet, and tree.
V.	3″	1.	This looks like bat wings—feet—ears—head.

I.	1.	[W] Looks like what I imagine a moon lizard looks like.
	2.	[W] Just face.
	3.	[W] Little lakes [S].
II.	1.	Palace far away. [*Broken walls?*] Zig zag like. [*edge detail*] [*Explosion?*] All the red and the fire going like this. I'm pretending the other red things aren't here.
III.	1.	Fire coming out like [*in gray projection center*] stick in fire.
	3.	Because center and . . . are wings—dark spots. [*Look like it if black?*] Probably.
IV.	1.	[*Monster?*] Feet so big and coming before him like walking like this [*demonstrates huge steps, legs high*], or this could be [*center projection* D] Empire State Building, and he's coming over and knocking it down.
V.	1.	Wings. He's coming. [*demonstrates*] Flying forward.

VI. 7″ 1. A space fox—
space wolf. I'm
imagining it.
Head—whiskers;
feet spread out
on the floor.
Someone killed
him. Layin' flat
on the floor like
a rug. Looks like
a rug 'cause he's
flattened out.
They cut him,
and this is fold-
ing from when
they folded him.
[*Is that the
whole of him?*]
Yeah, except for
toenails and eyes
and—here is
skin—smooth,
like my sweater—
like fur and they
smoothed it out.

VII. 14″ 1. Two little puppies standing on
a rock. Tail,
nose, goes in
here for his
eyes—here are
ears.

2. Also, it could
look like a giant
butterfly attack-
ing. And they're
attacking the
giant butterfly.
Have bouncers
and bounce on it.
They're like wild
puppies. [*Every
so often he swal-
lows his words so
E can't hear.*]

VIII. 5″ 1. Two tigers crawl-
ling up—monster
pushing them
down into a fire.
Tank holding
the fire.

VIII. 1. [*Fire?*] The
orange makes it
look like fire.
[*Look like mon-
ster?*] I don't
know. I just
thought of it be-
cause of tigers.
Maybe those
fingers are anten-
nae and can't see
eyes in head.

IX. 4"V   1. A plain design.

       V   2. 35" A pink water fountain with water coming up—pink water.

              3. Rocket blasting off; fire below in red, and this is the rocket coming out.

X.   6"   Too many things

   12"   1. Lions. I don't know what they're doing. Just lions, probably jumping off onto here.

            2. Space cows going up in a rocket to earth.

      V   3. Crocodiles.

      V   4. Men picking up a cow's head.

      V   5. A guy with giant arms, legs, face, head. Maybe a space Martian. I just thought up most of these. [*Limits: What is right color and shape?*] The bat. Maybe these men [*III*] in black clothes. Never heard of a pink tiger. I never saw a bright yellow lion.

TAT

1. Boy looking at a violin. [*throws card at* E—*very resistive*] He bought one up the street, and now he's examining it. He's thinking—dreaming, if he's gonna be very famous, put on a big show playing the violin. [*Does he become famous?*] Well, yes.

3 BM. [*Makes face*] A girl? Looks as if was dead or something. Looks like a knife over here. I can't make a story for that. Maybe she fell asleep while she was cutting with scissors [*and?*] I don't know. And—can't make a good story. [E *repeats: Dead? Knife?*] I can't think how it happened. Who can make up a story? I'll have to make a big beginning. Maybe she's a crook and she stole a person's diamonds—running all over town until she got to hideout and a man sneaked up behind her and killed her, and then she killed the man because you are licensed to kill someone. I think it's true—detectives are and police. [*License to kill?*] Someone has a license to kill—James Bond.

8 BM. Looks like a boy, and his father is having an operation in the hospital. No, looks like a man and a boxing fight. This boy won, and they are operating in the hospital on this man. He came to see him, see how well he is and shake hands. What's a rifle and a knife doing there? They must be crooks killing someone. I mean, there's a rifle—there's a knife. That's silly. What would a rifle be doing in a hospital? I don't know if it's a hospital or not. It's probably a secret hideout of crooks, and they are going to kill him if he doesn't show them trick plans of atomic bomb. [*Happens?*] Well, of course, the police save him.

13 B. Boy sittin' at door of log cabin eatin' an apple. Looks like—poor boy. He has no shoes and a dirty face. It's an old wooden house and it's chipped. He lives by the beach because there's sand. [*Do?*] He traveled and then found the old house on the sea shore and made it look a little better. He took a sponge out of the sea and made a bed. It's a lost island no one ever found. [*How come he found it?*] He got lost in a shipwreck. [*What about his parents?*] They're across the sea on different land. They never found him. [*Does he like it?*] I don't think he likes it. He never met them. He was a baby when the shipwreck came. [*How do they feel?*] They never saw the baby before. [*Do they miss him?*] They sent the whole navy to find him. [*How did he manage to survive?*] On board, he fell asleep; on shore sleeping. He survived by eating fish because he was about 8 years old and had matches so he could make a fire on boat and send signals out. [*Happens?*] Found his mother and father.

16. Can't. Ghost talking to a white cow on a very bright day.

12 M. Man ready to kidnap woman, putting hand over her face, uh, and he kills all the guards that try to get him, and FBI comes and makes a robot monster to take over them, and the man dies, and the robot breaks down before—and the FBI saves the girl.

7 BM. Captain Kangaroo talking to his son. That's all. [*What's he saying?*] Wouldn't you like to be on Captain Kangaroo? No, that's not the story. A judge in court talking to a man. The man tells if he's guilty or not. He's asking if the man is guilty, so he says yes, and the man is hanged in old days, and they take the wife and child and put them in a new home.

They're glad it's all over—the murdering and the trouble, that's why live happily ever after. [*Why kill him?*] For nothing—wanted to have some action—crook wanted action so said make a bet—I'll kill my son if you give me all your money. [*Who?*] Father, I mean the crook wanted to—crook killed boy for money—father was the crook, killed his own son for all the money the man had [*Man wanted it done?*] because he betted him.

6 BM. Haven't I seen this before in comics? This is Spiderman telling his aunt his identity that he was Spiderman—she didn't know that ever—he works for justice—always gets blamed for what crook does—but capture crooks who go to jail. [*Live with aunt?*] Yea. I don't know where his mother and father is.

18 GF. Get a happier one. I don't like to do all the killings.

Psychological Test Portrait

L: 8–6 Male

L is an 8-6 boy, the youngest of three sons. His mother died when he was 6. She had become ill during her pregnancy with him. His father, because of business needs, can spend only weekends at home. The family has relied on a variety of inconsistent caretakers.

He presented with major learning problems, repeating the second grade, and not showing any progress. He finds it difficult to sit still in school, and his behavior alternates between withdrawal and aggression. He has fears of being killed.

L is an attractive boy who related well, remained in his seat throughout the testing, and worked with effort, motivation, and determination to succeed. He spoke of his problems spontaneously, saying he has no friends, he cannot learn, and he wants help.

Cognitive Functioning

WISC: The outstanding discrepancy between Verbal and Performance IQ scores (51 points) immediately suggests a deficit in perceptual-motor functioning. The Full-Scale IQ of 109 is, therefore, misleading. It is clear in the Verbal subtests that L is an unusually intelligent youngster able to deal with concepts, language, and abstractions on a most superior level. It is in the areas of arithmetic and remembering digits that he experiences difficulties similar to his problems in the Performance subtests. His vocabulary is remarkable (cf. Similarities, 15, *antonyms*), and it is even more remarkable when one takes into account the difficulty he has in syntax (cf. his response to *Hat* compared to *Nuisance* in Vocabulary). He displays a superior fund of knowledge (cf. *Nitroglycerine* and *Cushion* in Vocabulary), and, although he typically begins his abstractions in Similarities on a concrete one-point level, he is able to develop a more general concept. Additionally in the Vocabulary section, item *Brave,* although one might find his response extremely humorous, L was very serious. In the WISC, he generally demonstrates a preferred cognitive strategy moving from the concrete to the more abstract. While this is to be expected developmentally at his age, his use of this style is excessive. L has a most primitive number sense, and is able to deal only serially and not in relationships. This concreteness of approach is again reflected in Block Design, where he cannot get the concept of the relationship of four blocks to a square to a pattern. Another major problem is his inability to sequence, seen in Digit Span, Picture Arrangement, Object Assembly, and Coding. The overall impression is of a very intelligent child struggling with a severe perceptual-motor problem and disturbance in the perception of spatial relationships.

B–G: Although this test is not used for diagnosis at this age, L's productions are outstandingly poor. He is unable to copy correctly even those designs that should be accomplished by 8 years of age and, in addition, is unable to retain the gestalt in A, 4, and 5, reducing them to a simple triangle, square, and circle shape. His overall organizational plan is confused, and again suggests his difficulty with spatial relationships. With all of this dysfunction, it is a testimony to L's superior intellect inasmuch as he is able to make contact on A and 4, and, moreover, demonstrates on item 6 his ability to learn by practice.

FD: L's drawings reflect his difficulty in producing an adequate body representation. They are primitive and even lack arms. This again confirms the hypothesis of a perceptual-motor deficit.

Rorschach: The unusual creativity expressed in *L*'s responses is commensurate with the very superior Verbal IQ. The Rorschach demonstrates his large fund of knowledge, ability to organize and integrate, and create original percepts. He has a large number of responses, excellent form level, and includes movement and elaborated descriptions.

In the instance of punning on Card I, the fact that this is unintentional on *L*'s part and is seriously presented is consistent with the concreteness seen already in the WISC.

TAT: This task was obviously a stress task for *L*. Under these conditions, his gifts of intellect and creativity break down, and he produces disorganized and repetitive themes with many instances of reverting to a concrete approach. The syntax of his language is confused, and he substitutes words without awareness, and alternates sex designation throughout. Stories are discontinuous, filled with unconnected associations, and end in midair. In light of his obvious disturbance in this task, his persistence is remarkable.

Summary Statement of Cognitive Functioning: *L* is a child with obviously superior intellectual abilities, but is handicapped by deficiency in the perceptual-motor sphere and perception of spatial relationships. He can also become disorganized cognitively when conflictual issues are aroused.

Dynamic Picture

WISC: Two major dynamic issues emerge in the WISC. One is seen in his fear of aggressive impulses (Similarities, 4 and 14; Comprehension, 4; Picture Completion, 15 and 17; Vocabulary, 5, 6, 8, 15, and his aside), and the other is seen in feelings of damage or inadequacy (Information, 14; Comprehension, 5; Vocabulary, 5, 6, 8, 15, 16; and Picture Completion, 15 and 17). The fact that his feelings of inadequacy are in part related to his perceptual-motor problem is obvious in the amount of encouragement that was necessary to help him maintain his effort on the Performance items. An additional concern emerges in Picture Completion, 19, where a most arbitrary imposition is made.

B–G: Nothing of a dynamic nature emerges in the Bender.

FD: The two issues in the WISC are suggested in the drawings, as the "hair" could be mistaken for a hole in the head, and the lack of arms reveals both his problems with aggression and feelings of inadequacy.

Rorschach: The same issues again emerge in the Rorschach, that is, aggression (II, IV, and X) and inadequacy (III and VIII), and by now these issues have become themes. Another issue is the sense of loss portrayed so poignantly in his response to VII.

TAT: Again, the themes of aggression and feelings of inadequacy are apparent in most of *L*'s stories. The sense of loss first seen in the Rorschach now is manifest throughout. Not only does the mother pass away (12 M), but now he is extremely concerned about the father's health. The sense of deprivation emerges in practically every story, which is obviously related to his sense of loss. The deprivations described are on the most primitive level of concern about lack of food and therefore suggest the central focus this feeling has for him. In this way, the usual sense of inadequacy found in learning disabled children becomes reinforced and intensifies his sense of unworthiness. In the 7 BM story, he develops the idea of the father's loss of pride in the son who cannot retain even the food he has, thus demonstrating the interconnection between the issue of basic nutriment and feelings of love and self-worth. (This was hinted at in the WISC, Picture Completion, 19).

Throughout the stories, also, is persistent alternating of sexual pronouns, testifying to *L*'s need to find a nurturing person of either sex, and the confused manner of presentation suggests the confusion between reality and fantasy. It is striking that this appears only in the TAT, indicating that this task elicits from *L* an admixture of real-life events in his feelings about interpersonal relationships.

Summary Statement of Dynamic Picture: *L* clearly presents his problems. He is concerned about the fate of aggression, whether directed by him or toward him. He has identity confusion in male–female roles as well as within his own perception of himself. His feelings of self-esteem are also undermined by his lack of a sense of competence and adequacy. His feelings of worthlessness are intensified by his profound experience of loss and deprivation.

Defenses

WISC: There are some subtle indications of distancing in some of *L*'s responses (Information, 13; Comprehension, 4), and some projection (Picture Completion, 10, 11, 12, 13, 15, 17, 18, 19, and 20). There is clearer evidence of avoidance in the oft-repeated desire to stop the Arithmetic and all of the Performance items. He manages to continue with *E*'s encouragement in several of the tasks. He also attempts to demonstrate that his difficulty in Performance items is a visual one (note recording on visual behavior). In light of his obviously painful experience in performing, it is remarkable that his attempts to avoid are so readily relinquished with *E*'s encouragement.

B–G: Since *L* experiences such great difficulty in producing these designs, it is striking that no other defensive stance takes place than his use of his peculiar visual behavior.

FD: *L* seems to try to avoid many issues through not including arms, ears, and mouths on his drawings. This perhaps speaks to his problems with inter-relationships he would like to avoid.

Rorschach: There is some evidence of secretiveness on *L*'s part in his percepts on I, V, and X. We speculate the defensive hiddenness is to protect his feelings of inadequacy or inferiority, but it is not clear from the content. It is clear, however, that when faced with traumatic stimuli, he seeks refuge in vague, amorphous responses (II, III, IX, and X). The only evidence for denial is seen in VIII, which would seem to be in response to the anxiety produced by the body percept.

TAT: The predominant defensive style in *L*'s stories is one of confusion and vagueness seen in the lack of organization of themes, the language regression, and the arbitrary sequencing of associations. His language improves remarkably when he assumes the stance of a storyteller and is not speaking for himself (12 M and 13 B). In addition, he projects blame on parents and other children for the lack of friendship and the lack of food. This is quite understandable in light of the inordinate sense of guilt portrayed in 12 M, which is followed by denial.

Also, throughout feelings of inadequacy seemed to be explained through physical illness or defect, which may harbinger the development of somatization as a defense.

Summary Statement of Defenses: *L* primarily relies on avoidance as a defense when he perceives himself in difficulty. This, however, is not rigidly maintained because it is easily relinquished with the intervention of another. We can see the suggestion of developing defenses in the occasional use of projection, the use of the more hysterical defenses of vagueness, secretiveness, and confusion, and regression in the more immature language productions of the younger child. It is a hallmark of his record, however, that he has no really adequately working defenses.

Affective Expression

WISC: Specifically, *L*'s mood on the WISC was pleasant as long as he dealt strictly with Verbal tasks. When faced with Arithmetic and Performance items, he became exceedingly tense (seen in his excessive activity) and unhappy.

B–G: Due to the struggle to produce on this task, *L* was very tense and unhappy.

FD: This was accomplished easily, and *L* seemed to feel good about it.

Rorchach: *L* was delighted with this task. He experienced difficulty only on Card VII. His problems with affective expression, however, were seen clearly in many responses (in the imagery of VII, as well as the response engendered by the red and black on II, the red in the third response on III, his first response to VIII, all of IX, and the beginning of X). Sadness is suggested in his response on VII and anger in II, IV, and X (3 and 4).

TAT: A pervasive feeling of despair, loneliness, sadness, and loss accompany the stories in the TAT. There is lip service paid to anger, but the depressive affect saturates all the content.

Summary Statement of Affective Expression: In spite of the demonstration of a wide range of affect, *L*'s predominant affect mode is one of sadness and despair.

Summary

L's feelings of inadequacy and ineptness produce frustration and despair at his inability to achieve in all areas, academic and social. He tends to blame himself and sees himself as unworthy. He projects blame for his failure on his parents, which is followed by anger that too much is expected of him, and he can never realize parental expectations. Therefore, he must always feel like a failure. This feeling is also seen in response to his mother's death, where he harbors anger with her for leaving him and, at the same time, feels much guilt over her death. He is fearful something terrible may happen to his father or himself. This feeling is sharpened when or if his father becomes more nurturing. His feelings of loss were exacerbated by his mother's death, but stem from a very early oral level.

   L is a child with superior intellectual endowment and a serious perceptual-motor dysfunction. His great feelings of inadequacy stem in part from this problem. In language arts his performance is remarkably good, intact, and available. On the other hand, in spatial orientation, his problems in perceptual-motor areas are so severe that learning in all areas appears to be an insurmountable task.

Diagnosis:

GAP:	Psychoneurotic Disorder, Depressive Type	
DSM III:	Axis I:	300.40 (Dysthymic Disorder)
	Axis II:	315.90 (Atypical Specific Developmental Disorder)
	Axis III:	Rule out neurological condition
	Axis IV:	6 (Extreme)
	Axis V:	6 (Very poor)

Therefore, *L* is seen to be a child with a neurotic adaptation to the problems presented by his perceptual-motor difficulties and the instability in his family situation since the onset of his mother's illness. Recommendation is made for a neurological evaluation, learning remediation, and psychotherapy. Prognosis is very hopeful in light of *L*'s intellectual abilities, motivation, trust in others, and awareness of his own pain.

Psychological Test Data
L: 8–6 Male

WISC

		Scaled Score
Verbal Tests		
Information		14
Comprehension		19
Arithmetic		10
Similarities		16
Vocabulary		17
(Digit Span)		(7)
	Total	76

Performance Tests		
Picture Completion		8 (1)
Picture Arrangement		7
Block Design		7
Object Assembly		6
Coding		9
	Total	37

	Scaled Score	IQ
Verbal Scale	76	133
Performance Scale	37	82
Full Scale	113	109

[*Throughout, he has to check and examine by tilting the surface. He looks out of the corner of his eye with head tilted.*]

Information

		Score
1.	Two	1
2.	Thumb	1
3.	Four	1
4.	Cow	1
5.	Fire? Get a pan or pot; put water in it, and put the fire on	1

6.	Grocery	1
7.	Five	1
8.	Seven	1
9.	Christopher Columbus	1
10.	Twelve	1
11.	Summer, spring, fall, winter	1
12.	I don't know	0
13.	Far away. I know this isn't it, but Florida	0
14.	Heart beats—takes your food and digests it.	1
15.	Because—like water, but it's lighter	1
16.	Don't know	0
17.	Fourth of July sparklers? The day we celebrate when they were made.	0
18.	Don't know	0
19.	About eight feet, no seven feet	0
20.	Should I guess? Rome?—No—I don't know	0
21.	1000	0
22.	Rome	0
23.	No	0
24.	10 hundred [Q] 1000 miles about; I never went there	1
25.	No	0
26.	No	0
27.	Thing what keeps temperature—red, goes up and down.	0

Total   13 (14)

Comprehension

Score

1.	Cut? Go to recreation office if no one was home and ask them for a bandage.	2
2.	I would pay for it.	2
3.	I would say thank you anyway, and I could go to another store.	2
4.	I would run so I wouldn't hit him. I wouldn't beat a little boy up, not four—I wouldn't run.	2
5.	Say stop—call police to stop them if they wouldn't listen to me.	1
6.	If start a fire brick won't burn, but on wood would burn up, and if wood, would fall down more easily—brick is stronger.	2
7.	Because then they'll hurt people and take things.	1
8.	Because they're smaller and should live a longer life, and women should be saved, too.	1
9.	Because sometimes you can make a mistake with cash, but on check can't.	1
10.	Because sometimes a beggar just needs money, but children's fund needs money for children.	1

11. Because if healthy and if get polio shot, will be strong and live longer.   0
12. Could be dried out good—good thread to make through cotton and won't rip easily.   2
13. Help president and mayor to do things.   0
14. If say something, it's not nice to not keep it. A friend wants to borrow a nickel then promises to pay it back and doesn't pay back; you'll get mad because you can't trust him.   2

           Total   19

Arithmetic

		Score
1.		1
2.		1
3.		1
4.	2	1
5.	6	1
6.	14	1
7.	7	0
8.	21	1
9.	19	0
10.	Don't know	0
11.	Don't know	0
12.	Don't know	0
	Total	7

[*Note: Counts quickly on fingers.*]

Similarities

		Score
1.	Sweet	1
2.	Arm	1
3.	Ladies	1
4.	Dangerous—sharp	1
5.	Both have pits and are fruit.	2
6.	Both have tails and whiskers, and they're both animals.	2
7.	Both have—are drinks and have stuff—bubbly stuff.	1
8.	Both are musical instruments.	2
9.	Coal is made out of paper, and you could write on the paper with the coal.	0
10.	One goes across and pound goes down.	0
11.	Scissors are made of metal, and copper is made of metal.	2
12.	Because when there's a lake there's surely mountains.	0
13.	In the sea	0
14.	No fighting for—all justice	0

15. Both antonyms—same but backwards—after got first, end up last. [*cannot explain, although seems to know*]   0
16. Both in twenties [*Repeated?*] 121 and 41 are together.   0
                                                          ———
                                       Total   13

Digit Span

F 4 + B 3   Total Score   7

Vocabulary

		Score
1.	A thing you ride on with two wheels.	2
2.	What you cut things with.	2
3.	Wear it so get warm on your head.	2
4.	To tell friend what you gotta do so you can't meet them then—and mail it to them.	2
5.	Say it snows and rains—use it so won't hit your head.	2
6.	Seat belt holds you back so have a cushion so you won't get hurt. Also like a pad, soft.	2
7.	Something you hammer into wood.	2
8.	An animal what has a horn and ears and feet what likes to kick you.	2
9.	Like a fur coat, keeps you warm, comes from dead animals.	2
10.	Something like a hard rock and worth a lot of money.	2
11.	Join a club and be friends with someone.	2
12.	Like on a card—a high—like spade of aces.	2
13.	Something to fight with.	2
14.	Like you won't go away from somebody, and you are bothering them.	2
15.	Let's say a donkey going to kick an old man, say 126, and he wants to live a long life, is brave and can live a long life.	0
16.	Like a kid says I can't do it—nonsense, can do it, but afraid to.	1
17.	Let's say win a battle and fighted for freedom.	2
18.	Like gamble money—like a saloon—card game lose or win.	2
19.	Dangerous explosive—like dynamite, but a liquid.	2
20.	Thing comes with glass—look through to see tiny thing no human eye could see.	2

21.	Money in France	1
22.	A story that teaches you a lesson	2
23.	No	0
24.	War thing—like camouflage	0
25.	I don't know.	0
26.	Like I seclude you in a game—let you be included. Are these walls fireproof?	0
27.	Like "Star-Spangled Banner" [*sings*]	0
28.	I don't know.	0
29.	I don't know.	0
30.	Like a thing in the sky—sun—once a year—sun that's eclipse.	0
31.	Don't know	0
32.	Don't know	0
33.	Can't be trustworthy.	0
	Total	40

Picture Completion

		Score
1.	These things [*occasionally looks at card from corner of eyes*]	1
2.	A leg	1
3.	Ear	1
4.	Mouth	1
5.	Whisker	1
6.	One of these	1
7.	Nail	1
8.	Spade	1
9.	One bigger than other—this thing goes [*demonstrates movement*]	0
10.	Man—no, one of these [*indicates pocket*]	0
11.	One of these on that side	0
12.	Screw driver	0
13.	Net	0
14.	This thing	1
15.	One of his arms	0
16.	Nothing really missing	0
17.	One of his arms	0
18.	A man is missing.	0
19.	Milk—the can that holds milk	0
20.	A tree	0
	Total	8 (9)

Picture Arrangement

	Time	Order	Score
A.		ABC	2
B.	39″	TOY	2
C.	29″	IONR	0
D.		[*Cannot do—then gets it, but overtime*]	0

[*Fight. E has to demonstrate and correct*]

1.	24″	FIRE	4
2.	19″	HGTU	0
3.	11″	QRST	5
4.	28″	EGFH	0
5.	21″	EPRCY	0
6.		EIRHFS	0
7.			0
		Total	13

Block Design

	Score
A.	2
B.	1
C.	2
1–7 [*Cannot do these at all*]	0
Total	5

[*Item 1: Enormous confusion—hit or miss turning of halves.*] Doesn't go, I can't do it. [*Only uses two until told to use all—enormous confusion and distress—cannot see parts at all.*]

[*Item 3: Uses Halves*] Can't do. [*With encouragement, will try*] Not sure if right. It looked hard on card.

Object Assembly

			Score
M	72″	[*Confused re: legs— back and forth*] One bigger than other. Can't do it. [*Puts legs wrong again. Suddenly gets it.*]	4
H	89″	[*Smiling*] I don't know this. [*Center omitted*]	4
F	180″	[*At time, hair pieces only*] [*Hit or miss. Can't recognize when correct*]	1
A		[*Hit or miss cannot do at all*]	0
		Total	9

Coding B	Total	22

[*Much extraneous movement in chair*]

Bender–Gestalt

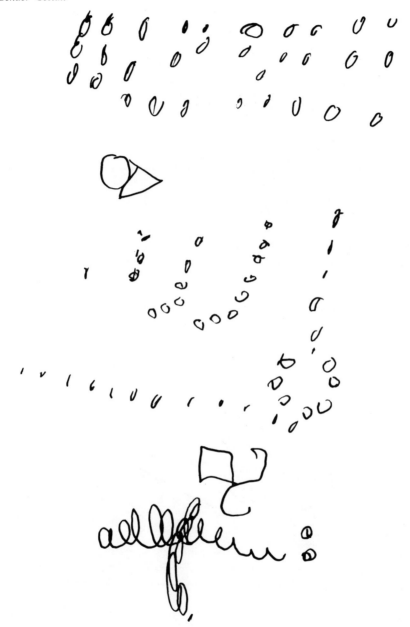

Figure Drawing

Rorschach

I.	8″	1. Looks like, kinda like a bat—not a baseball bat, but a regular, live bat, and it looks like . . .
		2. Bat man climbing up a window with this cape—hands looks like climbing —big cape so no one will see him.
II.	12″	1. Just dots—red dots. Looks like kinda bloodish.
		2. Round shape—black paint.
		3. Looks like kind of a turtle. [W] [*cuts off red*]
III.	3″	1. This looks like a butterfly. [D]
		2. Two people taking up a ball.
		3. Ink mark—like a tomato dripping [*upper red*]
IV.	3″	1. That looks like an ape. The ape is black and looks like that is a big ape. His head and his feet. He's fat. A thing down near his feet. He's mad—got shot. An ape can take four bullets before he falls down. Did you ever see King Kong?

V.	3"	1. Looks kinda like a ballet dancer with a suit. A big suit dancing [Q] a lady—looks like clothes around on side.
VI.	7"	1. This'll be a hard one. A violin of some kind. A big thing. A big guitar. [*indicates parts*]
VII.	42"V	1. Hard! Kinda looks like a big studio thing like a stage for people to dance on. Just an empty thing. A round empty stage.
VIII.	18"	1. Inside of a person. Looks like ribs—veins [*side animals*]. Rest I don't think would mean anything.
		2. It looks like here's a tiger and another tiger—a lake—they're going over a lake, and this half is the shadow of it. [*Lake?*] Looks like oil. Get rainbow and different colors, and this is the shadow.
IX.	27"	1. Looks like a collage—all different colors mixed together.
		2. Clouds—well, clouds are in this shape [*lower red*].
X.	3"	1. A masquerade party with all different shapes on walls—I don't know what it's called, but looks kind of like, well, shapes—collages—and cutouts.
		2. Red kind of wall.
		3. Bat [*blue center*] flying
		4. Fly—coming down will hit the wall, and the bat will chase him and eat him [*lower green*]. Bat's chasing him.
		5. Antennas
		6. Octopus [*side blue*]
		7. Two fish [*yellow*]

TAT

1. He's stuttering [*sic*] and doesn't want to anymore, but later he'll do it, and then his mother or father will test him to see what he knows, and he won't know too much because he won't be stuttering [*sic*] the violin. He thinks he did enough, but he didn't. [*How does he feel?*] Mad, because he doesn't want to, and if he doesn't he'll get in trouble. He wants to play, but he can't, so he gets in trouble. [*How trouble?*] Because he won't do it, and his father wants him to. [*Can't do, you said.*] Yeah, because too tired.

3 BM. He's crying and very mad. I think he got hurt, and can't do something what he wanted to because friend doesn't want to play with him. Friend would, but her mother wouldn't let him out, and he's mad because he had a date, and his friends won't like him anymore, because if had a date will just break it, and they already have a date with him today. Then he'll break the date because his mother won't let him out, and he can't call because he has no phone. [*Why not let him out?*] Did wrong, carried a scissors around and could have got hurt, and he will get the bad boy—a bad punishment, and he will get in trouble with his father for getting a scissors and carrying it, and he did carry the scissors around with him.

5. He—she—she won't go to get the milk and food. She wants to clean the house up. She is tired. She doesn't want to walk around because she does not want to go to outside now. Tomorrow she will get the milk and food for the children and herself, and his father, her husband, and [*is talking in staccato-like manner slowly for E to write it*] friends will come to supper and be nothing in the 'frigerator for food—nothing for food if they don't go out, and they won't go out because they want to play and play ball today. They will get it tomorrow, but tomorrow will be too late because we won't have anything for supper or breakfast or lunch for today or tomorrow. That is why. So please children go out. The end.

8 BM. He got new clothes today, and his father got hurt very badly, and he will get very sick if he doesn't go to the doctor today. [*Boy or father?*] Father will get very sick today, and he will get cancer or a very bad cold and he will go to the base hospital, and they might be able to save him from conking out. They might be able to save him from getting very sick. His son is very mad because he has been so nice to him to get the tie, shirt, socks, and pants for him and shoes, and he has been friends all his life with his father, and now he got very sick and they have to operate and get out what is ever wrong with him, or he will be very, but very, but very sick today, and he will go to home, even to tell his mother, and that is all.

16. Once upon a time there was a little boy. He was very sad because he did not have no money, and one day he went to the factory where his father works, but his father was not there. He went out for a coffee break, and he will get no food to eat, but then he got a very good idea too, because his father worked in the matzo factory he can ask one of the gentlemen if he may have a box of matzo balls because he loved them [*tells story of going to matzo factory in nursery school*] and he been very hungry and he will get something to eat after all. That's he liked matzo balls very much because he had them every day, except for two days didn't have any food because he went out and didn't come home. Out to play with big boys, but they would not let him play in the ball game. The end.

12 M. One day he had a bad cold. This lady, she'd been sick for many a day—"I'll be sick for now, you just leave and do your work," and he said, "If you want that, I will do that." [*What?*] I will go do that for him, and you have a very bad cold on your hands. You will get ammonia. [*sic!*] You should get a psychiatrist, I mean doctor to help you very much because you need a doctor to help you get better every day and he-she got better after all he said to she—I am good and fine, thank you, doctor, here is your money and leave us alone. One day she got sick again and passed away—then you should not of went outside—now look what happened—and he will have to get a maid to do the chores all around the house—and the man lived happily ever after. [*How come lived happily ever after?*] Because he got remarried. [*When?*] Forty hundred, no, four years ago. No one would live forty hundred years.

13 B. One day a boy named, we do not know, came over to our house. He was very sick and mad [*Why mad?*] Because he did not have no more friends, and he won't go out with no more friends, and he went out to play with the basketball but he went to the laundrymat [*sic!*] to get the clothes. One day he went to the laundrymat [*sic!*] but clothes were not there. I do not know what coulda happened to it, why I do not know what coulda happened to a little boy, to the clothes—and he went to machine where put clothes and get clothes back then he went to the house and gave the clothes to the rightful owner. The end of the story.

6 BM. One day a lady and man went out to have dinner when they came home felt sick and sad. They got tireder and tireder and sicker and sicker every day of going out. After went out one more day they got sick. One day they would not go out, and man said, "Why not?" "Because I feel like not going out, we used up so much money." [*Aside to E:* "I'm eating out today, too. I ate out for the last three weeks."] Next day they were great—would wanna go out for fortieth day of life—it cost too much money. Let's go out for dinner, lunch, and breakfast. One day they had seven hamburgers and when got home they had the baddest stomachache four persons could have. One day a person came over to the house to have supper, lunch, and dinner, and they would not have to eat out no more. The end.

7 BM. One day a person had a stomachache. He said he did not feel well, but his father had pride in him. He got good and better every day in the week. One day they went to church. He threw up by accident. Next day his father did not have no more pride for doing that. [*Didn't know it was accident?*] No, didn't. Next day got up and went to the church and father made him apologize to people at church and never should go back there again. He did it by accident he said to him. That is a lie. No, but then he believed him, and they were able to go back every church day. Next day they made up and went home. Next day he went to the church and went to school. He felt better, and he went back to church to say goodbye. The end of that church for him, he said the end to go back. The end. [*Much difficulty sitting still.*]

Psychological Test Portrait

M: 7–6 Male

M is a boy aged 7–6 who was referred because of enuresis and temper tantrums, which have been ongoing since approximately age 3. He also has problems in school.

He lives with his parents and is an only child.

He is cute and likable with large eyes. He was very concerned about his achievement, questioning E constantly as to how he was doing. This was an almost automatized behavior, since E 's feedback made no difference. He became distractible on different tasks, making peculiar noises and walking around the room.

Cognitive Functioning

WISC: M achieves a dull normal IQ score for both Verbal and Full Scale. His Performance score is average. There is little variation among the subtests with the exception of Object Assembly and Vocabulary. Generally, his answers are constricted, and he frequently makes no effort. Because of this, it is difficult to know if M has a greater potential than what he gives.

M has trouble in his language usage (Information, 5; Comprehension, 2 and 6; Similarities, 2 and 8; Vocabulary 5) on occasion. His difficulty is too inconsistent for us to specify its nature.

He shows trouble in concentration and attention (Digit Span, backwards; Arithmetic) as well as in shifting his orientation when faced with a new kind of problem (Arithmetic, 4; Similarities, 4 and 5; Picture Arrangement, D). He shows little ability to exercise critical judgment.

The low score in Object Assembly seems to be related in part to his assumption that E is "tricking" him (see *Dynamics*). There is an obvious discrepancy in M's ability to see the gestalt immediately (*horse, auto*) and inability to construct it (also see *Dynamics*).

B–G: The Bender productions are within M's age range and consistent with his achievement on the WISC. He shows impulsivity in his execution (A, 4, 5, 7, and 8), ommission (3), and substitution (5). This is in contrast to good organization and good control on some figures (A, 1, 6).

It was unclear in the WISC whether M had the cognitive energy available to him to achieve more. Here it becomes clearer that M can expend the extra attention and concentration to put out the effort necessary to achieve good results.

FD: M clearly has a concept of the body. There is some attempt to visualize the details of the body (and head) appropriately. The end product, however, leaves much to be desired (see *Dynamics*).

Rorschach: The Rorschach percepts are generally well organized and seen clearly. He is able to make good use of the structure of the blot, sees P's, and has original responses (IX, 1 and 2). He uses most of the determinants and has an adequate number of responses. All of this reflects M's ability to attend and elaborate in a task when he seemed to be comfortable. We, therefore, now see that he has a much greater cognitive potential than was evident in the WISC, but was somewhat suggested in the Bender. His language, again, is variable, but the variability tends to be from immature to mature usage.

TAT: *M* is able to produce only one logical story (Card 1) to the TAT cards. Otherwise, he gets lost in his own associations, losing both the card stimulus and his story sequence. There are several incidents of identity confusion (Cards 2, 4, 8 BM, and 12 M), and magical or arbitrary thinking persists throughout (with the exception of Card 1). His language is also arbitrary at times (Card 4, "war fight") and at other times immature (Card 8 BM).

Summary Statement of Cognitive Functioning: *M*'s cognitive functioning is extremely variable, seemingly dependent on the nature of the task. It seems all the more remarkable that his minimal performance in the WISC led to a normal IQ when there is evidence of his propensity for magical and arbitrary thinking. There is also evidence that he is capable of higher levels of cognitive achievement that his IQ would suggest.

Dynamic Picture

WISC: The persistent dynamic in the WISC is in *M*'s repetitive question, "Is it right?" One might assume that this reflects an inordinate need for re-assurance and support, but, in fact, this is not *M*'s intent. Rather, he seems to be using this phrase in a magical fashion (see *Defenses*), rather than as an ex-pression of a need to achieve.

There are suggestions of his extreme fear of aggression (Comprehension, 4, 6, and 7; Similarities, 4) which may be related to feelings of vulnerability seen in his inability to handle the Object Assembly in spite of his quick iden-tification of the whole.

M also feels himself in the position of being victimized or "tricked," as seen in the Object Assembly, which surely should add to his feelings of vulnerability.

B–G: The Bender shows *M*'s conflict between a need to do the right thing (A, counting on 1, 2, and 5) and a resistance to compliance (3 and 5). Other than this, no other dynamic is evident.

FD: The bizarre quality of the expression of vulnerability in *M*'s figures approaches the delusional. The idiosyncratic quality of each feature is in-comprehensible. For example, on the male figure, the 2 for an ear, the mouth, and the lines on the chin would seem to have meaning to *M*, but not to us. The bird-like limbs, the empty eyes, the strange ears (or lack of them) all suggest *M*'s fear of being unable to deal with the outside world. As in the male figure, there are also delusional qualities in the female figure—that is, the hair, lines on the face and body, and what appears to be a heart. Even *M*'s distinction between male and female is carried through strange elaborations between hair differences, eye differences, and details on the body. The amorphous quality of the body-contour line suggests *M*'s sense of himself as inadequate and unreliable.

Rorschach: As seen previously, the fear in *M*'s sense of vulnerability is clear in his Rorschach percepts (III, 1; VIII; and IX, aside). The conflict between the need to achieve and the intrusion of his own delusional thinking is clearly evident here (II; III, except 1a; IV, 2; VI, 1; VIII; and the aside on IX).

Although *M* has the sense of himself as a person (III), there is little clarity to this concept. His focus on hands (II, III) is as though he feels these to be the only body parts that can cope. Similarly, he produces clear symbolic sexual distinction between VI and VII, but does not utilize the popular figures in VII. In other words, *M* can entertain the concept of the person, but his definition is arbitrary. *M*'s unusual view of the body (III, VIII, and FDs) is also reflected in the concept of hiding in the bushes (IX). This seems to refer to concern about the unseen or the unknown, which bespeaks the increased sense of vulnerability in face of aggressive impulses.

TAT: *M*'s stories (other than Card 1) are filled with themes of aggression. Women and boys are good and are always in danger from real and fictional male villains. They are unable to ward off the murderous aggression, except when magical solutions occur. The extreme push to express aggression and the fear this engenders leads *M* to concoct arbitrary story lines as well as solutions. Although the theme of women and boys against aggressive men implies Oedipal concerns, *M* is dealing on a far more primitive level with fear for his own existence in face of malevolent forces. The only exception is the story to Card 1, where the boy is alone and able to cope with damage. All other stories portray the frighteningly dangerous nature of interpersonal relationships. There is no suggestion of nurturance or protectiveness in interactions between the nonvillainous people.

Summary Statement of Dynamic Picture: *M* is preoccupied with the threat of aggression to himself. He feels himself threatened by the manipulations of others and his own sense of vulnerability. He sees himself as being victimized by others' malevolent intents. There are conflicts on the basic level of reality versus fantasy, right and wrong, autonomy versus compliance, and maturity versus immaturity.

Defenses

WISC: The major defense seen in the WISC is denial. *M* either questions or states the rightness of his answers, regardless of their appropriateness. The other defense to emerge is projection when faced with the anxiety elicited by his vulnerability (in Object Assembly).

B–G: There is evidence for some ability for compulsivity in *M*'s attention to the correct numbers of dots and circles (1, 2, and 5). At the same time, he for some reason (fatigue, resistance) drops his compulsivity and uses more concrete and simple tactics (3, 5, and 7) to accomplish the task.

FD: In the drawings *M* uses denial and avoidance in unseeing eyes, unattached or absent ears, ineffective limbs, and undifferentiated bodies. An attempt at intellectualization is made in emphasizing the large heads and features. The idiosyncratic concern he has about his body is projected on the figures in their bizarre details.

Rorschach: Strikingly, *M* is able to utilize intellectualization (through the structure of the blot and the determinants) to create good percepts throughout the Rorschach. Although he attempts to avoid through vagueness in his initial responses to Cards I and II, this defense does not persist. In two instances (Cards I and V) we speculate that he uses the concreteness of the cardboard to protect himself from the experience of losing distance. The ability to intellectualize, however, is unstable, as upon questioning he becomes arbitrary and, on occasion, illogical (IV, 2). At other times this defense helps him to recover (III, 1a; VIII). There is a constriction in spontaneity, drive impulse, and interactions seen in the absence of *M, FM,* and limited *CF.*

TAT: *M*'s stories reflect the chaos that ensues when he cannot utilize even minimal defensive efforts. Although it is obvious that he is perceptually in contact with the original stimulus, his associations follow primary process principles.

Summary Statement of Defenses: Although *M* shows the ability to use intellectualization as a defense, it is not a reliable tactic for control over disturbing associations. Therefore, he often resorts to avoidance, denial, and attention to concrete details as ways of reducing the threat. When seemingly most threatened, he responds with projection. This can become so extreme that he can appear delusional on occasion.

Affective Expression

WISC: We can interpret from the nature of *M*'s questions and comments his extreme anxiety in response to the nature of this task. This anxiety was so great that nothing could reassure him.

B–G: The Bender suggests ambivalence in *M*'s affect. There is a willingness to comply and at the same time a resistance to putting forth the effort.

FD: *M*'s figures, bizarre as they are, still have a quality of *joie de vivre*. They convey the sense that he enjoyed the task.

Rorschach: The Rorschach is also filled with ambivalent affects. This is enacted in the way he deals with color—where he responds to the color, but is unable to integrate it in his percepts (II, 1; VIII). The one exception in IX seems to be permissible because of the concept of hiddenness.

TAT: As seen in the FDs, in spite of the nature of the content, *M* appears to enjoy this task. Notably, none of the characters is ascribed feelings, with the one exception of love (Card 4), but even here, he is confused and moves quickly into the aggressive theme.

Summary of Affective Expression: Generally, *M* is a very tense and anxious child. On occasion, despite the nature of the content, he appears to have good feelings about himself and the task.

Summary

M is an extremely frightened and tense child who is struggling to maintain reality contact. His fear of aggression seems sometimes to emanate from his concern over his own destructive potential and, at other times, is projected, leaving him afraid of others' intentions. This has particularly terrifying aspects because of its being within the context of a feeling of extreme body vulnerability and fragility. This state of terror leaves *M* with only the recourses of denial, avoidance, and, more generally, isolation from others. Even his fantasy is fraught with this terror, and the only relief is through magical solutions. The preoccupation with his fears extends into all areas, reducing the possibility of pleasure in intellectual achievement or in personal relationships. At times the intensity of these concerns becomes so great that it can produce delusional ideas.

With all of this, *M* is still able to maintain reality and makes efforts to please by compliance. He has some sense of himself as a person, and can use intellectual defenses well at times. *M*'s symptoms are obviously overdetermined, but definitely reflect his difficulties in control. In the same way that we cannot understand some of his repeated preoccupations (hands, hearts, idiosyncratic thinking), the meaning of his symptoms would, we hope, become clear in therapy with him.

Diagnosis:

GAP:	No appropriate diagnosis available
DSM III:	Axis I: 307.60 (Functional Enuresis)
	Axis II: 301.83 (Borderline Personality)
	Axis III: None
	Axis IV: 1 (None)
	Axis V: 5 (Poor)

M's concern with aggression is not on the primitive oral level seen in the psychotic. Moreover, he fluctuates between good and poor reality contact, but he never loses his awareness of reality. He is able at times to muster good defensive coping strategies, although at other times there are intrusions in their effectiveness. Although M does not express spontaneous joy or feelings of warmth for others, there is an ambivalent pleasure still available to him. This variable functioning in every area is consistent with a borderline diagnosis.

Therapy with M will not be easy, primarily because of his difficulty in relating. For treatment to progress, it would be necessary to have family participation. There is a moderately hopeful prognosis for M at this age, if indeed his family can be involved.

Psychological Test Data

M: 7–6 Male

WISC

		Scaled Score
Verbal Tests		
Information		8
Comprehension		9
Arithmetic		7
Similarities		9
Vocabulary		5
Digit Span		10
	Total	Prorated for 6 tests = 40

Performance Tests

Picture Completion	12
Picture Arrangement	10
Block Design	10
Object Assembly	5
Coding	10
Total	47

		Scaled Score	IQ
Verbal Scale	Prorated	40	87
Performance Scale		47	96
Full Scale		87	89

Information

		Score
1.		1
2.		1
3.		1
4.		1
5.	Put water in pan, and put on top of oven	1
6.	Grocery store	1
7.	Five	1
8.	I don't know.	0
9.	Lincoln	0
10.	I don't know.	0
11.	I don't know.	0
12.	I don't know.	0
	Total	7

[Note: *Usually asks if he is right.*]

Comprehension

		Score
1.	Put Band-Aid on it.	2
2.	Have to find it [?]	
	Tell him he lost it.	1
3.	Go to another store.	2
4.	I don't know. [?] Don't know.	0
5.	Tell him to stop. [?] Wave your hand.	1
6.	Brick better [?] stronger. [?]	
	Rain could break through wood.	
	Is that it—am I doing good	
	so far?	1
7.	'Cause they're bad. They steal. [?]	
	Hurt people.	0
8.	I don't know. Too hard.	0
9.	'Cause don't have enough money?	0
10.	I don't know.	0
	Total	7

Arithmetic

		Score
1.	9	1
2.		1
3.		1
4.	I don't know.	0
5.	6	1
6.	I don't know.	0
7.	I don't know.	0
8.	3¢	0
	Total	4

Similarities

		Score
1.	Sweet	1
2.	Feet [*repeat?*] feet	0
3.	Girls—ladies	1
4.	I don't know. Doing good?	0
5.	I don't know.	0
6.	Whiskers, feet, and eyes	1
7.	I don't know.	0
8.	They play—could do same tune—is that it? [*repeats*]	1
9.	Could burn.	1
10.	I don't know.	0
11.	I don't know.	0
12.	Water and mountain high—right—right—so far I'm right.	0
	Total	5

Digit Span:

F 6 + B 2   Total Score   8

Vocabulary

		Score
1.	Something you ride on with wheels [*?*] two wheels	2
2.	Something you cut with	2
3.	Wear it and hang it up [*Where?*] on head	2
4.	Mail it to somebody far away [*?*] that's all.	2
5.	In case it rains, put it under your head [*?*] not under. [*?*] You know, then put it in bathtub. [*?*] It's wet, you don't want it to go all over house.	0
6.	Sleep on it—rest on it.	1
7.	Bang it in wall, and it holds something up.	2
8.	I don't know.	0
9.	Like a fur coat [*?*] keeps you warm, and it's soft and furry.	1

10.	Something you wear [?]	
	I don't know.	0
11.	I don't know.	0
12.	I don't know.	0
13.	Something you saw with, wood.	0
14.	I don't know.	0
	Total	12

Picture Completion

		Score
1.		1
2.		1
3.		1
4.		1
5.		1
6.		1
7.		1
8.		1
9.	Hole should be bigger	0
10.	Buttonhole	1
11.	Other hand [*fin*]	0
12.	I don't know.	0
13.	I don't know.	0
14.	I don't know.	0
15.	I don't know.	0
	Total	9

Picture Arrangement

	Time	*Order*		*Score*
A.	4"	ABC	I'll do it!	2
B.	5"	TOY		2
C.	10"	IRON		2
D.	20"	BCA		0
[*Fight*]		XYZ	Is it right? [*repeats several times*]	
1.	44"	FIRE		4
2.	20"	THUG		4
3.	22"	QSTR		0
4.	30"	EHFG		0
			Total	14

Block Design

	Time	*Score*
A.	18"	2
B.	9"	2
C.	9"	2
1.	75"	0
2.	75"	0
	Total	6

[*Note: Repeatedly asks if he's right. Easily gives up on Block Design.*]

Object Assembly

	Time		*Score*
M	15"	See how good I am. You tried to trick me by putting it backwards.	3
H	180"	Horse! [*immediate*]	0
F	180"		1
A	180"	It's a car! [*immediate*] You try to trick me.	2
		Total	6

[*Note:* "I'm very good at puzzles, but this is much too hard for me."]

Coding A	Total Score	35

[*Makes peculiar noises—easily distracted several times*]

Bender–Gestalt

Figure Drawings

Rorschach

I.   5″   1. A painting—what I drawed. That's all.

               2. Looks like a bat. Is it? [?] Looks like one.

I.   2. Is it really a bat? [?] I'm asking you. [*Real bat?*] No, that's not what I mean. Wings [*side* D] eyes [*top* d] body [*center* D] [?] Just looks like one.

       1. [*Painting?*] Design. Is it a painting? [?] Just a design. [?] I don't know. Looks like it's painted on piece of cardboard.

II.   6″V   1. Looks like shape of flower. That's all.

II.   1. I don't know what kind. [?] I don't know. Just 'cause it has red stuff in it. [*everything in flower but* S] a. Looks like eagle, too, [W] legs [*red top*], eyes, [di, *red bottom*] wings, [*side* D] body in white part. [*looks like eagle?*] 'Cause of feet. b. Looks like hand, too, but not a lot. Two fingers [*top red*] [*places hand on card*].

III.   1. Looks like two persons, the inside of a person, or

              2. A woodpecker

III.   1. [*All usual parts except hands—hands are extended into red, center, joined.*] This is another hand. [*bottom center*] That's one hand, and this [*red*] is another.

       2. [*Woodpecker?*] I don't know. [*points to people*] a. Looks like chandelier hanging from wall [*top side red*] [?] 'Cause it's round and has things sticking up.

IV.   5″   1. That's a bat
      V   2. Looks like a
                spider.

V.   3″   1. This looks like a
                small bat.

              2. Looks like butterfly.
                This picture looks
                like butterfly.

VI.   20″ V   1. Looks like violin
                'cause it has that and
                this [*top extension
                and side projection*]

              2. Looks like machine
                gun. [*?*] Got handles.
                It just looks like
                machine gun.

VII.   8″   1. Looks like necklace because
                it's round—not exactly
                round. But could put it
                around your neck, and you
                could wear it. [*?*] Got big
                things—beads around it.
                [*Each segment is a bead.*]

VIII.   5″   1. This looks like inside of a
                body. The parts. Don't it
                look like it to you? Don't
                it? Different kind of col-
                ors. Part of head [*very top
                projection*] neck, attached
                to arms [*usual animals*],
                heart [*center d*], part of
                body [*bottom pink and
                orange*]. [*Where see
                something like this?*] If you
                see a skeleton, it looks like
                it. [*?*] I don't know. [*See
                inside of body?*] X-ray
                machine. [*?*] This is.

IV.   1. Bat, wings, head
                [*bottom center*]
                [*looks like bat?*] I
                don't know—just
                looks like it.

  V   2. [*Spider?*] Looks
                like spider, too. [*?*]
                I don't know. [*Why
                look like spider?*]
                'Cause it has wings,
                and it's shaped like
                it. [*Spider have
                wings?*] Yeah. [*Fly
                too?*] They do.

V.   2. Butterfly, 'cause it
                has wings, and it's
                shaped like it.

           1. [*Bat?*] Looks like
                small bat. Like a de-
                sign, too. [*?*] Wings
                and shaped like it.
                It can fly. [*?*] No,
                this is cardboard.

VI.   1. [*Violin?*] String part
                and handle. Old
                violin. [*?*] 'Cause
                it's gray [*?*] Some
                are, and some are
                brown, too.

           2. [*Handles?*] [*side*] I
                don't know.

IX.   Looks like inside of—   IX.
15″

1. Looks like giant
bird, no.
2. Looks like robot
hiding in bushes.
Looks like giant
bird, too.

1. Bird hiding in bushes
[*each orange* D *is
wing, body in center,
no detail to head*]
[*Why hiding?*] I
don't know. Maybe
just wants to.
2. Green bushes—
orange arms and
body [*light green*]
He got power pack
on that makes him
fly. Smoke comes
out here [*pink is
smoke*]. [*Hiding?*]
I don't know.
Maybe wants to
scare another robot
away.

X.   5″   1. Looks like picture of
spiders. Lots of
spiders.
2. Looks like eagle and
smaller eagle.

X.   1. [*Spiders?*] [*blue side
area*] Yellow stuff.
[*side*]
2. [*Eagle?*] Pink and
green. [*top*] [*?*] Just
'cause it has wings.
[*Parts?*] No.
a. Fish [*top brown*]
b. Shark [*bottom
green*]
c. Turtle [*brown
center*]

TAT

1. Boy sitting down, and he had violin. It was broken. [*?*] He couldn't play it. [*?*] He tried to
fix it, and then he fixed it, and that's the end. [*Feel?*] Happy. [*?*] 'Cause his violin is fixed.
2. Girl lost in a desert, and there are bad people, and then she lived on a farm in the country.
The man was bad, and she couldn't take it any longer. Suddenly she wanted to go—to
ride a horse. The man stopped her 'cause you can't get outa here—that's what the man
said. That's all. [*End?*] She went back in house, and she saw an apple and was a prince.
The witch turned a prince into a house, and then she married the prince. The end.
6 GF. Girl sleep down on the bed, and then this man came along and wanted to kill her. He was
smoking a pipe, and he had knife in his hand. Lady said to get off her—herself. Secret
passageway and man left and button over there, and she pressed it, and door went back
and was a tunnel. Ghosts down there, and she made herself up like a ghost, and when
man came she frightened man away. End. [*Why kill her?*] I don't know. [*?*] I don't know.
3 BM. Boy—man had a gun—wait . . . and man shooted boy with gun, and he was dead. He
wanted the jewels. [*?*] Robber. [*Dead boy in picture?*] Yeah. Robber wanted combination to safe. Put water in boy's face and woke him up. He got fake teeth, you
know—those that look sharp—when man put water on him, he scared him away, and
that's the end.
4. Man loved, no—lady loved the man and was a war fight, and man had to go fight [*?*] the
bad people. Lady try to stop him, but he couldn't and just went. Ten men out there who
almost shot him, but he still ain't dead. He took machine gun and weapon and went out
with army clothing. One of men shot him, and he got dead. In couple of months he woke
up and was saved. And that's the end.

7 BM. Can't make up a story. [?] Can't think of any. Can't do it. [*keeps asking what* E *is writing.*]

  15. He was a vampire, and this girl came along. He looks like a robot, but he ain't. Somebody shot him one day—he looks like statue—man in the war with bad men. Bad man shot the good people. The police came, but couldn't arrest him. [?] Couldn't see him because he took some kind of pill. He was still there. Somebody shot him with fire. Only fire could hurt him. He got shot with fire, and he's dead. The end.

8 BM. This is part of this story [*No. 15*]. Took him to doctor to get well. Had to stay in hospital ten weeks. The boy was his father. They had to take out the bullet. He was OK after ten weeks. He had to go into a wheelchair. He had bullet in chest and leg. Boy pushed him on wheelchair, and then somebody shot him ten times in chest and leg. He died, and that's the end.

12 M. This is Frankenstein, and lady was sleeping. Frankenstein waked him up. He had a mask and wasn't really Frankenstein. She's trying to get out. Man killed lady, and another lady came with her and was in the room. Frankenstein killed other lady, and they lived happily ever after. That's the end.

Psychological Test Portrait

N: 8–8 Female

N is an 8–8 girl, an only child, referred by her mother for the following problems. She is sexually preoccupied, frequently masturbates, has facial tics, low frustration tolerance, no real friends, nightmares, and sucks her thumb. Her parents were separated, and she was able to get along better with her father. Her father reported that the facial tics diminished the longer she was absent from the mother.

She is a round-faced girl of average size, who clutched her lunch box to her. When E moved the box to another table, she checked it carefully every so often as if to ensure that all was intact. She compulsively talked, verbalizing her difficulties, performance, and actions. As things became more difficult, she became more voluble. She went to her lunch box (prepared by her father) which contained a large bag of hearts with "I love you" on them and a thermos of juice. As she took only one candy at a time, she had to get up frequently. As she vigorously sucked, she began to rock in her seat, snap her fingers, and hum with a euphoric-like expression. Her arm movements and verbal affect became somewhat flamboyant and more dramatic. On a couple of occasions she interjected arbitrary statements, for example, "My teacher is kooky. She can't control the class, but not too bad. She didn't commit suicide, and went on with it."

Cognitive Functioning

WISC: N's above-average IQ of 115 is misleading, as it does not tell us the superior level she performs on the Verbal tests and the just average score in the Performance. The 26-point discrepancy would raise the question of a learning disability first. Rather, there is a great deal of variability between and within tests. Also, there is confusion and disorganization in her approach to solving tasks. The hallmark of the total WISC is the unusual and idiosyncratic flavor of most of her responses and her reasoning. Therefore, the WISC suggests a child with peculiar ideation.

In spite of her strange associations, she is able to offer good and accurate responses as long as she does not get too involved in the content. She is able to verbalize a good awareness of social expectations, can handle abstractions easily, and has excellent language knowledge. Her method of computation in Arithmetic suggests she was unable to concentrate on the presented problem and rather confabulated her own problem. This intrusion may be responsible for her low score on Digit Span, backwards, also. In a way that we do not understand, the tasks of Arithmetic, Picture Completion, Picture Arrangement, and Object Assembly triggered either unusual anxiety or strange associations that led to highly unusual approaches. In spite of this, she still works hard and sometimes achieves some success (for example, the face in Object Assembly).

B–G: Although N is only 8, the productions in the Bender suggest the absence of perceptual-motor difficulties. It also confirms disorganization in her approach and strange combinations of elements (2, 5, first rendition of 6).

FD: Strange elements again appear in the drawings. The girl has only one elaborated eyebrow, which is outstanding when one looks at the care with which the eyelashes are drawn. The nostril is odd, and in addition she has tears. The body stops at the bottom of the page without legs or feet. The extreme size of the head in relation to the body is notable. The boy's body also stops at the bottom of the page, and his body is inscrutable.

Rorschach: In spite of the bizarre associations in N's responses, she does manage to produce populars and utilize the structure of the blots. Furthermore, she produces thirty-six responses, many organized W's, and, generally, conveys a sense of intellectual energy.

TAT: In spite of the obvious thought disorder, N constructs elaborate stories with plots, beginnings, middles, and ends; assigns feelings to the characters; and, initially, starts off each story in response to the picture (with the exception of 3 BM). She is able to incorporate a sophisticated knowledge of the world, and, also, to display remarkable spelling for her age and excellent use of phonics. There is perceptual denial in Cards 1 and 8 GF, and she perceptually combines the two last cards (2 and 7 GF).

Summary Statement of Cognitive Functioning: N's cognitive functioning is very susceptible to the intrusions of her idiosyncratic associations, illogical assumptions, and unrealistic interpretations. Although her language at times has a poetic flavor, it is arbitrarily composed of concrete and meaningless juxtapositions. In spite of this great difficulty, she still reveals an extraordinary intelligence with evidence of having learned a great deal.

Dynamic Picture

WISC: In certain WISC items, N already demonstrates a concern with body vulnerability (Comprehension, 6 and 8; Vocabulary, 5; Similarities, 11) and body integrity (Information, 14; Picture Completion, 13, 14, 15, 18, 19, and 20; Picture Arrangement, E, F, G, and H, the difficulty experienced in the Object Assembly). Also, her concern with aggression emerges (Vocabulary, 13, 18, 22, and 24; Picture Arrangement, *FISHER*).

B–G: The Bender does not reveal any dynamic considerations.

FD: Body vulnerability is revealed in the drawings in the fragile body of the girl and her tears, and in the boy through his glasses and distorted body.

Rorschach: N's Rorschach percepts show an inordinate preoccupation with body mutilation, oral incorporation, and death. The autistic interpretation of the functioning of the body and its parts reflects a delusional system about the body. In addition, the aggressive content is of a sadistic nature. One can see that N is disturbed on the most primitive level of oral trust in her pseudopoetic responses of "a shock-proof sound note" (VIII) and "bridge of death" (X).

TAT: Sadistic themes occur again in the stories to the TAT in 3 BM, 2, and 7 GF, and body distortions appear in the stories to 16, 2, and 7 GF. Although there is an emphasis on love, marriage, having children (8 GF, 16, 4), and family relationships (1, 3 BM, 2, and 7 GF), the development of the stories demonstrates that N is not at a phallic-Oedipal level.

Summary Statement of Dynamic Picture: N is inordinately preoccupied with thoughts and fears of annihilation. She provides information suggesting a delusional system about the body and feelings of extreme vulnerability. This is related to her sadistic impulses and fears of oral incorporation. Although she has a facade of social comprehension and relatedness, it is very superficial, as her autistic associations must emerge.

Defenses

WISC: When N experiences difficulty on WISC items, she can become concrete (Information, 13) or projects her own disordered reasoning on the test item (Information, 14, 15; Arithmetic; Picture Completion, 1; Picture Arrangement, 1; Object Assembly). She tries to use oral reassurance (sucking on candies) and avoidance (having to leave the test item to get the candy) as ways of coping with her experience of difficulty. In the B–D she projects blame on the task and on E by stating that structure had not been provided.

B–G: Compulsive attempts are seen in efforts to count the dots or loops and reproduce the number correctly. Her compulsivity, however, is interfered with by a seeming inability to maintain the necessary concentration.

FD: The content of the drawings suggests N's wish to control the body via ideation. She also avoids detailing any body part below the shoulders. There is also the suggestion of a paranoid-like defense in the ears on the boy and the eyes in both figures.

Rorschach: The major defense seen in the Rorschach is in N's attempt to establish a paranoid stance. This fails again and again because of the loss of distance between her percept and herself, and it becomes interwoven in a delusional system. Her anger mounts toward E, who seems to become the responsible party for her distress. Her inordinate push for all-inclusive W's to establish control also fails.

TAT: Somehow, the TAT offered N the opportunity to feel in total control of the task and of E. She, therefore, is euphoric as she dictates her stories to E and is eager to correct and criticize E. In this way she maintains cognitive structure and does not lose distance as seen in the Rorschach. We speculate that the nature of the instruction to "tell a story" provided her with a socially acceptable format for her fantasy (that is, like her statement needing a "frame" in the B–D).

Summary Statement of Defense: Although N uses different defenses, none of them is adequate for preventing the intrusion and expression of her disturbing ideas. She uses avoidance and can become compulsive, but mainly she attempts to handle distressing material through projection. She is unable to maintain the paranoid position she seeks, however, because she is unable to distinguish between the materials and herself.

Affective Expression

WISC: Generally, N's mood was pleasant and conforming throughout the Verbal items. In the Performance items, although she tried hard, she experienced a great deal of anger at the test items. She seemed to attempt to mask her anger at times through singing, humming, and sucking her candies.

B–G: N worked on the designs with effort and did not seem to be at all distressed in this task.

FD: This task was a pleasure for N, seemingly because E did not make demands, and she felt in total control.

Rorschach: In addition to the nature of the blots in this test, E's questions made N increasingly upset and angry. She again attempted to deny her anger by singing (Cards V and VIII) and by spending an excessive amount of time unwrapping her candies (Card VII).

TAT: As on the FD, N's mood was happy and gay, as if the task itself were a cathartic experience for her.

Summary Statement of Affective Expression: N seemed capable of only two moods. She was happy, and sometimes euphoric, when she sensed herself in charge. When she experienced herself as being controlled by the other (in this case, E), she became angry.

Summary

Due to the nature of N's disturbance, there are certain aspects to be highlighted. The paramount one is her thought disorder. This intrudes in all areas of functioning. At times there is a pseudopoetic quality to her verbalizations, there are many logical contradictions, there is an autistic delusional system with respect to the body, there are peculiar verbalizations, confusion between animate and inanimate, loss of distance, and syncretistic thinking. This leads to a totally egocentric perception and relationship to the world.

One aspect of N's idiosyncratic thinking to be highlighted is her need to incorporate two totally different percepts (sometimes opposites) into a single unit. She does this on a thinking, perceptual, and motor level. It is seen most explicitly in her drawing of the female between the left and right sides of the body. We do not know what this means, but it seems very significant because of its pervasiveness.

N demonstrates an awareness of socially appropriate behavior. This awareness, however, is most superficial. She attempts to deny her idiosyncratic thoughts and her sudden anger responses by withdrawing from the interpersonal realm and engaging in autistic-like behavior.

Diagnosis:

GAP:	Schizophreniform psychotic disorder
DSM III:	Axis I: 295.32 (Schizophrenic Disorder Paranoid Type)
	Axis II: None

        Axis III: None
        Axis IV: 5 (Severe)
        Axis V: 4 (Fair)

   N should benefit from intensive individual psychotherapy. Her parents
need to be involved in corollary treatment to help them not use N in their
ongoing struggle. It is quite possible, given the degree of disturbance, the extent of the parental discord, and the advent of adolescence, that N would re-
quire residential treatment.

Psychological Test Data
N: 8–8 Female

WISC

	Scaled Score
Verbal Tests	
Information	13
Comprehension	17
Arithmetic	9
Similarities	16
Vocabulary	16
(Digit Span)	(13)
Total	71

	Scaled Score
Performance Tests	
Picture Completion	8
Picture Arrangement	9
Block Design	11
Object Assembly	9
Coding	13
Total	50

	Scaled Score	IQ
Verbal Scale	71	126
Performance	50	100
Full Scale	121	115

Information

		Score
1.	Two	1
2.	Thumb	1
3.	Four	1
4.	Cow	1
5.	Boil it—water in pot and heat up stove	1

6.	Grocery	1
7.	Five	1
8.	Seven	1
9.	Columbus	1
10.	Twelve	1
11.	Spring, fall, summer, winter	1
12.	Red	1
13.	Behind a cloud or a mountain	0
14.	Thinks—holds up your intestines	0
15.	Because oil is really oil, because stays on top, because it has globs and—light water or heavy water, any water—I know what it is—take a Sardo bath with the moisture in it.	0
16.	I don't know.	0
17.	Independence Day	1
18.	I don't know.	0
19.	Six feet, three inches	0
20.	In Mexico.	0
21.	Five	0
22.	Turkey	0
23.	France	0
24.	Seventy-five	0
25.	No	0
26.	No	0
27.	No	0
28.	No	0
29.	No	0
30.	No	0

Total   13

Comprehension

Score

1.	Put a Band-Aid; spray it; wash it.	2
2.	Should either replace and you always say I'm sorry, forgive me.	2
3.	Go to another store, and if they didn't have it, go to another store.	2
4.	You shouldn't hit her because you're much stronger than her.	2
5.	You should immediately pick up a stick and say, "watch out," scream, and set off any kind of thing. [*excitedly*]	2
6.	Brick is harder—stay up longer and brick is harder—can crack wood in two, but brick very hard to crack in two.	1
7.	Because they're very mean, and they should take a bit of their own medicine.	1
8.	Because much, much more delicate than men. Men can survive better than children and women can.	1
9.	Because by check have more time to pay it, but cash give it right away—wait till time is over to pay	0

10. Because organized charity doesn't go around begging—beggar could be a drunk and may want a drink, and organized charity you can trust.   2
11. Before he gets it—be sure he's healthy and not sick.   0
12. I don't know.   0
13. I don't know what a senator is— because they help us.   0
14. Because it's very important to keep a promise—it's cheating other person if say going to and don't. That's being a big liar and cheater.   2

             Total   17

Arithmetic

	Answers	Score
1.		1
2.		1
3.		1
4.	2	1
5.	6	1
6.	14	1
7.	7	1
8.	20¢	0
9.	19	0
10.	17	0
11.	25 days	0
12.	73¢	0
13.	—	0
14.	$1.00	0
15.	40¢	1
	Total	7 (8)

Similarities

		Score
1.		
2.		
3.		
4.		4
5.	Both fruits	2
6.	Both animals	2
7.	Both something to drink—usually strong. Both bitter or something.	1
8.	Both musical instruments—hard to play	2
9.	Both useful—draw on paper with coal	0
10.	Both with feet and have arithmetic in them	0
11.	Both very strong—hard to break and useful around house	1
12.	They go together with their view	0

13.	Both something you would cook with	1
14.	Both for independence and peace	1
15.	Both have to do with numbers—if form circle, they'll meet.	0
16.	Both numbers	0
	Total	14

Digit Span

F 7 + B 3   Total Score   10

Vocabulary

		Score
1.	Something with four—two wheels—ride around.	2
2.	Something to cut steak with—all kinds—steak knife, butter knife—to cut into.	2
3.	Something to wear on your head.	2
4.	Something you get from someone—gives you a note.	2
5.	When you have a rainstorm, it's to protect you or can have a sunny day to keep things from your eyes.	2
6.	All kinds—sitting cushion, sewing cushion to put pins in, cat's cushion [*etcetera*]	2
7.	A sharp tool like a pin for holding bird houses, or things together and has head on to stop or end it.	2
8.	A dumb, slow animal in Mexico, stubborn, will kick you.	2
9.	Usually from a fox or an animal—lot of money.	2
10.	That's real valuable—sparkly and it's a birthstone.	2
11.	To join a club—come along with us, let's join the fun, or join even bad things.	2
12.	On a card—something in a palace like kings and queens of spade.	2
13.	Usually used, not today, sharp instrument, shield to it—for dragons, your enemies, try to stick it in—never really a dragon—if were, stick in where it breathes fire.	2
14.	Someone that's bothered you, say they're a big nuisance. Sometimes call them a noods.	2
15.	Someone that's a hero—fight something dangerous—my father brave or something.	2
16.	Someone do silly things.	2
17.	A brave person—someone that saves someone and they had swords.	2

18.	Make a bet—play cards for money and shoot you if you cheat.	2
19.	I don't know.	0
20.	Have little things—you see the germs and things—become bigger, and you can study them.	2
21.	Money in Mexico.	1
22.	Old story—not usually true—something of a dragon or something.	2
23.	I think it's a country.	0
24.	A big war—a bomb, and they've had espionage in Germany.	0
25.	I don't know.	0
26.	No	0
27	No	0
28.	No	0
29.	No	0
30.	No	0
31.	No	0
32.	A shell	0
	Total	41

Picture Completion

		Score
1.	Some of fracks [*indicates correctly*]	1
2.	Leg	1
3.	Ear	1
4.	Mouth	1
5.	Other side of whiskers	1
6.	Other one of those to hold door	1
7.	Nail	1
8.	One spade	1
9.	I have no idea.	0
10.	Buttons	0
11.	Fin from other side	0
12.	It's hammer—also wood to put it in	0
13.	Probably a leg	0
14.	Wing from the other side	0
15.	An ear and shoulder	0
16.	Red line down middle	0
17.	Button to the buttonhole	0
18.	Someone holding it up	0
19.	Its udders	0
20.	A door	0
	Total	8

Picture Arrangement

	Time	Order		Score
A.				
B.				
C.				
D.				8
[*Fight*]		XYZ	The wife is always getting mad.	

1.	22″	FIRE		4
2.	17″	TGHU	Doorman there and he says, "Oh, I'm just on my own window, just moved in." Seems young to be a burglar.	0
3.	18″	QRST	Planting—growing	4
4.	31″	EFGH		4
5.	26″	PRCYE	Ends home in bed	0
6.	75″	ESFHIR	He ends up sad—going on his way—quit—and then was relaxing time.	0
7.	37″	MASRTE	Umbrella got lost.	0
			Total	20

[*Brought huge bag of candy with her lunch. Took some at No. 5, and sang and hummed as she sucked.*]

Block Design

	Time		*Score*
A.			2
B.			2
C.			2
1.	26″		4
2.	31″		0
3.	50″		0
4.	30″		4
5.	OT		0
6.	OT		0
		Total	14

Object Assembly

	Time		*Score*
M	18″	A human	5
H	31″	[*Recognized immediately, all correct, but legs reversed*]	5
F	180″	[*Hair pieces, nose and mouth*]	3
A	180″	[*Front three pieces done; Rest is confused—then gets all at 5'*]	3
		Total	16

Coding B   Total Score   36

Bender–Gestalt

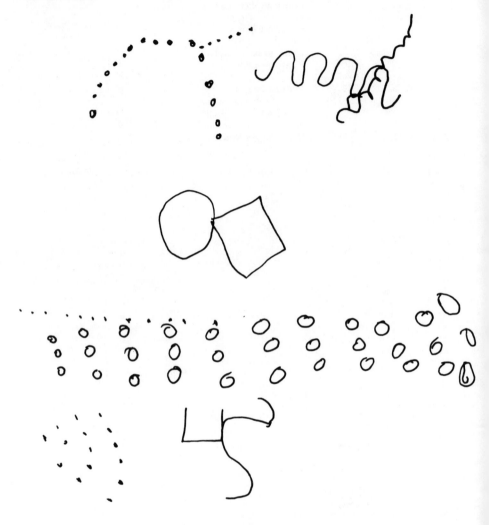

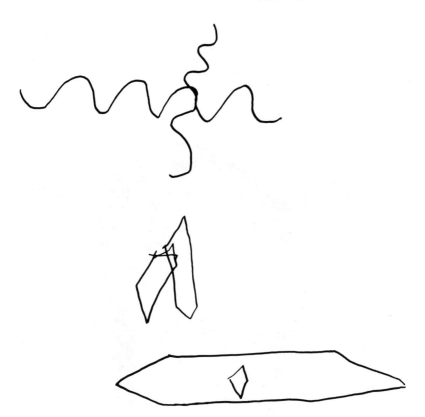

Figure Drawing

Girl or boy? [*Either*] I always draw pictures differently. [*then describes variation in terms of hair style*] This way [*filling in hair*] takes a long time. [*Hair finished before features drawn in.*]

    Any kind of a picture of a person? [*Mean?*] Make her crying or something like that—That's her dress coming down to end of page. [*sees dirt on paper—tries to rub off hands on skirt*] My hands are dirty.

[*Boy?*]
[*Very cooperative—willing—spontaneous. Again head outline drawn first followed by hair. Humming as works on hair.*] Football outfit—he didn't take his glasses off to play football.

Rorschach

I. 2" 1. Bat [W]

II. 5" 1. A moth

2. Friendly creature [W]

3. Upside down, it's a terrifying creature [W]

2. Sort of a monster [W] [*looks on back*] four-eyed—two-nosed.

III. 6" 1. A spider [*deep sighs*]
2. The bones by an old thing

3. A bow [*center* C]

I. 1. Wings—holes in him—a holely bat— seems to be two holes in it—and it seems to be leaning forward saying, "I'm gonna eat you." Looks like a deadly animal.

2. Four-eyed monster and two-nosed— beauty of the wings. [*Mean?*] Has beautiful wings. Looks like just gonna get you.

II. 1. Well, usually a moth is wide, and it's got a dividing line right here and here. [S] Looks like its body was cut out.

2. Two creatures— friendly but looks deathly because of the red blood—if it was moving the in- testines would move along. [*All red is the intestines.*]

3. Look at those big things coming out and feet, big feet coming out behind it. Looks like com- ing to suck your blood because in here the profiles. [*indicates inner shading*] Looks like sucked in blood, sucks in blood with its two tubes.

III. 1. Don't really see it.
2. Of a prehistoric thing because not exactly attached and look at sharp little teeth coming out of it.

3. Well, doesn't look like a bow—looks like these two little creatures just tied the bow because hands fit in there. It's shaped like.

4. Two friends talking
   to each other.

5. Two monkeys. [*side
   C*]

IV. 10″ 1. Two feet.

V.   2. Historical monster.
             [*W*] That's it.

V.   7″   1. A bat

2. Two crocodile heads

3. A wing-wing bird—big
   wings and little body.

VI. 3″   1. Lizard cat [*W*]
          2. An unknown creature,
             head up here
          3. A body bird [*1, 2, and
             3 were given as if all
             one response.*]

4. Beaks, tails—
   creatures talking to
   each other.

5. They got a long tail
   and hands and seem
   to be looking that
   way toward where
   you are sitting.

IV. 1. Clown's feet—because
        feet and shoes are
        big.

2. Has a big head, and
   these two little
   things seem to be
   spitting poison—
   wings and body—
   wing thing—rear
   end here. [*Q*]
   There's blood on it.

V.   1. Well, long wings,
        legs sticking out,
        looks just like a
        bat—it ate a royal
        person—like they
        say they're blue-
        blooded—I don't be-
        lieve it, but could
        imaginate in world
        of fantasy—but if
        you hit it you see
        blue blood around
        here [*hits card*].

2. You notice big head
   and long narrow
   mouth, and have
   that kind of edge
   and that bump
   around the mouth.
   [*singing*]

3. Look at the size of
   those wings on one
   little bit of
   things—floating
   right through the
   air—seems to have
   no trouble. [*Much
   erasing on blot with
   pencil eraser*]

VI. 1. Whiskers coming out
        of its body—thin—
        two eyes and whiskers
        that come out of it
        so I called it the cat.

2. [*W*] Look at lizard,
   the cat, the wings,
   and the big-sized
   body on it—it's a

"hard to live thing" because how would you like it if you had big thing sticking in back of you to carry and to fly. Want to fly and have big thing sticking in back of you for life—attached—to lizard cat—big body—hard to live thing-part that would be hard to live with.

VII. 2" 1. Two little animals having a little talk or fight.
2. A castle [*center* D]
V 3. Gate [W]

VII. 1. Little rabbits having a fight—talking it over.
2. Way far away.
3. Whole arch and someone right there [*presses eraser to center* S] would be crossing it. [*deliberate movements to open candy—as though rigidly controlling anger*]

VIII. 3" 1. Gophers

VIII. 1. Seem to be walking on a rock and water [*indicating half of blot*] and you see the reflection and top of water where it divides—exact fuzzy reflection.

2. Rocket

2. Point—seems to be dropping other parts and becoming capsule. Point made it look like a rocket—already in sky and we're becoming to have a missile. [*humming*]

3. Reflection of the water, see, somebody can climb in there.
4. A shock-proof sound note. [Q] Things seem to be shocking and still—earth quiet.

3. [*included in 1.*]

4. [W] People seem to be still—world is still. [Q] Does that look like its vibration? Sure doesn't look like it's moving—shock—still—people

					fuzzy—everything blurred. [*Why shock-proof sound note?*] No one seems to be falling through floor to death—shock-proof—water-proof—they won't die.
		5. Long-haired strange bird.			5. Don't really see a bird in it—world of fantasy again—long hair in top gray and rest a bird. [*Q*] Doesn't look like a bird.
IX.	9″	1. Kooky reflections—creatures—monstrous. Tongue sticking out, has an eye.	IX.		1. [*W*] Reflections because down here, too. Looks like this. [*moves hand in outward shaky way*] Horrible one has tongue out.
X.	3″	1. Crabs	X.		1. Long things seem to look like crabs—sticking out—and has things sticking out of the things that are sticking out. You understand?
		2. Bird–fox–head.			2. Well, long beak bird fox head rounds, slick eyes. [*fox head rounds?*] Well, fox would look like that—high cheeks, long jaw bones, [*slick eyes?*] very sharp, can see what they're not supposed to see. [*Before lunch, she drew an eye chart—a very difficult one—and tested her vision.*] They can see quite a lot—are half asleep now—they're slick and slim and seem to know what's going on around here, and he has nothing to fear of now, and he seem to know was going to be in for a big surprise, but now those people are in for a big surprise.

3.	Tweet-tweet bird	3.	It's going tweet-tweet—it's got two sides of its beak—tweet-tweet. What floor do you live on at home? They didn't have as many robbers when you were a child, but then they didn't have as many good shots. I guess some good and bad.
4.	Fire birds	4.	[*Fire birds?*] They had some sort of secret, you can't see wings, but they have yellow like fire.
5.	Animals	5.	Creepy animals—look like they're creeping up on you.
6.	Bridge of death	6.	[*Bridge of death?*] Because all these things are deathly, and they form a bridge, and the bridge is death, and no matter how you put it, you find same word coming out of my mouth. [*Deathly?*] Everything but the tweet-tweet bird. [*Why deathly?*] Because looks like going to get you all except tweet-tweet bird, but if it was, would be worse because usually the nicer looking the more mean they are.

TAT

1. Once upon a time—little boy is Tommy—one day he sat down, and he began to invent something. It was metal. He had quite a lot of metal. Tommy was a strong boy, so he could bend this metal. Then once—well, he began to invent—he bent his metal, and he had straight metal and crooked metal, and then he took some paint and painted a face on the front of it. He put some wheels on it, and it would

move. He went out to the store, and he bought a little siren so when it moved it would make a sound—zink, zink, zzzink—went the little truck.

Though Tommy did not call it a truck—he called it a Loolie bus—but he went downstairs and he played with it, [*looks to back of card*] and his mother and father got mad—so they said, "Tommy! Where did you get that awful thing?" He said, "Mother, Father, I made it." His father in a loud voice said, "You made a terrible thing like that, you ought to be ashamed of yourself." So tears began to fall from Tommy's eyes. After spending all my money, this is what I get!

His conscience slowly drifted and said, "Don't fear, Tommy, you'll get better results." Tommy sighed. Downstairs mother and father were saying, "Maybe we were too hard on Tommy. That was a good thing." But it was too late! Tommy had already got rid of the Loolie bus. Parents ran up to him and said they were sorry. So Tommy went out of his house. Quickly he went where he threw it and there it was. Lucky for Tommy he got it back very happily. The End.

5. Once upon a time there lived a woman. Her name was Mrs. Goo Four Tee. Now one day Mrs. Goo ran out of her house. I mean—say, into her living room. She thought she heard a little old noise nibbling on her door or on her furniture. Yes indeedy, there it was—a burglar and a mouse. She screamed, "Oh, dear!" She ran out of her house and called the police. They came and arrested the burglar, and they choked the mouse. That wasn't a nice thing to do. The End.

[*From here on, N dictates to E including spelling, punctuation, parentheses, etcetera.*]

8 GF. Once upon a time there was a girl—her name was Annishka Zipzealdin Vitzkup. She was German. She was beautiful, very beautiful but she did not have any parents [so] she was unhappy she did not have anyone to love. One day she met this boy—his name was Lauretesny Goosetray Yeastin. He was 16 years old [and] Annishka was 15 years old [and] (they loved each other). They went out (and they hugged and kissed and hugged and kissed) and they married when old enough. Annishka became Annishka Zipzealdin Yeastin. Annishka gave birth to seventeen children, it was hard but yet she managed and children grew up as pretty as Annishka. Good Nacht.

[*What is she thinking there? E points to picture.*] If only she had her parents, she's sad.

3 BM. The Crime of Lady Bushe. Once upon a time [*N walks around room*] there was a girl and her name was Barbaretta Bushe. She was a young girl at 19—very happy—she had three brothers [*She is now pacing up and down room.*] and her family and brothers and she lived together in Sweden. Her brothers' names were Jushloo B, Ratsday B, Ogneeshin B. *J* was 16, *R* was 17, and *O* was 20.

One day *O* got a new car. [*pacing faster*] It was a new car. It was a Tootack car. [*no longer looking at picture*] It was a beauty. A good big car. It had two backs and enough for three to sit in the front. One day *O* was driving in his car when there was a car accident. Draw a picture of car looking like this. [*drew picture on E's pad*]

He's holding the wheel. He fell forward with glass shattering in every sort of direction. He's died. He was killed in the most painful way, glass was stuck all over his face and stabbed in his heart. His brains were stuffed and shattered with glass. They spread the news and Barbaretta heard it. Again, I want you to draw a picture when I say draw. She came out with her head down and hand over her head. [*shows E a picture to draw*] She screamed and cried. "Mother! Mother! *O* was killed in a shattering glass accident with his new car. It shattered in every place of his body and he died in pain forceness. Unfortunately, we have lost a body in our family."

Next week was *B*'s birthday. It was a sunny day. [*put in picture*] It was a happy day for everyone but *B*. It was still mourning for her brother. Then it occurred to other people what a sad day it would be. They lowered their heads and sighed—brought packages to *B*. They wished her luck in which of her brother—not the witch that's gonna come over and kill you—in which for her brother. [*put in a picture*] The End.

16. What kind of trick is that? Can I draw a picture on board? [*Yes*] Mean I can skip this if I want to, but I don't. I want to take my proper test. [*drawing a face on writing pad*] A strange kind of a story, half animal like a myth—long nails sticking out of him. Dots all around and circles it—shower for him [*dots*] the world for him [N *draws several concentric varicolored circles touching at head and foot.*] has his tail.

The name of the story is The Silly World.

Once upon a time [*begins a prancing movement*] there was a boy—man, rather. His name was Furry Tail Mr. McCloud. He was sort of a myth. He was made up of both Greek mythology and was also true and here. He was (half monkey) and half man. He had a long tail and he had two monkey feet sticking out of his big feet with toes [N *adds to drawing*], man's top, monkey's bottom. He knew about this. He had hair on his leg [*adds to drawing*] big grumpily hair on his legs—well, he had one problem. He only had shorts to wear, but he had one friend that wouldn't laugh if he knew and he knew of this problem—reason he had this problem was his mother liked gorillas and she married one. Well, he called his friend up and he asked him to go to the store, to let him borrow a pair of his pants and he would go to the store and buy some decent ones. So he went to the store and said to him, "I'll go to men's room with my own locker and my own room and key." He tried it on and bought seventeen of them. I mean twenty of them. They all fit and he paid man $20.00, no 28, no I'll change that to $40 [*much overlay on circle*]. He went home and wore them and got a job and earned a lot of money—he got $100.00 a week. After he collected $1,000.00 he went to store again and had to buy shirts and socks and men's suspenders, no garters. He had one problem: he had that tail—and went to friend and said—since you had a young chimp and tried to keep him as your son and got him into school—this is all fantasy, you know—and you trained him how to talk and which knowing you so well—how did you hide his tail? His friend said, "Well—it was easy. I took butter and slipped it on all over. Three packs." Mr. McCloud wrote it down—buy three packs of butter—schmear them on the top of your tail. [N *repeats three times*] and pull your tail to the side, then put your pants over 'em and—then you hide your tail—your tail is hidden—he said, "Thank you, my friend, and I'll do just that." He went to the store and he bought all the stuff that he needed and he looked like a man. His feet were quite big, had another problem there, how to fit monkey feet into human shoes. Went to a store in Loolang where people had quite big feet because they walked the desert with heavy shoes that flattened them out and were warmed by the sun that filled them out and he bought sixteen pairs of shoes and left. All he needed was brush to comb the hair on his head. Had a lot—it hung down the middle of his face like that [*puts on drawing*]. He brushed his hair back into a curl like that—his ears were big, too, another problem so went to doctor and asked for operation on his ears. They took bits of his ears off [*pacing*] into regular man-sized ears—and he looked like a real man but again had a problem. He had a drop of fur on his nose. Had to shave it off and friend said put Vaseline on it and shave it. It will never grow back for a long time and when it does, you know what to do. He was a man but had one bitsy little problem, before becoming a regular man. Go to hairdresser to fix his hair as a man would—living as an ape, he pushed and slashed it—he had no manners, but now he was a man with proper hairdo pushed back in proper way—

He went out and he met a girl. She asked to marry him, but what was he to say, his not being a regular man? What was he going to say? He took a checkup with her, gave her an engagement ring—they had to take a checkup together. The minute she saw the hair she screamed. He explained he was really half-half. She still loved him and married him. They had children and they were one quarter half-half. He took care of them as of himself and when they got married, they got half of half children and when they married, they didn't have any kind of human children and it went back to seventeen years—seventeen marriages until all about monkey business was lost and they had monkey children. How could they understand? The friend of this man's really parents were killed and it was a young child and he gave them all information (the friend did) and when older they told them way back they had half ape in your family and he had a father gorilla and you got monkey children. Can this be published in a book? You got monkey children and that was the end of that roar.

4. He doesn't love her that's what it looks like. She loves him—really looks like someone starting a fight and she's saying, "No, don't go," and he's saying, "You stay here, you've been in enough trouble together."

2. & 7 GF. [N *wants to mix these together.*]

The Braid on a Girl. Once upon a time—girl named Mathilda lived on a farm and was very unhappy. She was 7. She lived in big house. Every day she would sit by the fire and hold her baby doll and her nursing maid Leila would read to her. Years went by. She had long, long hair. It reached one inch down off her shoulder and she never cut it. She was now 13. She lived on a big farm. She used to come home from school and see her brothers working. She was beautiful, yet still with long braid, and it reached her waist. This time yet she wore in a ponytail which hair was it brushed thoroughly every day. It was beautiful hair and two years went by. She was growing up. Now her hair reached the bottom of her bottom in a braid. She grew up with it. It was beautiful until one day there was a fire. She was still and almost paralyzed for five seconds. It was a hot farm and her brothers didn't agree with that long braid. It looks like maid here reading from the Bible. She stood paralyzed for five seconds. And her brother cut it off up high where boys' hair would be. She cried, she combed it, and now she is 43 and it reaches her thighs. What is the moral to this story?

The longer your hair, the prettier you are.

6
The 9- to 12-Year-Old

Developmental Expectations

By 9, children have transferred their primary interests to the world outside of the family. After 10, we consider them to be in the prepubescent phase of development, which will continue until puberty at 12.

Cognitive Functioning. As the concrete operational stage of cognitive development has been mastered, children at this age are ready to begin to deal with more abstract thinking and begin to grapple with the laws of logic. Similarly, they now begin to comprehend moral issues on a more abstract level—that is, understanding the value of laws governing human intercourse.

This is the period when knowledge begins to be appreciated for its own intrinsic worth. Also, hobbies and extracurricular activities develop that may, indeed, become life-long interests. Along with the refinement of muscle coordination, children can now begin to envision their skills at performing with musical instruments, dance, athletics, or more fine motor activities such as knitting and model building. This is also the time when reading skills enable the development of a life-long enjoyment of literature. Boys and girls of this age prefer structure and take pleasure in having a routine to follow. They also can now enjoy developing their own plans.

There is a striking change during these years as children in this age group begin to grasp humor at the adult level, although they still cling to the earlier humor they so enjoyed.

Dynamic Picture. Similar to the previous age group, the dynamic development of prepubescent children has not been well delineated. Along with interest in peers and others outside the family comes some rebelliousness and a judgmental stance toward the parents. This comes in conjunction with increasing independence and a need to define the self as separate and distinct. Identification with the peer group is critically important because the child's self-esteem is at stake. The parents can serve as buffers and confidants as the child struggles with relationships in the peer group, but cannot criticize the group or its members, because the child then feels devalued. Slowly during this time there is a beginning transition from feelings of disgust and distaste for the opposite sex to an interest in one another. This more often than not is expressed in playful "fighting," in which the girl will complain about being hurt, while at the same time delighting in the boy's attention.

Defenses. Internalization of defenses continues into this period and becomes solidified. The character style of a particular child is more clearly visible and is not so fluctuating as in earlier years. Due to this solidification, children are now in a position to begin to understand themselves. They now have the ability to examine their behavior and to be self-critical and to some degree predictive. For the first time, they have a view of themselves that is more commensurate with reality.

Affective Expression. This is the age of the giggles. Anything can set off giggling spasms in both boys and girls. In contrast, they do not resort to tears as previously. The giggling seems to express both a sense of camaraderie with peers as well as an appreciation for the ludicrous. Feelings between friends are intense and pleasurable during this time, and even when there is disappointment, attempts are made and are usually successful to recover the good relationship. This is a period of well-being and easy recovery from experiences of sadness or pain.

Normal Expectations on Tests

Intelligence Testing. Consistency is expected in both *intra*test and *inter*test functioning. Due to the age limitations of the WISC, this age group falls in the middle, therefore permitting the 9- to 12-year-old a greater range in the difficulty of items per subtest.

Bender-Gestalt. By this age the figures can be reproduced accurately (with the exceptions of 3, 6, and 7, which should be accomplished by age 11). Children with visual-motor difficulties should demonstrate compensatory coping by this time.

Projectives. The FDs should exhibit a well-developed body concept by this age. Also, there should be interest in adding embellishments of clothing and adornments, and occasionally identifying the figures by having them carry objects (for example, school books or a football).

In the Rorschach, determinants at this age show an increase in number of responses (fifteen to twenty), at least three *M*'s (*FM* becomes more equivalent to *M*), *m* should be rare, *c* could be present, there should be at least two

FC's, *FC* should be as high as *CF*, and there should be no *C*. Normal for this age is the presence of *CF* and *FM*, indicating the capacity for spontaneity. *H* should approach *A* in number. There should be at least five *P*'s. *FK* may put in an appearance, but is not necessarily expected. One can find a greater use of *D* and *d* and the ability to organize an integrated *W*. At this time, *F* approaches fifty to sixty percent of determinants.

TAT stories are given in two styles at this time. One type is the perfunctory story that meets all the requirements of the instruction. The other type is the expansively elaborated story told with great enthusiasm and pleasure.

Representative psychological test interpretations and psychological test batteries for children within this age range now follow. The raw test data from the psychological test battery follow the discussion of each child so that easy reference can be made to the examples selected for illustration of the interpretations. We include examples of children diagnosed as having a reactive disorder, being mildly disturbed, moderately disturbed, and severely disturbed, in order to demonstrate how a psychological portrait is developed. Each child's tests are analyzed, interpreted, and concluded with an integrated summary.

As stated before, the summary is not a complete report, but represents the salient features leading to the diagnostic portrait.

Psychological Test Portrait

O: **10–11 Male**

O is a 10–11 boy who was referred because of behavior difficulties at school, which seemed to be reactive to a distressful home situation. He is his alcoholic mother's caretaker, as his father spends increasingly more time away from home.

He is a handsome, well-built boy who was adopted in infancy. He is an only child.

He related very well and had a good sense of humor. His strong need to achieve led him to work in a goal-directed manner with concise, but complete, responses. He was careful and accurate, cooperative, and enjoyed the tasks. He is left-handed and well coordinated.

Cognitive Functioning

WISC: O achieves a very superior verbal, performance, and total IQ. All functions are outstanding. The Digit Span represents the single area of difficulty he experiences in which sustained concentration was not maintained. This is also reflected in the lowest of his Performance scores—that is, in Coding. He had received a Full-Scale IQ of 119 (Verbal, 118; Performance, 117) two and one-half years previously. Since only this information was available, we can speculate that O may have had a more widespread difficulty in concentration and/or attention at that time.

B–G: The figures are well executed and, with the exception of the placement of A, are well organized on the paper. The use of a line to separate B–G drawing 5 from drawing 3 and subsequent numbering shows us that O is aware of a tendency to collision and structures himself to prevent it. He overlooks a figure in his need to number, which suggests the same trouble seen in his concentration or attention in the WISC.

FD: The FDs come across very well in spite of the fact that they are not that well executed. They convey a sense of vigorous real people in assertive action with feelings. Difficulty in critical judgment is seen in his lack of accurate planning for the size of his figures. (This is particularly true with the female.) In light of the fact that he is perfectly capable of representing a three-dimensional view, it is even more striking that he cannot solve a simple problem of size and spatial relationships.

Rorschach: O uses unusual energy in this task. In contrast to the problem we saw before, he concentrates and attends to even the tiniest details on each blot. Within this restricted range, he demonstrates creativity equal to his intellectual ability. He also displays the same excellent language usage and fund of information seen before. The acuity of his percepts and productivity are remarkable. With all of this available energy, it is striking that O seems reluctant to try for integrated W's.

TAT: O's concise stories are related to the card stimulus and are complete. In only one instance (18 BM) does his thinking become tangential. The overall quality, however, does not reveal the intellect and creativity seen in the WISC and the Rorschach. There is the suggestion that this is due to the intrusion of unpleasant thoughts and feelings.

Summary Statement of Cognitive Functioning: O is able to perform across the board on a very superior level. His only difficulties appear in moments of disturbance in his concentration and attention, which seem to be related to dynamic issues.

Dynamic Picture

WISC: There are few dynamic intrusions in the WISC. There are some suggestions of problems over aggression (Information, 5; Comprehension, 6 and 7) and oral dependency (Information, 14; Comprehension, 7 and 9).

B–G: The hallmark of O's B–G is its immaturity. He prefers circles to dots, is expansive, and arbitrarily puts a separation between two figures that appear to have collided.

FD: Again, O is expansive in his drawings and reveals a very immature body concept. This immaturity is also seen in little sex differentiation, although he does assign a stereotyped masculine role to the male. The conflict between maturing and the pull of immaturity is seen in the more sophisticated drawing of a profile with such poorly defined bodies.

Rorschach: The problem of O's conflict between growth and wishing to remain small and dependent is seen throughout the Rorschach (for example, in card VI, 5, and VIII, 5, versus III, 4, and X, 5). This is indeed an uphill struggle for him (IV, 4 and 5; V, 3; X, 5). Unresolved oral dependency needs and wishes (I, 3 and 4; II, 2) conflict with the threat of aggression (III, 2 and 5; VI, 2; VII, 1; IX, 3; X, 2), and, if one is not protected, it could boomerang (V, 6). O's sense of body vulnerability is on a phallic level. His need to fragment body parts seems to be in keeping with his fear of aggression from within or directed toward him from others. He is left feeling very precarious in the world, as he eloquently describes in IV, 6. He can allow himself a full range of impulses and wishes so long as he restricts his area of attention. He is too frightened to look at, or attempt to integrate, the whole.

TAT: The stories to the TAT portray the outcome of O's conflict between dependency and aggressivity. People die, go crazy, or are left lonely, and even one of his most arbitrary stories (18 BM) seems to convey a feeling of no escape from death. There are slips in O's stories (7 BM, 6 BM), which are the result of his confusion in roles between the man and the boy, or the wife and the mother.

Summary Statement of Dynamic Picture: It is clear that O struggles between a wish for dependency and the need to assume an aggressive independent stance. This conflict can intrude in all areas when it is seemingly provoked by the stimuli. His confusion in role identification is seen in the pressure to assume adult roles while the longing to be dependent is still present.

Defenses

WISC: O's intellect functions freely and exceedingly well. There are only minor instances of intrusions, which do not disrupt him.

B–G: Here O's intellect does not hold up to the task, and he shows regressive ways of coping. He counters with a compulsive technique (numbering) and sacrifices accuracy in achieving structure.

FD: The head is obviously of paramount importance here and is best realized. He would like to control unexpressed body impulses through intellectualization, but is not successful. He, therefore, avoids details of body integration, while at the same time paying compulsive attention to some embellishments.

Rorschach: The impact of the blot seems to have led O to attend obsessively and compulsively to primarily small details. This effectively results in an avoidance of the W. Although his intellect shows clearly in his small detail percepts, he often regressed to produce immature content. The inhibition in spontaneity (seen in the lack of CF and almost equal FM to M) and the limited interaction in his M and lack of interaction in FM speak to a developing isolation. This is also testified to in the M:C ratio.

TAT: The nature of this task resulted in O's greatest failure in mobilizing adaptive defensive strategies. He demonstrates an obsessive preoccupation with death as a resolution, rarely punctuated by the success of the hero. His associations can become arbitrary as he attempts to use regressive tactics (Card 3 BM), rationalization (Cards 7 BM and 12 M), grandiosity (Card 13 B), denial (Cards 8 BM and 16), and compulsive specifications of details (Cards 12 M and 18 BM). Finally, he becomes so upset by the task he resorts to a sarcastic denigration of his own ideas (Cards 13 B and 6 BM).

Summary Statement of Defenses: O's major successful defenses are intellectualization, obsessiveness, and compulsivity. When unable to make use of his intellectual defenses, he regresses and produces more immature responses. At the same time there is evidence of the developing use of isolation to avoid response to affect. When he cannot mobilize isolation he demonstrates a wide array of unsuccessful defensive tactics.

Affective Expression

WISC: O's affect was pleasant throughout the WISC, as he enjoyed the test and his performance. Even the few difficulties he encountered did not upset him.

B–G: Affect throughout the Bender was neutral. Again, although he ran into trouble, he was not upset or discouraged by it.

FD: O felt insecure about his ability to draw, but worked doggedly to satisfy the request. The figures seem purposeful with a pleasant mien.

Rorschach: O thoroughly enjoyed this test, but the content produces a minimum of color. In addition, there are several *m* and four *FK*'s reflecting a great deal of inner tension and anxiety. This state seems similar to the description of tension in IV, 6, as well as the effort in IV, 4 and 5, and V, 3. O seemed to enjoy this test because of its intellectual demand, whereas the fragmentation and content (referred to previously) reveal a very tense boy.

TAT: O's affect throughout his stories was neutral. The content, however, reveals his belief that if one is not successful (interestingly enough, without any accompanying pleasure), one is left lonely, despairing, and hopeless.

Summary Statement of Affective Expression: Generally, O maintains neutral affect throughout the testing. However, the content of his responses belied this calm demeanor, as it reveals a great deal of inner tension and despair.

Summary

O is a child of very superior intellect, with an array of defenses, who seems happy only when faced with intellectual challenge. He is very frightened, anxious, and tense in relation to others and in relation to his own inner self. He fears aggression from outside as well as the potential from within. This leaves him feeling hopeless, helpless, and at the mercy of unknown depriving forces. The struggle to contain his own impulses and gain gratification for dependency needs leaves him particularly vulnerable, and on occasion he can explode. This, in turn, frightens him even more.

Diagnosis:

GAP:	Reactive disorder	
DSM III:	Axis I:	309.28 (Adjustment Disorder with Mixed Emotional Features)
	Axis II:	None
	Axis III:	None
	Axis IV:	5 (Severe)
	Axis V:	4 (Fair)

O is at a phallic level of development with strong motivation to achieve and to please. He, therefore, is an excellent candidate for treatment if the environment can cooperate. This, in conjunction with his diagnosis of reactive disorder, suggests a hopeful future. If the environment proves to be intractable, consideration will have to be given to placing O in a boarding-school setting with concomitant psychotherapy.

Psychological Test Data
O: 10–11 Male

WISC

		Scaled Score
Verbal Tests		
Information		16
Comprehension		19
Arithmetic		14
Similarities		17
Vocabulary		18
(Digit Span)		(9)
	Total	84

Performance Tests		
Picture Completion		14
Picture Arrangement		14
Block Design		15
Object Assembly		16
Coding		12
	Total	71

	Scaled Score	IQ
Verbal Scale	84	143
Performance Scale	71	129
Full Scale	155	140

Information

		Score
1.	Two	1
2.	Thumb	1
3.	Four	1
4.	Cow	1
5.	Steam it with fire	1
6.	Grocery	1
7.	Five	1
8.	Seven	1

9.	Christopher Columbus	1
10.	Twelve	1
11.	Summer, winter, spring, fall	1
12.	Green	0
13.	West	1
14.	I know why—your food, it like dissolves—digestion	1
15.	It's light	1
16.	Shakespeare	1
17.	Declaration of Independence	1
18.	Collect on delivery	1
19.	Five or six feet	0
20.	South America	1
21.	I don't know.	0
22.	Rome, I think. Not sure.	0
23.	I don't know.	0
24.	About 900 miles	1
25.	October twelfth. Not sure.	0
26.	Byrd	1
27.	Weather meter for pressure of air	1
28.	Don't know	0
29.	Don't know	0
30.	Don't know	0
	Total	21

Comprehension

		Score
1.	Wash it, then—I'm a Cub Scout—in book, put a sterile bandage on it.	2
2.	Pay for it	2
3.	Go to another store	2
4.	Try to stop it. Wouldn't hurt him.	2
5.	Try to stop it. Hold up hands or show some signal.	1
6.	Wood burn down easier, and hurricane could just demolish it.	2
7.	They could hurt people and would rob, so not good. You'd run out of money.	1
8.	Because they are weaker and might not be able to survive. Men are stronger.	1
9.	Won't have enough to go around; have to keep going to bank to get cash.	1
10.	Organization charity do more with it; have more uses. Beggar only for self, and the beggar could work.	2
11.	Well, see—some men might not be eligible to do the job	1
12.	They have it—comfortable; doesn't cost very much	1
13.	So they can represent the states	1
14.	If don't keep it, won't tell you a secret again, so don't trust you.	2
	Total	21

Arithmetic

		Score
1.		1
2.		1
3.		1
4.	2	1
5.	6	1
6.	14	1
7.	7	1
8.	21¢	1
9.	14	1
10.	13¢	0
11.	9	1
12.	10¢	1
13.	62	0
14.	$1.20	0
15.	55¢	1
16.	9	0
	Total	12

Similarities

		Score
1–4.		4
5.	Have a pit inside—grow on trees, and are fruit	2
6.	Four-legged animals	2
7.	Liquor	2
8.	Instruments—stringed instruments	2
9.	Don't know	0
10.	Measuring	2
11.	They're metal	2
12.	Both have a bottom	0
13.	An ocean—are in ocean	0
14.	For the law—have to be free governments	1
15.	A place in a game or a race	2
16.	Numbers	0
	Total	19

Digit Span

F 5 + B 4   Total Score   9

Vocabulary

		Score
1.	Two-wheeled vehicles	2
2.	A sharp object for cutting	2
3.	To wear out—on your head	2
4.	Message sent by mail	2
5.	Object for when raining to protect you from water	2

6.	Soft thing for comfort—sit on	2
7.	Something to hold something tight by hammering [etcetera]	2
8.	Animal for carrying heavy load	2
9.	A soft, light—soft skin from an animal	2
10.	Valuable stone	2
11.	To put together	2
12.	A gardening tool	2
13.	A weapon—war weapon	2
14.	Troublemaker—something that bothers you	2
15.	To—somebody who is daring	2
16.	Make believe—not true	2
17.	Man who has been very brave and skillful	2
18.	Sometimes against the law. Game, with cards and money	2
19.	Very sensitive liquid that can blow up	2
20.	For seeing little things like molecules	2
21.	English coin	2
22.	Story telling—a lesson	2
23.	A place where bells are hung	2
24.	Spies	2
25.	A verse of a song	2
26.	Keep in one place—like chained—closed in	2
27.	Don't know	0
28.	Don't know	0
29.	Go back	2
30.	Don't know	0
31.	Don't know	0
32.	Don't know	0
33.	Don't know	0
34.	Don't know	0
35.	A nighttime prayer or service held at camp	2
36.	No	0
37.	No	0
38.	No	0
39.	No	0
40.	No	0

Total   54 (56)

Picture Completion

		Score
1.	Things here	1
2.	Leg	1
3.	Ear	1
4.	Mouth	1
5.	Whiskers	1
6.	Other brace	1
7.	Fingernail	1
8.	Spade	1
9.	Nut to hold together	1
10.	Holes for buttons	1

11. I don't know		0
12. Line on top—dent		1
13. Can't see		0
14. This thing		1
15. Don't know		0
16. Mercury moving down here		1
17. Hole other side		0
18. Don't see anything		0
19. Doesn't have two things on this foot		1
20. Don't know		0
	Total	14

Picture Arrangement

	Time	Order	Score
A–D			8
[*Fight*]		XYZ	
1.	7"	FIRE	6
2.	9"	THUG	6
3.	6"	QRST	6
4.	16"	EFGH	4
5.	19"	EPRCY	0
6.	45"	FSIHER	4
7.	32"	MASTER	4
		Total	38

Block Design

	Time	Score
A–C.		6
1.	15"	6
2.	26"	4
3.	14"	7
4.	16"	5
5.	84"	4
6.	81"	4
7.	115"	4
	Total	40

Object Assembly

	Time	Score
M	8"	7
H	20"	8
F	69"	7
A	31"	7
	Total	29

Coding B	Total Score	43

Bender-Gestalt

A. [*Rotates paper*]
1. [*Circles—fills in*]
2. [*Fills in circles initially, then leaves them open. Counts.*]
3. [*Circles*]
4. [*Curves from point down each side*]
5. [*Circles. Collides with 3. Makes line to divide. Numbers them—omitting 1 and making A 1.*]
6. [*Well, fluidly done*]
7. [*Erases to make angle clearer on cross. Does crossed one in one continuous sweep.*]

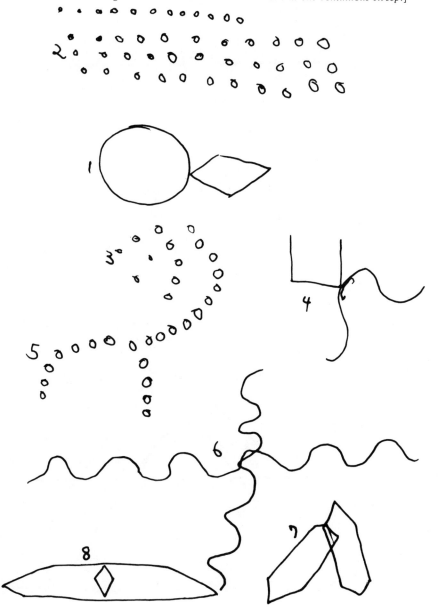

Figure Drawing

[*Man: Makes in profile—strange leg extensions as though unattached—carrying a football, then adds second arm out from back—fills in features—details on clothes.*]

[*Woman: Makes slotted eye first, then makes it bigger and rounder. Hair and head large. Curly hair, much emphasis on hair. Profile again.*]

Rorschach

I. 2″   1. Looks like an insect, a butter-fly. [W] Claws.

I.   1. Wings—claws like—muted.

2. A wolf's nose and eyes

2. Nose of it—shape of it and size of mouth and mean-looking eyes.

3. Looks like a mountain, like flat top ones in Mexico. Could I move it around?

3. Like a starting and goes up—far away.

a. I just saw antlers here.

V 4. Like an island all together in the ocean with little lakes. [S]

4. The design of it—peninsula and here [*indicates outline*] and looks like little lakes.

II. 19″V 1. Antennas of a bug. Needle in head of a bug—head of a bug. A bug.

II.   1. [*Looks like a bug?*] Wings, legs, shape of it.

< 2. This looks like mouth of a bird.

2. Design of it—open, too.

3. Husky leg of a bear.

V a. Nose and head here—a young deer with antlers just growing.

3. Slant of it—hair on it—paw there.

4. Paw of a dog.

4. A little whitish and hairy [*edge*] and shape of it.

5. Two peninsulas

5. Long jets out.

6. A rabbit—same on other side.

6. Tail of it; bushy; and ears of it—paws, legs in a running position and a little whitish. [*indicates shading*]

III. 8″ 1. Leg of an elk. I can see a lot of things.

III.   1. Because of hoof.

2. Face with mouth of a spider

2. Teeth in mouth and big, black eyes.

3. Seahorse—head, tail.

3. Skinny, has jaggedy parts like seahorse and head shape.

4. Head of a baby chicken.

4. Pointed beak shape of it and eye in it.

5. Wide open mouth and eye. Head of a bear.

5. Because mouth open, teeth sticking out and eye.

6. A butterfly

7. A funny-looking high heel

IV.   3″   1. Two giant feet—a
           giant—arms, head
           [W] [*after 5″*]
           I see an . . . thing
           can put down on
           giant—ears.
      V   2. Snail's head.
      < 3. Head of eagle.

4. Oh, I see—like a
   heavy pack on man's
   back—arm sticking
   out, leg here.
5. Army men trying to
   get up to top of hill
   here.
< 6. A balanced hill;
     balanced mountain;
     very sensitive—if
     somebody steps on
     it, might crumble.
7. Bridges—rope
   bridges—at high
   places to walk over.
< 8. Eye of an animal.

V.   2″   1. A butterfly—whole
           thing. Legs, anten-
           nas, wings.
         2. A *V*—the legs are
           shaped like a *V*.
         3. This looks like a
           farmer trying to get
           up the hill with
           plow. [*hump is
           plow, hill ahead*]
         4. The space looks like
           leg of lamb or horse.
      V 5. A gulch or a
           gully.
      < 6. If take all the points
           off, [*projections*]
           looks like a
           boomerang.

VI. 6″   1. A bear rug—legs—
           just up to here [W].
           On almost all I see
           heads or something
           of animal.

6. Wings and body.
   [*Look as much like if
   black?*] No, the color.

7. Pointed part here,
   and heel

IV.   1. Because so big—go-
          ing down for a
          jump.

2. Antennas—outline
   of it.
3. Has the outside
   shape like a bald
   eagle.

6. Big arch of it—a lit-
   tle part sticking out—
   so weak.

V.   1. Looks like it's flying.

5. Deep down

VI. 1. Legs—darkness of it—
         flat, some hairy.

2. [*Top D*] This part looks like a bird.

2. Wings—looks like somebody shot through the wings—has a hole, and head looks like a bird.

3. A mountain here
4. Mainland and light-colored water.
5. Car with luggage on top then a trailer traveling. [*tiny* dd]
6. A hiking pole [*center* d]
7. Two eyes

VII.   7″   1. An Indian with mouth open and feather, and he's pointing his arm behind him.
2. Eye, nose, mouth—is open— head of an animal.

V ∧ V   3. This way, looks like elephant head with trunk and eye.
4. A lion's head

V   5. A beaver with his big tail.

VII.

5. Tail looks flat, and it looks hairy. Just finished building the dam, he's standing on part of it—and water.

VIII.   3″   1. Right away I see an animal, a lion, walking across a ledge to the other side.
2. Antlers and head of a deer.
< 3. Prehistoric animal's head.
4. An insect with huge wings
5. Ledges and stalagmites

VIII.

2. The jaggedy part of it [*edge detail*]
3. Size of it—chin.
4. Just there—wings big.
5. The way it was going down [*indicates shading*] looks more real because light color.

IX.   11″   1. An antler—two antlers
< 2. A man, arm sticking out trying to pick up something.

IX.   1. Jagged part again.

2. Trying to pick up— looks more like a lady trying to pick up some clothes or wash them. There's a board to rub them against to get it clean.

		3.	All of pink is a running elephant and ears sticking up—head part only there.			
		4.	Two eyes and like a trunk; an elephant's head—all the light green.			
		5.	Man's head			
		6.	A man conducting.			
		7.	An animal—ram, head down, legs, tail			
		8.	Bear's head			

X 3″ 1. A crab   X.   1. Legs—grabbing for something and missed.

     2. Two crabs trying to get a skinny fish.

V   3. A man, two legs, body, and head standing there.   3. Just there

V   4. Dragon's heads   4. Nose and back of head, design.

< 5. Baby chicken walking up the rocks.

V   6. A jumping over water—head turned other way trying to get to another piece of land. Looks like a deer sort of, or maybe a dog. A dog.   6. Body and legs, and color of it.

     7. Small head and big antlers.

     8. Two men playing with a ball to keep it in air—have hands behind back like soccer, can't use hands.

< 9. Watermelon.   9. Roundness and the color.

<10. Buffalo.   10. Head big.

TAT

1. Boy got a violin for birthday present. Thinking what he'll do with it. Later maybe he becomes a musician. That's all I know. [*Want to be a musician?*] Yes, he likes music.

3 BM. He's sad because his mother just died, and he's thinking of what he'll do in future; who he'll live with. Crying. Later on maybe he goes crazy because he's so unhappy and lonely. [*Does being unhappy and lonely make you crazy? Tells story of van Gogh.*]

5. Mother comes to see if done doing homework, or maybe visiting a friend and time to go home, and she was looking for him. [*Happens?*] Find them in garage playing. [*And?*] They go home.

8 BM. These are crooks trying to kill a man. Have a rifle in it—and boy, he's blind and can't see what they're doing—going to take the gun [*the robbers*] when they're finished [*Finished what?*] Killing man and boy, he [*boy*] doesn't see what's happening, so they get him. He's blind and can't see.

16. Movie screen—were playing a movie. Film broke and blacked out, so this is what screen looks like now. [*What was the movie about?*] War scene—having World War II. All of a sudden, film broke.

12 M. Doctor coming in—going to feel head to see if he's warm. He's been very ill three or four days now. He's unconscious right now. Wouldn't eat or anything. Didn't feel good. [*Happens?*] Doctor takes temperature and he has 105 degrees. Next day dies. [*Nobody could help him?*] Was some new illness never knew before and didn't know what to do for it. [*Parents feel?*] They're very upset.

7 BM. This is man coming to work and late. Boss looking at him, asked why late, and getting mad. He said, "I didn't get up on time." Later gets fired. Then gets another job as a grocery boy. Then grows up and gets married. Man gets a job in a gasoline station and never got fired from that job yet.

18 BM. This man is getting robbed, and when wakes up is in hospital. Tries to escape, but can't Later goes on a jungle safari and on safari gets crushed by a boa constrictor. Fifteen-and-a-half-inch boa, no feet; boa constrictor three inches thick. Then he dies.

13 B. This boy—pioneer days and in his wood home and lonely. His brother just died. Very lonely sitting outside. Later becomes president of Texas, Sam Houston. Quick one. He had a very quick life.

6 BM. Man, father, and that's his mother and wife, they just had a divorce, and mother very upset, and he's sad and said, "I'm gonna get married again and have a much pleasanter life." Later after that, he got married. His wife became a movie star, and they didn't get a divorce. That's end of story. Very touching. Touching.

Psychological Test Portrait

P: 11–2 Female

P is an 11–2 girl who is excessively rivalrous with her younger brother, is "fresh" to her parents, has an eating problem, and is very sensitive about her height (tall). She also is shy and timid, unhappy, withdrawn, and has poor coordination.

P is a pleasant-looking, neatly groomed, dark-haired, tall, thin girl who wears glasses. In the testing sessions she was friendly, spontaneous, and talkative. She strongly resisted the work, although she obviously wanted to have E approve of her. Any attempt on E's part to elicit motivation by either encouragement or challenge was interpreted as undue pressure and met with passive resistance.

Cognitive Functioning

WISC: P achieves a very superior total IQ of 131, and her Verbal IQ of 138 is commensurate with this total IQ. The 21-point discrepancy between her Verbal and Performance IQ (of 117) should be considered. The 117 IQ in and of itself is above average. It is necessary to ask the question, however, why someone who achieves a Verbal IQ of 138 cannot perform in a commensurate fashion on the Performance items. In examining the subtests we see several reasons why she achieves lowered scores. These reasons will be elaborated under *Dynamics* and *Defenses*, as there is no evidence of any cognitive disability in the perceptual-motor sphere. As Digit Span and Coding are her lowest scores (with the exception of Picture Arrangement), we can speculate that the rote nature of these tasks interferes with her employing maximal cognitive attention to make the effort to achieve. With regard to her lowest score of 9 on Picture Arrangement, however, another explanation is needed. It would be appropriate to question whether this lowered score reflects a disturbance in her comprehension of social interactions. When we compare this to her score of 16 attained on Comprehension, we have to assume that the particular items she failed demonstrate an interference in her superior cognitive abilities when there is a particular pull for intrusions of a dynamic nature.

B–G: *P* is obviously able to reproduce the designs accurately. She also organizes her approach in an efficient manner. For some reason, perhaps because of her left-handedness or visual difficulties, her designs were executed with her tilting her head close to the paper. This may explain the extent of the angulation on items 2, 4, and 5, rather than its being caused by a motor problem.

FD: *P*'s drawings are well proportioned, placed well on the page, and are age appropriate for both content and developmental expectations.

Rorschach: In keeping with *P*'s superior intellect, the Rorschach shows a large number of *R*, excellent *F* +, and full use of determinants and locations. In addition, she describes her percepts accurately and precisely. With the quality of her intellectual ability, it is surprising that there are so few creative responses.

TAT: *P* tells complete stories with a good sequential sense. Her stories accurately reflect the pictures. Again, it is surprising that she is unable to develop more creative content.

Summary Statement of Cognitive Functioning: P demonstrates through the different tests a very superior cognitive ego function. Her difficulties in achieving her potential are seen as related to dynamic and defensive issues rather than to perceptual-motor discoordination, or to memory or language problems. Whatever problems she experiences appear in the areas of concentration and motivation. This indeed may also be related to the lack of any particularly creative use of her intellect in the projective testing.

Dynamic Picture

WISC: Despite her superior score (16) on Information, *P* is unable to respond to Information item 14 correctly, producing an unusually immature response. The significance of the pull of the question and her personalized response therefore alerts us to her concern with her body. This is supported by item 19 on Information, in which she contributes personal information while achieving an accurate response. Immaturity can also be interpreted from her mistaking profiles as whole faces, as seen in Picture Completion, 15 and 17, and her difficulty with the face on Object Assembly. Comprehension item 3 states her feelings of dependency needs clearly. Although *P* exhibits a superior understanding of rules governing social behaviors, she is not able to utilize this ability when the task requires demonstrating knowledge of social interaction (Picture Arrangement). In this task she does not gain time bonuses on easy items, makes a simple error on item 5, and seemingly does not understand the interaction in 6 and 7. These last failures seem to reflect *P*'s wish to remain childlike in the face of adult issues or concerns. In addition, more age-appropriate concerns are seen in responses hinting at sexual concerns (Comprehension, 8; Similarities, 7) as well as aggression (Vocabulary, 13).

B–G: Given the fact that *P* worked with concentrated effort on the B–G, it is surprising that her overall production is not commensurate with what we would expect from her age and ability. This suggests that this task elicited a more childlike response on her part due to the rote nature of the task and need to comply with *E*'s directions (cf. Digit Span and Coding).

FD: *P*'s drawings are well proportioned and generally well executed. Concern over body vulnerability may be inferred from the sketch line she uses as well as the way she positions the hands. The conflict between dependence and independence is stated clearly (see comments) in her response to the request to draw. This is also evident in her drawing the feet facing at right angles to the body and the fact that buttons are the only embellishment she adds to the clothing.

Rorschach: *P*'s prepubertal concern with her body (both pubescent changes and developing sexuality) are seen in her percepts of females, "lady" (I, 1), "earrings" (IV, 1), "lady in fancy dress" (IV, 2), "girl" (VI, 1), "girl's hair" (X, 4), "mermaid" (X, 5). Her concern about her height would seem to determine the unusual percepts of the lady in Card IV, 2. This emphasis has a narcissistic flavor, as there is an overdetermined preoccupation with her concept of herself as an adult female. Also present is the conflicting wish to remain a little girl, seen in her more childlike percepts of ducks (I, 2), elephants (II, 1), hair bow (III, a), elves (VII, 1), bunny rabbit (VII, 4). The torn shoes (IV, 3) and the broken butterfly (VIII, 3) suggest that this conflict is not without fear of damage.

Although *P* initially gives popular responses to Cards II and III, they are followed by aggressive percepts. As the effect of the stimulus *red* is repeated in Card III, anger breaks through in her association of "twisted them." There is the suggestion that when *P* becomes aware of possible sexual feeings she becomes uncomfortable and responds angrily (IV, 3).

TAT: The story to 7 GF reflects *P*'s conflict between growing up and remaining a little girl. In this story she resolves the dilemma by remaining young. For the first time we get a view of the way *P* experiences her mother. She seems to feel her mother to be detached (7 GF), withholding (18 GF), and demanding (5, 16). We can presume that this description of the mothering figure speaks to her feelings of not being supported. *P*'s fear and fascination with men is shown in her aggressive handling of the man in 8 GF and in making the man the aggressor, as in the story of the thief of a precious pearl (9 GF). The discomfort occasioned by her aggressive feelings and ideas leads to an unusual perseveration from Card 8 GF to Card 3 GF and confusion in Card 9 GF.

Summary Statement of Dynamic Picture: In all the tests we see *P*'s struggle with the conflicts of growing up versus remaining a small girl. She shows a narcissistic preoccupation in her sense of adult femininity. Her expressed concern about her height may be a reflection of unconscious fears regarding damage to her body. When *P* allows her aggression to emerge, it is most clearly directed toward men, and there is accompanying angry affect.

Defenses

WISC: The major defense seen in the WISC that *P* has working for her is her compulsivity. This enables her to be precise and exact. The evidences of regression (Information, 14, 19, and 28; Comprehension, 3, 11, and 13; Similarities, 15 and 16), therefore, are startling when they appear. In addition, she uses avoidance throughout the test whenever she experienced the least difficulty. This was most clearly seen on the Vocabulary, where there were repetitions of "I can't describe it," "I don't know," and so forth, and in Picture Arrangement, where she made simple errors, putting forth minimal effort.

B–G: Again, *P* uses compulsivity seen in her precision in counting dots and curves before she starts. Regression is noted on 1, 4, 5, 6, 7, and 8. Avoidance is suggested in her putting her head to the paper so that *E* cannot see what she is doing.

FD: Compulsivity does not work in this task, where *P* allows a transparency in the girl's hair and has the feet at right angles to the body. She approaches the drawing by a regressive question and goes on to defend herself against possible criticism by belittling her ability. In this way she seems to be attempting to avoid the anticipation of failure.

Rorschach: *P*'s compulsivity leads to well-defined and precise percepts. With the exception of the integrated responses (I, 1; III, 1; V, 1; VI, 1), *P* produces a childlike Rorschach with the emphasis on the enumeration of parts. This use of regression is also seen in her anthropomorphizing of animals, "ducks singing" (I, 2) and "elephants . . . hissing" (II, 1). There is evidence of isolation of affect in her limited coping with color stimuli and, also, in limiting herself on occasion to perceiving parts of the body (V, 3; VIII, 5; X, 4).

TAT: Interestingly enough, obsessiveness appears for the first time in *P*'s TAT stories to 7 GF and 4. She also obsessively persists in continuing her theme from 8 GF to Card 3 GF. It is unusual for a defense to put in a singular appearance in a testing protocol, and we, therefore, must presume that the stimuli of these cards and her associations called forth this doubting and perseverating with respect to the dynamics involved. We would hypothesize that this suggests another defense available to *P* at a more mature level of functioning and may be the style in which she is developing.

She attempts to deny the impact of her aggressive ideas by smiling, giggling, and sarcasm (8 GF) and also her aggressive feelings toward the card and *E* (16). Otherwise, in this task we do not see evidence of compulsivity, regression, or avoidance.

Summary Statement of Defenses: P's predominant defensive maneuvers in these tests are compulsivity, regression, and avoidance. She also makes use of denial, isolation of affect, and obsessiveness to a lesser degree.

Affective Expression

WISC: For the most part *P* worked hard and with pleasure at success in the WISC. When items seemed difficult to her, she either tried to engage *E* in conversation, or became annoyed at *E*'s pressure to try.

B–G: *P* performed this task in a most matter of fact manner.

FD: In spite of *P*'s apology about this task, she obviously enjoyed drawing and was pleased with her productions. The drawings, though pleasant, reflect less enjoyment than she expressed. The smile is constricted, and the eyes appear concerned.

Rorschach: *P* enjoyed the Rorschach. She took pleasure in finding things and gradually elaborated more and more. For some reason she did not experience *E* as pressuring her in this task, rather responding easily and freely to the questions. Predominantly, her percepts were of a benign nature, and when she used color, it was used appropriately.

TAT: *P* enjoyed this task as much as the Rorschach. She took pleasure in her stories, and the affects expressed in the stories are generally positive.

Summary of Affective Expression: Despite the displeasure *P* expressed when *E* was perceived as demanding, *P*'s overall affect was one of pleasure throughout the testing.

Summary

P is a young girl with very superior intelligence who does not show major disturbances in her cognitive functioning.

Her problems, rather, are related to the conflicts she experiences related to her developmental level. The presenting problems of shyness, withdrawal, and unhappiness reflect her inability to cope with her age-appropriate conflicts. She avoids and withdraws from her peer group. Within the family she appears to feel deprived and unloved, which leaves her feeling angry.

Although her conscious preoccupation is with her height, basically *P* feels very inadequate about herself. In much of the test data, this feeling of inadequacy is conveyed in a sense of vulnerability as well as a fear of body damage. She does not feel herself up to the task of pubescence and yearns to return to the role of the little girl. Her anger at home seems to reflect her feeling that she is not allowed to remain a little girl and that her mother is demanding of more mature behavior. At the same time that she feels the push of pubescence, seemingly experienced as too much too soon (as experienced in her concern over her height), she experiences her mother as withholding of support. Her father would not seem to be of help, as she experiences males as figures she has to diminish and minimize or be the frightened recipient of their aggression. This conflict between her physiological drives, her wish to remain little, and her inability to experience her parents as supportive leads sexuality to be a frightening mystery that attracts and repels her. In addition, she is struggling to maintain a stance against expectations of others to behave in a more mature fashion. This gives her a narcissistic flavor. Her own sense of inadequacy and poor self-esteem in comparison with her peers, as well as her unwillingness to compete and/or move ahead leaves her with little sense of gratification.

Thus, we see a girl who has all the potential for growth—an array of defenses, a capacity to relate, a sense of self, reality orientation, and the ability to use her good intellect. All the same, she is struggling with conflicts that her defenses are inadequate to handle.

Her sense of inadequacy produces a narcissistic preoccupation with herself and a view of others as depriving. These concerns preclude the use of her superior intelligence creatively.

Diagnosis:

GAP:	Psychoneurotic disorder, depressive type with manifestations of anxiety type
DSM III:	Axis I: 300.40 (Dysthymic Disorder)
	313.00 (Overanxious Disorder)
	Axis II: None
	Axis III: None
	Axis IV: 1 (None)
	Axis V: 4 (Fair)

We recommend that *P* receive psychotherapy. We feel she would benefit from individual, group, and/or family modalities. Due to her strengths, prognosis with psychotherapy is excellent.

Psychological Test Data

P: 11–2 Female

WISC

		Scaled Score
Verbal Tests		
Information		16
Comprehension		16
Arithmetic		16
Similarities		19
Vocabulary		13
(Digit Span)		(12)
	Total	80

Performance Tests		
Picture Completion		13
Picture Arrangement		9
Block Design		15
Object Assembly		13
Coding		12
	Total	62

	Scaled Score	IQ
Verbal Scale	80	138
Performance Scale	62	117
Full Scale	142	131

[*Overall resistive to effort or concentration; difficult to elicit real effort. What she understands quickly is done easily, but where effort or study is required, there is much resistance. Passive anger at pressure.*]

Information

		Score
1.	Two	1
2.	Thumb	1
3.	Four	1
4.	Cow	1
5.	Heat it	1
6.	Grocery	1
7.	Five	1
8.	Seven	1
9.	Columbus	1
10.	Twelve	1
11.	Winter, spring, summer, autumn	1
12.	Red	1
13.	I think—the west—not sure.	1
14.	Stores food. [Q] Makes me hungry.	0
15.	Because it's lighter than water	1
16.	Shakespeare	1
17.	Independence	1
18.	I don't know.	0
19.	My family is tall, so I'll say six feet. [*Repeat Q*] five feet, nine inches. I know a lot of short people.	1
20.	S.A.	1
21.	2,000	1
22.	Athens	1
23.	Soy beans—not sure.	0
24.	About 500 miles	0
25.	First Monday in September	1
26.	No	0
27.	A weather instrument	1
28.	Something to do with gliffs [*sic!*]. Don't know.	0
29.	No	0
30.	No	0
	Total	22

Comprehension

		Score
1.	Put a bandage on it.	2
2.	Buy them a new one.	2
3.	Tell my mother—she'll probably send me to another store.	1
4.	Try to stop it.	1
5.	Get a red flag and wave it to stop train.	2
6.	Because it's stronger and safer because wood could be struck by lightening.	2
7.	So they don't do any more crimes.	1
8.	Children are going to be future generation, and women can have babies.	1
9.	By mail? Because money can get lost, and checks can't use except proper destination.	1

10. Because organized charity would do something worthwhile with it. Beggar keep to self and not do worthwhile thing with it. 1
11. So be sure that the people are all right. 0
12. Strong, cool. 2
13. So they can get the best for our country or city or state. 1
14. Because you want people to think you're trustful. 2

Total 19

Arithmetic

	Score
1–3.	3
4. 2	1
5. 6	1
6. 14	1
7. 7	1
8. 21¢	1
9. 14	1
10. 18	1
11. 9	1
12. 10¢	1
13. 54	1
14. 40¢	1
15. 50¢	0
16. $2	0
Total	14

[*Reads fluidly. When can't do something immediately, tries to say can't do it.*]

Similarities

	Score
1–4.	4
5. Both fruit	2
6. Animals	2
7. Both drinks—minors can't drink it, get drunk	2
8. Both instruments—stringed instruments	2
9. Come from natural resource—wood	2
10. Both measures	2
11. Both metal	2
12. Both physical features of land	2
13. Both minerals	1
14. Both right things	1
15. Both like numbers	0
16. Both numbers	0
Total	22

Digit Span

F 6 + B 5   Total Score   11

Vocabulary

		Score
1.	A two-wheeled riding vehicle	2
2.	I don't get it. [*thought* E *said ninth*] Instrument for cutting.	2
3.	Something to wear on your head	2
4.	Can't describe—something receive by mail and a letter, in the other sense, is a sound.	2
5.	Something to keep you dry in rain.	2
6.	Soft pad for usually furniture	2
7.	Part of body; [*points to fingernail*] iron something or other	2
8.	An animal	2
9.	Fir or fur? Skin of an animal.	2
10.	Coal aged thousands of years—cut, then shines.	2
11.	Can't describe it. Get together.	2
12.	Something used for gardening—turn soil with it.	2
13.	Long and skinny metal—sharp, used for killing people [*Tries to avoid—"can't describe it," etcetera*]	2
14.	My nuisance—a pest	2
15.	Courageous	2
16.	Something that doesn't make sense	2
17.	Person who's done something courageous	2
18.	Take a chance	2
19.	Never heard of it	0
20.	It magnifies blood or bacteria	1
21.	English money	2
22.	Story	2
23.	Don't know	0
24.	No	0
25.	Verse, part of a song	2
26.	No	0
27.	No	0
28.	No	0
29.	No	0
30.	No	0
	Total	43

Picture Completion

		Score
1.	Tooth	1
2.	Leg	1
3.	An ear	1
4.	Mouth	1
5.	Whisker	1
6.	One of these	1
7.	Nail	1
8.	A spade	1
9.	Nail to hold together	1

10.	Buttonholes	1
11.	Fin on top	1
12.	Screw thing on top	1
13.	Antennas	1
14.	Don't know—claw—extra on here, not here	1
15.	Half his face, [*laughs*] let's see, nothing except half his face.	0
16.	Degree sign—doesn't have freezing mark.	0
17.	One of his ears	0
18.	Could be something like rain, but don't think that's it.	0
19.	I don't know.	0
20.	I don't Know.	0
	Total	14

Picture Arrangement

	Time	Order	Score
A–D.			8
[*Fight*]		XYZ	
1.	10″	FIRE	6
2.	37″	THUG	4
3.	11″	QRST	5
4.	22″	EFGH	4
5.	16″	EPRCY	0
6.	46″	SFIHER	0
7.	65″	MSATER	0
		Total	27

Block Design

	Time	Score
A–C.		6
1.	6″	7
2.	21″	4
3.	18″	6
4.	13″	6
5.	61″	5
6.	141″	4
7.	90″	5
	Total	43

Object Assembly

	Time	Score
M	12″	6
H	18″	8
F	112″	6
A	45″	6
	Total	26

Coding B   Total Score   43

Bender–Gestalt

[Left handed]

A. *[Head to paper. Well done.]*
1. *[Counts before beginning, then right through.]*
2. *[Again counts twice before beginning, then through.]*
3. *[Looks as does—no direct counting—well angled.]*
4. *[Well done.]*
5. *[Again counts dots first and then does it.]* Not very shapely.
6. *[Counts curves.]*
7. *[Examines card as draws.]*
8. *[Examines card as draws.]*

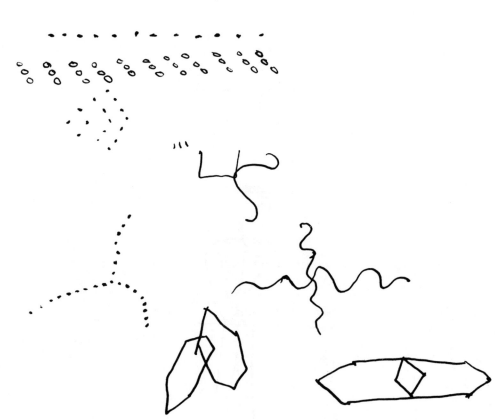

Figure Drawing

[*Person*]: Real person? Like you or my mother? [*Eyes almost to the sheet of paper—body bent over the paper.*] Easier to draw close for me. My drawings are usually horrible. [*Finishes up to waist—then hands, hair, face—then to skirt—to legs.*] That's supposed to be me.

[*Boy*]: I can't draw boy very well. Girl is easier. [*With boy, head raised from paper so E can see the sheet, and for most of time she maintains normal distance. Outline all the way done, although hands put at ends of arms as finishes the outline.*]

Rorschach

I.	7″	1.	Two clowns and a lady in middle.	I.	1.	Hats make them look like clowns. [*Lady?*] Because of her skirt—dancing—three together.
	V	2.	Two ducks singing.		2.	Ducks because of bills
II.	2″	1.	Two elephants	II.	1.	Trunks—the ears—they're feet—trunks up—seem to be kissing each other.
		2.	Two guns—pistols.		2.	Shape
III.	3″	1.	Two people playing ball with two balls—boys and . . .			
		2.	Looks like somebody had rifles and twisted them [*upper red*]	III.	2.	Remind me of shape of rifles but are wiggly, but are bent or curved all over.
		3.	Butterfly here.		3.	Wings. Also looks like a hair bow. [*As much like a butterfly if black?*] No. I think it's partly the color.
IV.	8″	1.	Two earrings—I mean ears.	IV.	1.	Shape—not attached.
		2.	Lady in fancy dress, long evening gown and feet in back like her partner.		2.	Just reminded me. Can only see partner's feet in background. I see the front of her way feet are pointing.
		3.	Torn shoes		3.	[*Torn?*] Shape reminded me of shoes, but ragged edges, so has to be torn.
V.	5″	1.	Butterfly with wings, too long for it.	V.	1.	Wings. [*Mounted—flying, etcetera?*] Mounted.
		2.	Martian with antennas sticking up.		2.	Because of antennas—Martian—standing.
		3.	Feet—leg of a person		3.	Shape
VI.	14″V	1.	Two people—two people spreading hands out, and here are their legs.	VI.	1.	Faces and shape—my imagination—girls—looks like a skirt.
VII.	3″	1.	Two elves here	VII	1.	Looks like elves—shape, color and shading—because, because, looks like they're dancing—arms.
		2.	Two feathers		2.	Ragged edges

		3. Butterfly		3. Flying
		4. Bunny rabbit		4. Looks fuzzy and ears —just 'cause they look fuzzy and the ears—not the shape.
VIII.	3″	1. Bears	VIII.	1. Shape—climbing
		2. Mountain [*top* D]		2. Shape, just shape.
		3. Broken butterfly [*center blue*]		3. 'Cause over here looks like wings are coming off.
		4. Parakeet [*side animals*]		4. Tail—beak.
	V	5. Two hands		5. Outstretched because of fingers.
		6. Butterfly		6. Colors—mounted.
IX.	17″	1. Lobsters [*top* D]	IX.	1. Color, shape, claws.
		2. Rainbow [dr]		2. Because of its colors. [Q] Far away.
X.	2″	1. Octopus [*side blue*]	X.	1. Legs—even though more than eight.
		2. Bugs		2. Just looks like bugs —no special reason.
	V	3. Thermometer		3. Because looks like darker here and lighter there, so.
		4. Girl's hair		4. Flipped at bottom— just hair.
		5. Two mermaids		5. Here is the bottom and it's yellow, and mermaids in movies have blond head— head up—like doing a push-up like I do with back curved like this.
		6. Two more bugs		6. Just looks like bugs —these two.
		7. Wishbone		7. Color and shape.

TAT

1. Well, before, before boy was trying to get ideas for his music. Now he's getting ideas, and later he's going to play that piece. (*Ideas?*) He's going to make up a piece. [*Talented?*] Better be because I don't like stories about untalented people.

7 GF. I don't know if this is supposed to be a baby or a doll. I don't know if this is supposed to be a mother or a friend. Before the girls were playing. Now they're thinking of another game to play, and later they're going to play that game. [*Feel?*] Feel good. [*Suppose it's a mother?*] Mother looking at girl's new doll. That's all.

5. Before mother cleaned up the room. Now she's double checking. [*What?*] The room, and later she's gonna have company. [*Why check?*] Wanted it to be perfect for her company.

8 GF. Before mother was told something. Now the la—the mother is thinking about it. Later she's gonna find out rest of story. [*What told?*] One of neighbors died or something. She's gonna find out how. [*How?*] Ask some other neighbors what happened. [*What did happen?*] He was in an auto crash [*smile*] and he got killed. [*giggle*] Bright side of things, I always think like that. [*Feel?*] Sad, because that was a good neighbor.

16. [*Giggles*] Well, before there was wallpaper on the wall. Now it is painted, and later it's gonna get dirty. You showed me the picture.

3 GF. I have to continue with this. [*Refers to 8 GF.*] Uh, well, before the lady was told that neighbor had died, now she found out how, and later she's gonna be sad. [*Not sad now?*] A little sad.

12 F. Before lady went to museum, now she saw that picture [*rear female*] and later she's gonna get inspired by it and draw another picture.

18 GF. Before robber came into house. Bright side of things again. Now trying to get lady to tell her where precious jewel is, and later the police are going to get the robber. [*Did she get the jewel?*] Nope. [*How come?*] Because the lady wouldn't tell her. [*Why didn't lady tell her?*] Because it was a precious jewel and she wanted it and because it belonged to her. [*She wasn't afraid?*] Yes, she was afraid, but she controlled herself. [*Who called police?*] She screamed.

9 GF. Before started out on the mystery. Now looking for clues and later going to solve the mystery and don't ask me what the mystery is. [*I'm going to.*] Umm, the mystery was, umm, why the town kept hearing strange noises at night. [*What kind of noises?*] Eerie noises of a ghost haunting the ocean—and that's one of noises—other was bell at night that no one could find. So the girls looked and found bell buried in hollow tree and noises from ocean was only two men looking for oysters because was one oyster that had a precious pearl in it. Those are only two noises. Those two men were also ringing bell to make town suspicious and scare them so wouldn't call police. [*They were thieves?*] Not really thieves, but wanted the precious pearl. [*Why didn't they just do it quietly?*] Because might be some night walkers, people taking walk along ocean, and if heard weird noises, would be afraid to go there.

4. Well, before, the man loved the girl, but girl didn't love the man. Now the girl loves the man, but man doesn't love the girl, and later they're gonna get married. [*How come?*] I don't know. They're feeling happy.

Psychological Test Portrait

Q: 9–5 Female

Q is a 9–5 girl who was referred for frequent stomachaches on school days, nervousness, difficulty in making friends, and getting upset if things did not go right. There is a constant conflict at home over her wanting to watch television and not do her homework. The mother brought her after finding no medical reason for the stomachaches.

Q lives with her mother and younger brother. Her parents are separated, but she sees her father regularly.

She is a tall, well-built girl with short hair. She is very well dressed. She smiles easily and relates well to E. Q has a bite plate in her mouth, which makes her feel that she sounds silly when she talks.

Cognitive Functioning

WISC: Q has a very superior IQ with unusual verbal ability. She, for the most part, has very sophisticated language development, remarkable social judgment, excellent abstract reasoning, and very superior fund of knowledge and arithmetical ability. In contrast, her Performance score was just above average, leaving a 35-point discrepancy to be explained. This discrepancy does not appear to be caused by a visual-motor problem. In examining the

Performance subtests, we see that she performs inconsistently and loses time credits because of slowness. Therefore, we will look for an understanding of this extreme disparity in her defenses against dynamic issues.

B–G: Q's figures are clearly reproduced and well organized on the paper. However, she shows some difficulties. She realized some of her errors and was able to compensate. It is as if the use of framing on A and 1 enables her to retain an appropriate spatial orientation for organization. In 3 and 6, she utilized another technique. Still, there are moments when she does not make the extra effort required to improve her drawing (A, 2, 5, 6, and 7). The type of error she makes does not reveal visual-motor difficulties.

FD: Similarly to the overall organization in the B–G, Q's FDs at first glance appear well proportioned, sexually differentiated, and pleasant. Upon close examination difficulties in execution are seen. In the drawing of the female she cannot differentiate shoulders from arms, and she draws the arms out of the neck with no hands. This is in contrast to her ability to differentiate legs and shoes. In the drawing of the male there are parallel lines down the front of the shirt without any indication of whether there should be buttons. There are no fingers and no ears, in spite of the attention she pays to the shoes and particularly the ties. All of this suggest fluctuation in her attention and autocritical judgment.

Rorschach: For the most part Q maintains good F in her percepts, provides several P's and a few good FC's. These determinants, however, produce only a stereotyped-like protocol rather than what could be anticipated from her very superior level on the WISC. Even the language use, so superior in the WISC, fails in this task, and she uses vague, immature, and simple descriptions. Similarly, her use of bats and butterflies (Cards I, II, IV, and V), although suitable percepts, are simple organizations of the blots. As already seen in the B–G and FD, Q's overall protocol looks good. It is again on closer scrutiny that one sees the arbitrariness of many of her productions, bespeaking the lack of application of critical effort.

TAT: Superficially, Q, as in all previous tests, conforms to the instructions and to the test stimuli. She sees what others see and elaborates a well-organized story. Her language is erratic, varying from simple and immature usage to introducing more sophisticated phrases. The arbitrary quality seen in the Rorschach is repeated here in her own restructuring of the instructions to give a story that justifies the picture (7 GF, 5, 3 BM, 8 GF, and 4).

Summary Statement of Cognitive Functioning: The most striking aspects of Q's cognitive functioning are seen in the inconsistencies in attention, concentration, autocritical judgment, and language usage. In spite of these inconsistencies, she demonstrates a very superior intellectual capacity and potential.

Dynamic Picture

WISC: There is little evidence of specific dynamic issues in Q's performance on the WISC, which is seemingly why she does so well. There are hints of her body concerns (Information, 14 and 19; Comprehension, 8; Picture Completion, 14, 15, and 19), and preoccupation with money (Comprehension, 9; Arithmetic, 13). Otherwise, the intrusions are seen in the intratest inconsistencies and the slowed effort on the Performance items.

B–G: The effort at framing and placing guide marks in the B–G suggests Q's feelings of inadequacy or, at least, insecurity in doing this task.

FD: The same insecurity is seen in the erasures in the FD, to the point of redoing the whole female figure. Although Q shows good sex differentiation, this is not to say that she is not conflicted over sexual impulses. She cannot complete the hands on the female, makes the eyes on both figures hooded, and omits the fly and the ears on the male figure. The eyes are particularly strange, and may have some specific meaning to her. Concerns about the body are expressed in her sketchy and shading lines on both figures.

Rorschach: As manifested before, Q is concerned about body integrity (I, 2; III, 3; VI, 3; VII, 2 and 3; VIII, 4; IX, 1) and impulses toward voyeurism (I, 3; III, 3; VII, 3; IX, 1 and 2; X, 5 and 6). For the first time, aggression toward E and/or the task appears (that is, inverting each card with the exception of VI, where she states how it should be changed, and her remark to E on II, 3). Most important, however, we begin to see manifestations of conflict over merging (III; IV, 2; V, 2; VI, 3; VII, 2; VIII, 4; X, 7). This is clearly the result of a threat to her narcissism, which in turn leads to the arbitrary nature of her responses (II, 3; VI, 3; X, 7).

TAT: The major dynamic theme to emerge in the TAT stories is Q's sense of deprivation. Children do not get what they want from people who seem insensitive to their needs. This seems to arise out of Q's narcissistic orientation that others should somehow know what is wanted and provide it. To have this expectation, one must have the sense of a symbiotic-like relationship to the mother or parents. Since others cannot magically respond to unrevealed needs, Q is continually left feeling deprived. Her solution is to use magical thinking to counter these feelings and to satisfy her needs. One solution is seen in her preoccupation with money (Cards 8 GF and 16). These stories are remarkable in the persistence of this theme to the exclusion of any concern about sexual, aggressive, or competitive strivings.

Summary Statement of Dynamic Picture: Q's preoccupation with her feelings of deprivation, which stems from an expectation of narcissistic entitlement, is a persistent theme throughout the tests. This precludes any interest in more age-appropriate concerns with sexuality, aggressivity, or competitiveness.

Defenses

WISC: Q's intellectual defenses work well for her in the Verbal tests, even though there are indications of regression (Information, 14; Comprehension, 3; Similarities, 5 and 9). In the Performance tests, however, as her attention fluctuates, she fails to gain important time credit. This is thought to be the result of a diminution in her efforts, preoccupied as she is with fantasying. Her susceptibility to constriction in her energy output is related to idiosyncratic meanings different tasks have for her.

B–G: Q utilizes compulsivity to enable her to maintain a structure for her drawings (A, 1, 3, 6). Even though she is able to do this, the regressive pull is strong enough to produce errors.

FD: Q's compulsive defenses work well in the drawings in achieving reasonable figures overall. Denial is seen in the content of the drawings in the masked eyes, missing ears, missing hands, and missing fly. It is as if Q withdraws from sensory contact with others, even to the extent of erasing her original female profile with arms extended to produce the constriction seen in the final picture.

Rorschach: Q works her way through her percepts compulsively, explaining vagueness and precisely detailing what is missing or what is there. Regression is evidenced throughout in content and in language use. The same sense of withdrawal through isolation seen in the FDs appears here in the lack of M's and the lack of any interaction. The push to express some of her ideas makes her use projection most unsuccessfully (II, 3; IV, 2; VI, 3; X, 7). With all these efforts at compulsivity, regression, isolation, and projection, her language still reveals the intrusion of psychotic ideation.

TAT: The TAT stories reveal the same defensive attempts at compulsivity, regression, isolation, and projection as seen in the Rorschach. They are effective and fail in the same way, and psychotic ideation is introduced in her language and story content. Furthermore, she does reveal strategies for achieving her own ends via somatization, deceit, and improbable rationalizations.

Summary Statement of Defenses: Although Q utilizes a wide array of defenses—compulsivity, regression, isolation, projection, constriction, improbable rationalizations, and somatization—she is unable to prevent the expression of narcissistic concerns and psychotic ideation. Intellectualization and compulsivity are the only defenses that are effective when she is faced with structured tasks.

Affective Expression

WISC: When Q found test items difficult (Arithmetic; Digit Span, backwards; and all Performance items), she became anxious. This anxiety interfered with her achievement, as she became rigid and more concrete. Otherwise, her affect was neutral throughout.

B–G: The nature of this perceptual-motor task made Q quite anxious. The disruptive effect of anxiety breaks through her defense in A and 3, but she does recover.

FD: Although Q erased a great deal and explained that she was not good at drawing "whole bodies," she complied to the task demands easily. Her drawings reveal affectless people who resemble wooden puppets more than real people.

Rorschach: Q enjoyed the task and felt free to elaborate her percepts. The amount of m would seem to indicate that she is struggling with a great deal of inner tension. Similarly, although she sees pleasant and pretty colors, she ends the Rorschach with "stormy colors" that are mixed up and connected, although she does not want them to be. Her percepts are devoid of any expression of feelings.

TAT: Q really enjoyed this task, and she said, "this could go on and on" (Card 16). Despite this, there was no expression of positive feelings or interactions between people. Instead, there was always a searching theme for better gifts, supplies, or parents.

Summary Statement of Affective Expression: For the most part, Q presented herself with neutral affect. There was evidence of anxiety when she experienced difficulty that could become disruptive to her performance. Otherwise, although she appeared to enjoy some tests, her responses were devoid of any meaningful affective interaction.

Summary

Although Q has a very superior intellectual ability, the profound disturbance with which she struggles precludes realization of her potential. She is in conflict on the most primitive level of a narcissistic dilemma that leaves her always feeling deprived and unhappy. She has to use her intellectual energies to ameliorate these feelings. These feelings emanate from a conviction that others deliberately withhold gratification from her. As a result, positive human interactions hold little nurturance, and she views human intercourse as a battleground for realizing her own wishes.

Therefore, Q is a child who is isolated, projects ill will onto others, and regresses into more primitive and magical solutions to try to find some relief. This cannot work, and she is left feeling unhappy, frightened, endangered, vulnerable, and tense.

Of most concern in this protocol is Q's resorting to regression and magical thinking as a solution to her problems. Although she has not yet developed a clear-cut thought disorder, there is much evidence that this is the direction in which she is moving.

Diagnosis:

GAP:	Isolated Personality	
DSM III:	Axis I:	V61.20 (Parent-child Problem)
	Axis II:	313.22 (Schizoid Disorder of Childhood with Paranoid Traits)
	Axis III:	None
	Axis IV:	4 (Moderate)
	Axis V:	4 (Fair)

Q is a borderline child with paranoid orientation who is in need of treatment. Because of her inability to trust others, establishing a therapeutic alliance will be difficult and take some time. If such an alliance can be achieved, prognosis is hopeful.

Psychological Test Data

Q: 9–5 Female

WISC

	Scaled Score
Verbal Tests	
Information	16
Comprehension	20
Arithmetic	16
Similarities	18
Vocabulary	20
(Digit Span)	(12)
Total	90

Performance Tests

Picture Completion		10 (12)
Picture Arrangement		11
Block Design		12
Object Assembly		11
Coding		15
	Total	59

	Scaled Score	IQ
Verbal Scale	90	150
Performance Scale	59	113
Full Scale	149	136

Information

		Score
1.	Two	1
2.	Thumb	1
3.	Four	1
4.	Cow	1
5.	Heat it	1
6.	Grocery	1
7.	Five	1
8.	Seven	1
9.	Christopher Columbus	1
10.	Twelve	1
11.	Spring, winter, summer, fall	1
12.	Red	1
13.	In the West	1
14.	Mean? What does it do? [RQ] Digests food.	1
15.	Can't soak into water	0
16.	Shakespeare	1
17.	Independence Day	1
18.	I don't know	0
19.	Five feet, guess, or four feet, five inches	0
20.	Is that a place? I don't know.	0
21.	2,000	1
22.	Rome	0
23.	I don't know.	0
24.	1,000 miles	1
25.	In October—not sure, no, isn't October	0
26.	I don't know.	0
27.	Know what it is. Yes. Wait till I—to show how fast or what pressure or how strong wind is.	0
28.	No	0
29.	No	0
30.	No	0
	Total	18

Comprehension

		Score
1.	First thing I'd do is wash it and put Band-Aid on.	2

2.	Pay for it.	2
3.	I'd just return home, or I'd go to another store.	2
4.	Not hit back—not pay attention	2
5.	I'd tell somebody and hope they would know what to do—or yell out.	1
6.	Brick is stronger, and I think brick is fireproof, and wood certainly isn't.	2
7.	So they won't go and rob somebody else—rob or murder.	1
8.	Men are stronger—women more delicate	1
9.	For person paying it to, or yourself? Can have more money with you if don't use it—or if something happens, you'll be responsible if they claim you didn't pay, but can prove it by writing a check.	2
10.	Because sometimes beggar might not need it, but charity needs it for clothes and stuff—beggar might be a robber.	1
11.	Like take tests? They want a person who's good at the job.	1
12.	No other material would get this kind of texture—smooth.	1
13.	Because the people want the best they can have because we wouldn't be organized if we didn't have them—be no law and wouldn't be taking care of things like criminals.	1
14.	First of all, person would feel very bad if you don't, and when promise that's giving your word of honor you are going to do it.	2
	Total	21

Arithmetic

[*Note: Anxiety causes confusion of reasoning and some perseveration on Arithmetic. Perseveration takes form of concern about money from one question to the next.*]

		Score
1.		1
2.		1
3.	1	
4.	2	1
5.	6	1
6.	14	1
7.	7	1
8.	21¢	1
9.	14	1
10.		0
11.	9	1
12.	10¢	1
13.	A dollar, a dollar, 8; no, that's wrong. [Q *repeats question*] 72¢, but has to be another third. That's hard.	0

14.	40¢		1
15.	60¢		0
16.	$54		0
		Total	12

Similarities

			Score
1–4.			4
5.	Both come in summer; taste a little alike; same shapes; in same family of color.		1
6.	Both animals		2
7.	Liquor		2
8.	Instruments—string		2
9.	Both things in the world. Only thing I can think of.		0
10.	Both type of measurement.		2
11.	Both made of same material—metal		2
12.	Not synthetic—are from nature		2
13.	Both nature, too. Can't think of anything else.		0
14.	Both freedom like.		1
15.	Both at ends.		1
16.	Both numbers		0
		Total	19

Digit Span

F 7 + B 3	Total Score	10

Vocabulary

		Score
1.	A thing you ride on.	2
2.	Something you cut something with	2
3.	Something you wear on your head	2
4.	Write to someone and tell them what you want to say	2
5.	Thing use to protect self from rain	2
6.	Something you sit on like a pillow on sofas and things like that	2
7.	Something put two things together by hammering in it	2
8.	Animal	2
9.	The outside skin you see in [*sic!*] an animal	2
10.	Valuable stone or a shape	2
11.	If put together or if joining a club, go into it and are a member	2
12.	Something used for digging	2
13.	Long knife used for duels	2
14.	Someone who's a big pest—doesn't have to be person—anything that's annoying you.	2

15.	Not afriad—have courage	2
16.	Something that doesn't make sense	2
17.	Something [*sic!*] who's done something big and good—rescues	2
18.	People play poker, and use money in game to lose or win	2
19.	Something like bombs—it explodes	1
20.	Thing you look through to see things you can't see with naked eye	2
21.	Coin from France or England it is	2
22.	Story that's not true—like a myth	2
23.	Don't know	0
24.	Like a spy	2
25.	Part of a song	2
26.	Don't know	0
27.	Something that, when put it on something it has a lot of things on it—and shiny	2
28.	Never heard of it	0
29.	No	0
30.	Something bad happened to you	2
31.	No	0
32.	No	0
33.	No	0
34.	Praying mantis—a bug or insect	2
35.	Like praying—have vesper services late afternoon	2
36.	No	0
37.	No	0
38.	No	0
39.	No	0
40.	No	0
	Total	55

Picture Completion

		Score
1.	One of spikes	1
2.	A leg	1
3.	An ear	1
4.	Mouth	1
5.	Side whiskers	1
6.	Hinge	1
7.	Nail	1
8.	A spade	1
9.	A thing that connects two parts together	1
10.	Buttonholes	1
11.	A fin, no, don't know	0
12.	Nothing missing—hammer to hammer it down	0
13.	If insect supposed to have more legs—I don't know.	0
14.	Side feathers	0
15.	Wrinkles, no rest of face, like two eyes, rest of mouth, and other ear—oh, oh, other side of jacket.	0

16. Hard! [*time studying*] Oh! mercury at
    bottom.   1
17. Doesn't go in here   1
18. No.   0
19. Things they milk   0
20. House looks dark, and sun is out.
    Looks like night because of shadow.   0
                                        Total   10(12)

Picture Arrangement

	Time	Order	Score
A–D.			8
[*Fight*]		[*Examines these carefully before proceeding*]	
		XYZ	
1.	11″	FIRE	5
2.	12″	THUG	5
3.	17″	QRST	4
4.	13″	EFGH	5
5.	51″	EPRCY	0
6.	53″	EHISFR	0
7.	73″	MTSEAR	0
		Total	27

Block Design

	Time	Score
A–C.		6
1.	23″	4
2.	123″	0
3.	73″	4
4.	34″	4
5.	80″	4
6.	[*Gives up—15″ overtime*]	0
7.	[*At time, none correct*]	0
	Total	22

Coding B   Total Score   46

Bender–Gestalt

A.   [*Rotates paper ninety degrees*]
1.   [*Counts dots*]
2.   [*Erases second group*] Supposed to be more slanty.
3.   [*Carefully matches hers to those on card*] Those [*on card*] look more round than mine.
4.
5.   [*Counts carefully*]
6.
7.   [*Each figure drawn in one continuous line*]
8.   [*Outer figure drawn in one continuous line*]

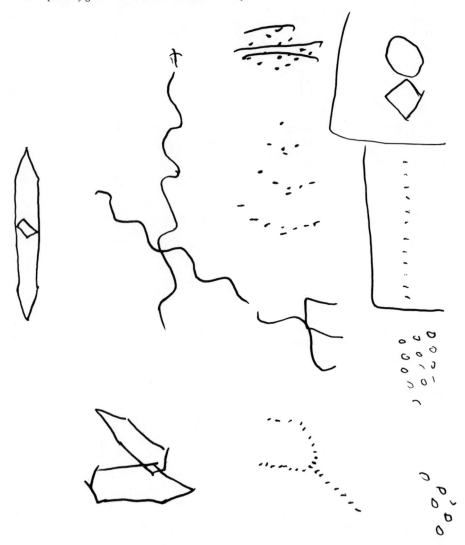

Figure Drawing

[*Female: Much erasure—does a profile. Body before face, although face shape is there without top of head. Erases whole top of body, makes firmer lines. Makes it full front, although original drawing of profile very well drawn and proportioned. Difficulty with feet again—adjusts waist—then to face—erasusres—finishes female.*] Not too good.

[Male]: Can I just draw faces? I'm not too good at drawing whole body. [E *asks for whole.*] Okay. [*Again, much erasure*]

Rorschach

\

I.	3″	1.	A bat [W]	I.	1.	Well, the wings, little head, little hands—wings out in the air.
	V	2.	Chair, arms, back [W]		2.	Don't see the seat of chair—that's the back, and this is where you put your hands over here [*points to arms on chair she's sitting on*]
	V	3.	Pumpkin cut into face. Mostly I see bat.		3.	[*Pumpkin?*] Whole thing is dark, and when look into it seems very light and bright. [*describing three dimensional view*]
II.	6″	1.	Butterfly—not exactly [*without upper two reds*]	II.	1.	Because looks like spreading of the wings. Don't really picture as butterfly, but shape is like a butterfly.
	V	2.	Horseshoe crab [*lower red*]		2.	Because all the things sticking out of it and the shape.
		3.	Map of U.S. without this part and this part [*reds*] [*looks on back surreptiously*]		3.	Shape of it—has all indented things [*shading*] and don't think you could follow, and when I think of map of U.S., I think of shape like that.
III.	3″	1.	I see a cat's face [W] when first look at it. Whole thing could be cat's face, and that could be a bow on it.	III.	1.	This is the cat face [*W—covers red tops*] without this. I don't know what made me think of it, but on TV that's the shape of it—ears, nose.
		2.	Or, bow all by itself. Looks like a bow.		2.	[*Bow?*] Looks exactly like a bow—has sides and parts where connects both of them. [*As much like if black?*] Yeah, because shape, but red gives it more color, more like a bow.
	V	3.	Monster bird, two big eyes, hands,		3.	Eyes, hands, and just the body that

mouth, and could be
the bow on it.

goes about to its
waistline. [*Mouth?*]
No mouth, that lit-
tle thing, nose, but I
don't see a mouth.

IV.   4″V   1. A different type
bat

IV.   1. Wings look like a
bat. This bat like
that because when I
picture a bat, be-
cause practically all
looks like different
kinds of bat. [*Flying
like first one?*]
Yeah, it is.

2. Dog, ears bent over,
two legs.

2. [*Dog?*] Ears and foot
put together. Floppy
ears and big feet—
head shape except
that part. [*covers
center projection*]
No face but that is
head. [*vaguely*]

V.   2″   1. Another bat. Still
looks like bat to me.

V.   1. This looks like a bat
because of wings and
antennas—flying, too

V   2. This way looks
like butterfly—no,
like a bat, too, but
sorta like a butterfly.

2. Same thing.

VI.   12″   1. Whiskers and also
only . . .
2. This is a head.

VI.   1. Pointed out and
thin like whiskers.
2. Because shape—be-
cause was round,
and if those were
whiskers, would be
a head. Whiskers
are part of head put
together. [*in main
performance,
separates the two
responses*]

3. If would come up
close together [W]
[*pushes at D with
hands as though
bringing it together*]
I might see a cat.

3. If was standing up,
no piece there [*cen-
ter column*] and
whiskers there—and
those would be the
legs. Supposed to be
four legs on cat. I
only have two here,
but it's imaginary.
[W] [*Whole?*]
Umhum, if you put
it together.

VII.   4″V   1. Like a bear doing
a dance [W]

VII.   1. Hands, feet, head.
[*Body?*] This part, I
guess. [*runs hand
over center S*]

V	2.	Islands breaking off—part of land—not exactly, just see them—not this. [*cuts off lower* D]			2.	Out, coming out from that—islands here just coming out. Don't see any water. [*Again, she has to cover part of blot she is not using*]
	3.	Dancers—no heads—dress, feet [*covers parts of blot not using*]			3.	Yeah, lady dancers.
	4.	Elephant's head			4.	See the trunk? [*Anything else?*] Not really. I don't think shape too much, because the shape is is not round like an elephant.
VIII.	9″	1.	Little animals crawling.	VIII.	1.	[*Again covers all but animals*] Head. Can even make out eyes and nose a little bit, and then they have the four legs.
		2.	Like a design to me.		2.	Just whole thing. A design. Well, there are pretty colors. Just looks like a design.
		3.	Mountain		3.	Pointed like a mountain. That's about all. Always when I think of a mountain, looks like a triangle.
		4.	Looks like two pieces of paper or cloth tearing away [*blue* D]		4.	See little ends there and see it separating, and down there it's together. It's cloth because paper wouldn't have ragged ends sticking out—not like that.
V		5.	Butterfly [*lower* D]		5.	[*Again covers*] Pretty. Colors were pretty and shape of wings.
IX.	9″	1.	A buffalo that green thing.	IX.	1.	Ducking its head and looks like buffalo usually does. Whole body except no legs. That's head, and that's body.
V		2.	Monster with two eyes, and that's the orange thing—a cape coming over.		2.	Cape resting on him, over his shoulders, and instead of his eyelids closing down, they close to side.

X.	5″	1. Crabs	X.	1. Just the feelings [*sic!*] of crabs and claws. [*moves hands in claw-like motion at E*] [*Doing?*] Because that's what looks like. [*squirming in chair*]
		2. The whole looks like a seashore.		2. [*Seashore?*] All animals from sea and waves.
		3. Lobster		3. All clawy—and shape there.
		4. Sand crab		4. Looked small and had little claws on it.
	V	5. Two little fish		5. One big eye and little point on back.
		6. Flying fish with wings		6. Little fish, big wings. Look sort of like capey wings because so big and floppy.
		7. Waves		7. Sort of going upward—looks like stormy colors. When get there, mixed with the blue, see as get here, see connecting these two? [*blue center*] Not exactly connecting, touching both of them. I didn't want it to be connecting. Stormy colors—red mixed with the blue at end—looks like pushing upward like a wave.

TAT

1. Well, um, this is a boy who just received a violin as a birthday gift, and he doesn't want a violin and is very sad and gloomy about it. [*Do?*] So he's just sitting there wishing he didn't get it, and his mother and father said, "We're just going to get you one big present that's very good, not junky," and he got one big present that he didn't like. [*Do about it?*] Can't do anything. Can't tell mother he doesn't like it because he's already told mother he wanted to play the violin very much. It was a long time ago, when went to concert. Changed his mind because had friends who played and said had a horrible, ugly teacher and had to practice a lot and they didn't like it. [*Do?*] Well, so he, umm, days pass by and tries to throw hints to mother about how he doesn't want to play it. One day mother said now you are going to take lessons. Evidently mother didn't know he didn't like it. And so day came that when he had to take first lesson and he felt very gloomy, but after school when he came home ready to take his lesson, and said to mother, "I'm not feeling well." Mother said, "You're feeling perfectly well. It's just you're a little scared at your first violin lesson." So he, um, said that, "But I *really* don't feel well." Mother said, "You feel well." So it turned out he was really very sick. So he was sick one week or so, and mother said not be able to take lessons because have to

make up schoolwork, so have to wait for lessons, and boy pretended was sad and gloomy, but he was secretly very happy. So, his mother had to get him a new present because the violin was a birthday present. Instead of one big one, had to get a lot of little junky things like guns and airplanes and other things boys are interested in. The End.

7 GF. [*Thinking*] Okay. Once upon a time was a little girl, and her mother was reading her a book she wasn't the least bit interested in, and so her mother got angry she wasn't listening, because this book was very important and teaching her lessons. And so, meanwhile, she had always wanted a special doll, so her mother said, "Don't you want to listen to this book? What do you want?" She said, "I want a doll." Mother said, "But you have so many dolls already." The little girl said, "I know, but I want a special kind of doll." So her mother went into the room and slammed the door. Meanwhile, the little girl had been saving up for this doll, because knew her mother's not going to get it for her. So little girl went into room, counted her money, and had just right amount of money to buy the doll. So she crept quietly out of the room, opened door, and went out down to store and bought the doll—and just as she returned home, opening the package the doll came in, her mother burst into her room. Had just enough time to slide doll under bed, because didn't want mother to know she had the doll. So mother said, "I've had enough of this nonsense. You're going to forget about the doll and come in here and listen to this book." So, the, uh, the girl went into the living room and listened to mother blab away about the book, and quietly she crept back into her room and got the doll, and she quietly crept back into the seat, and she is holding the doll, and this is a picture where she's quietly holding the doll and mother is reading.

5. Mrs. B lived on, a, Cherry Tree Lane Post Avenue. One night when in her apartment late at night about eleven o'clock, Mrs. B was reading in bed. Now, about this time of night, she heard weird little things—noises in her living room—and never dared to go in at night. Every night at this time she heard weird things. One night, Mrs. B was reading and finally decided, "I'm going into that living room and find out who's in there, or what's making that noise." Mrs. B was surprised at her comment, because she knew she would never go into that living room as long as someone was in there, but she did. She silently opened door to living room, and here's a picture of the opening door. [*What see?*] I never thought about that. Have to think about it. She saw nothing, but a little mouse scratching at the door. [*Do?*] She laughed and picked the mouse up and put it in cage. She had the mouse and it evidently got loose every night. She saw there was a bobby pin next to the cage, and the mouse could easily pick bobby pin up and somehow open the cage.

3 BM. Oh, God. Hard. Okay. One day a girl was walking home from singing lessons and choir practice, going to sing in a concert in one week, so it was a very hot day in July. As she walked in, opened door, everything started to become black, and she was just about to faint and, uh, she did, but recovered in about two seconds exactly and took a cold shower, because so hot, and that's her, just about to faint.

16. Any story? Okay. Mary and her brother, Michael, lived in a cabin at end of a big town. She, her brother, and mother and father were very poor, but other people in town were pretty rich. In fact, a couple of them were millionaires. One morning when Mary was coming home for lunch, Michael was standing at the door, who had already beaten her in. He said, "There's a cheese sandwhich on table and a cookie for dessert, but don't take any milk." Mary knew that they couldn't—were too poor to have milk three times a day. Could only have it at supper and sometimes at breakfast. This story taken place a long time ago. So, she took her mug and went outside to water bucket and dipped mug into it. Water was the beverage they usually had at lunch. [*rocking in chair*] This could go on and on. After lunch, raced brother back to school and found that dinner was already on the table. Had baked beans and franks. That was what usually had because too poor to have roast beef, except once in a while. They had one advantage that rich people in town did not. There was an apple orchard two miles away and a peach orchard about two miles down from the apple orchard, and growing all around were lots of wild berries that weren't poisonous. No one owned these orchards so much, and Mary often went down and picked bushels of fruit—apples, peaches, and

berries. This way got more fruit for free. Other people in town didn't know that this fruit was so good. Thought would have worms or other things, so always bought fruit at stores so they had the whole orchards and berries to themselves.

12 F. This looks like a fairy tale. One day, no once upon a time, there was a young man who lived with an old witch. Many times he tried to escape the witch and return to own family, but the witch had always caught him. One day when tried to escape, just as nearing the door, stood frozen, realized witch had followed him all along, so he tried many more times to escape, but witch was either following him or in her power. She knew where he was [*Why didn't live with family?*] One day was going through the woods, was tired, and went to sleep for a while. He rested against a cave. The cave was the witch's, and she captured him, and ever since then for about five years he had been living with the witch. [*Family feel?*] Well, he only had a mother, father, and one brother. This brother was a stepbrother who was very mean to him and same age, but two years before he started to live with witch, this brother left and went and got his own family. His mother and father had always told him never to stop and rest in the woods because not only were there witches, but spooks and phantoms, and things like that, but they only came out at night. Mother and father, of course, felt very sad, but never knew what happened to him. His mother thought that spooks of forest got-ten him, and father said, "No, I told that boy many times not to go in forest after dark or to sleep in forest. I think he ran away and got his own family. But mother would never believe that, and father would never believe that the spooks got him. [*Happens?*] He has to live with witch the rest of his life. One day the witch died—no, not that— went on a trip, so the boy escaped, but when returned home, another family was living in his old house. The family told him that people who lived here had left to search for a son who'd suddenly disappeared. The boy was sad, and had no choice except to go and get a family of his own.

8 GF. One day there was a great artist. Um, he had traveled all over the world to find five girls to pose in five different positions. For each painting would get $14,000 and pro-mised each of girls they would get half of it, $7,000. He picked up most beautiful girls he could find, and one was posed in three positions. Here's the picture of that girl.

4. Once upon a time there was a big circus. There were lots of people in the circus. There was one lady and her husband. The lady enjoyed being in the circus, but the husband did not. One day the husband said, "I'm leaving this circus for good." Wife tried to talk him into being back in the circus because she loved circus, but he didn't. But she could not. That's when trying to persuade him back into the circus. [*Does she stay?*] Yes, she stayed, but husband didn't. [*Ever see each other again?*] Yes, he comes to see the cir-cuses. Likes to see them, but hated being in them. [*Almost never see each other?*] I guess so. She was bareback rider and on trapeze, and he was another trapezist or whatever you call them. [*Why didn't she leave, too?*] Because loved the circus so much, and just wanted to stay.

Psychological Test Portrait

R: 10–8 Male

R is a 10–8 boy who was referred because of "withdrawn social relationships" and showing "no effort in doing school work" in fifth grade. He is the only child of divorced parents. He lives with his mother and rarely sees his father.

He is a fair, thin child of average height who wore glasses for the morn-ing session, but refused to put them on after lunch. Although he is an attrac-tive child, his unrelated quality precluded seeing him as pleasing. He walked down the hall with arms crossed, and his only communication to E was to ask if she had a radio so he could hear the World Series game, since baseball is very important to him. *E* said no, pointing out that he would be finished before the game started. He talked a great deal about his love for baseball and that women have no interest in it. The talk was confused and confusing, and he made flagrant errors—for example, that the Yankees were playing the World Series, which was not true that year.

R went out to check with his mother several times during the testing session. At one point, he said that she had just told him that she was going to marry again. "Someone," he said, "she is going out with steady, and I, too, am going steady with him."

Cognitive Functioning

WISC: *R* has a very superior intellect in all areas of cognitive functioning. His areas of unusual abilities are in spatial relationships, computation, and abstractive ability. Generally, his language is superior, as is his fund of knowledge and memory. Occasionally his language surprisingly regresses (Vocabulary, 22; Comprehension, 14) to more immature formulations. Although *R* has excellent understanding of social expectations, he has some difficulty in understanding interpersonal interactions. Despite the remarkable demonstration of rote memory on Digit Span, there are lapses in Coding, where visual-motor coordination is required.

B–G: Although *R*'s Bender is benign in the overall production, there are many subtle indications of lapses in his concentration and/or motor performance (namely, spacing on 1 and 2; dashes on 1, 3, and 5; open circles on 2; tails on A, 7, and 8; perseveration on 6; and variations in pencil intensity in 3 and 5.)

FD: *R*'s drawings illustrate problems in body concept. In addition, his motor execution shows variations in line intensity, control, and lapses.

Rorschach: *R* works hard on this task, is able to identify the locations of his percepts, attempts to take the whole blot into account, and is able to communicate his images. *R* has a most idiosyncratic way of perceiving the world. Even in his one *P* (Card V), he adds unusual aspects, detracting from this usual percept. He is unable to maintain discrete *D*'s or *W*'s because the syncretistic way in which his mind works leads to confabulatory *W*'s. For a 10-year-old there is also a notable lack of *H, M,* and *FC,* suggesting his egocentric perception of the world. Personal concerns emerge (see *Dynamics*), which lead to loss of distance. His language erratically varies from the very mature to confused communication and poor syntax.

TAT: As in the Rorschach, R loses distance and shows little interest in human interactions (with the exceptions of 10, 12 M, and 18 BM). On the other hand, his language does not vary so much as in the Rorschach, and he even comes up with a pun (18 BM). He is able to respond to the stimulus of the picture with a somewhat cohesive story.

Summary Statement of Cognitive Functioning: R's very superior intellectual abilities are frequently disrupted so that he can surprisingly show regression in his language and idiosyncratic perceptions of the world. Due to these intrusions, it is difficult to predict where or when he will be able to realize his potential.

Dynamic Picture

WISC: R responds very well to the structured nature of the WISC, which enables him to deal with the task in a realistic fashion. Dynamic suggestions emerge only a few times (Comprehension, 14; Vocabulary, 15, 17, and 19; Picture Completion, 10 and 15) in response to issues of vulnerability and fears in relation to rejection.

B–G: As in the WISC, the structure of this task as well as the lack of any affective stimulus helps R maintain his reality.

FD: One's initial impression of R's figures is that they resemble embryos in terms of the proportion of head to body and the amorphous nature of the body and limbs. At the same time, the fact that he makes profiles as well as characterizing the faces as old represents the lack of conflict and the lack of awareness of two severely discrepant perceptions of self. Each aspect appears to have a life of its own with no possibility (and, indeed, no wish on his part) of integration. Although we do not usually predict from figure drawings alone, these drawings clearly suggest that R's behavior will be widely discrepant and, therefore, inappropriate. A further conjecture is that the void between these two aspects leaves R with a sense of emptiness. Specific bizarre attributes of the drawing suggest a dangerous aspect to the female with her claw-like left hand, a peculiar rendition of the mouths with 3-like symbols, the contrast between the dangling arms and the outstretched arms, the feet pointing in opposite directions to each other, and, finally, the suggestion that the two figures are mirroring each other.

Rorschach: The two major themes throughout the Rorschach are R's inordinate preoccupation with body integrity and primitive aggressive mutilation. He is unable to integrate a whole body, being preoccupied with missing heads, invisible bodies, and/or body parts. The same emptiness seen in the FDs is repeated in his percepts of skin and/or skeletons. Even when able to see what others see (*P*'s), they are damaged or distorted. *R*'s concern with aggressive impulses is on the most primitive level of oral aggression or body mutilation. His identification with these impulses is seen in the loss of distance (in I and VI) and with body parts (VII and X). His peculiar treatment of eyes (X) and ears (V) suggests an inordinate concern with these sensory organs. There is also evidence of a struggle with a conflict over merging in *R*'s inability to resist combining images that do not belong together. Also, he is preoccupied with halves, which led him at times to search almost frantically for the other part (VI).

TAT: Again, it is clear that the major themes with *R* are body integrity and primitive aggression. There is something wrong with objects or people (1, 3 BM, 8 BM, 12, 18 BM, and 10) in all but two stories. And even in one of these, someone is stealing (5). The story to 18 BM is one of pure sadistic mutilation to which he associates a pun. In addition, we clearly see *R*'s struggle with symbiosis again (3 BM, 18 BM).

Summary Statement of Dynamic Picture: *R*'s primary problem is the inability to maintain a separate identity. He experiences himself continually pulled with the wish to merge and the threat it presents. This is expressed in an inordinate preoccupation with body integrity and impulses at the most primitive level of oral aggression and mutilation.

Defenses

WISC: *R*'s intellectual defenses stand him in good stead so that he is able to perform at an excellent level in this structured situation. There are rare intrusions or disruptions in his functioning.

B–G: *R*'s intellectual defenses hold up well here with only occasional lapses in his performance.

FD: There is an overall paucity of good working defenses other than intellectualization (see large heads). He erases and corrects many times, but still ends up with a poorly executed representation of the human form.

Rorschach: Aside from *R*'s intellectual defenses, which enable him to stay with the structure of the cards, the defenses we see are all pathological. He uses contamination, confabulation, overuse of tiny details, projection, internal-external confusion, and arbitrary explanations of relationships of body parts—all of which together suggest a delusional system. The loss of distance (seen in VI) has the implication that E or the material itself is tricking him. This in conjunction with the emphasis placed on eyes and ears suggests a paranoid delusional system.

TAT: R gives short stories in the TAT, seemingly because he projects onto E or the materials that they are tricking him. This projection is relinquished only when he becomes involved in sadistic tales of body mutilation. He attempts to minimize the brutal content through resorting to the use of intellectualization—that is, punning. His stories are not only short in length, but also he perseverates the content (1 to 3 BM, 8 BM to 12 M to 10).

Summary Statement of Defenses: R's reliance on intellectualization produces more often than not a seeming conformity to reality. If the task at hand produces no affective response, he can perform well. Otherwise, he is at the mercy of pathological defenses.

Affective Expression

WISC: R was challenged by this intellectual task and was pleased with his success.

B–G: R perceived this as an intellectual task and therefore approached it as a neutral demand.

FD: The only evidence of distress in this task was the many erasures R made in his drawings.

Rorschach: R enjoyed this test because he seemed to see each card as a challenge for him to figure out the trick that either the card or E was playing on him. On the limits, he became distressed in response to his feeling that E was tricking him as she made specific demands on him.

TAT: R's affect in the TAT was labile. He moved from fury to conciliation. His anger, again, seemed related to experiencing E as demanding, therefore, controlling him. He wanted to please, but could not tolerate his feelings of being controlled.

Summary Statement of Affective Expression: R's affective response is continually governed by his distorted perceptions of the world about him. His need to disguise his anger in order to placate leads to lability in his affective expression. He seems to experience pleasure or neutral affect only when he sees himself as in control.

Summary

R experiences the external world as dangerous and threatening. He is preoccupied with terrifying ideas stemming from oral aggressive and sadistic impulses, and needs to withdraw from others because he projects these very same impulses onto others. This also serves as his one means of control over these impulses. He vacillates between appeasing others and becoming angry at them for eliciting these frightening impulses. For R a symbiotic attachment offers the only possibility of closeness, but is equally terrifying. All of this leaves him unaware of what is appropriate and available for relationships.

The one area of competence that R demonstrates is his intellectual ability. It is fortunate that R has such a superior intellect and can maintain it, for the most part, free from the preoccupation of his pathology.

Diagnosis:

GAP:	Schizophreniform Psychotic Disorder
DSM III:	Axis I: 295.12 (Schizophrenic Disorder, Disorganized Type, Chronic)
	Axis II: Paranoid traits
	Axis III: None
	Axis IV: 5 (Severe)
	Axis V: 5 (Poor)

R is a severely disturbed child who is diagnosed as a schizophrenic with paranoid features. He needs extensive psychotherapy. His family situation has to be evaluated in terms of whether his treatment should be as an outpatient or an inpatient.

His prognosis is very poor. In addition, the imminence of puberty offers the possibility that the tenuous control he has will break down.

Psychological Test Data
R: 10–8 Male

WISC

	Scaled Score
Verbal Tests	
Information	14 (16)
Comprehension	16
Arithmetic	18
Similarities	18
Vocabulary	13
(Digit Span)	(16)
Total	79

Performance Tests

Picture Completion		15
Picture Arrangement		13
Block Design		18
Object Assembly		16
Coding		13
	Total	75

	Scaled Score	IQ
Verbal Scale	79	137
Performance Scale	75	135
Full Scale	154	139

Information

		Score
1.	Two	1
2.	Thumb	1
3.	Four	1
4.	Cow—goat	1
5.	Heat it	1
6.	Grocery	1
7.	Five	1
8.	Seven	1
9.	Real one was Leif Ericson, also Columbus	1
10.	Twelve	1
11.	Summer, fall, spring, winter [*reads from test form upside down*]	1
12.	Red	1
13.	West	1
14.	Digests food	1
15.	Air—it's lighter	1
16.	Shakespeare	1
17.	Independence of America; signed Independence	1
18.	No	0
19.	Six feet	0
20.	South America	1
21.	2,000	1
22.	Rome, [*laughs*] don't think right	0
23.	That one I don't know.	0
24.	Around 300 miles.	0
25.	It's movable—first Monday of October; no, November.	0
26.	I forget his name—but was English.	0
27.	I don't know—wait, air pressure— measures it.	1
28.	That one I don't know.	0
29.	Chinese king	1
30.	No	0
	Total	19 (21)

Comprehension

		Score
1.	Let it bleed then bandage it.	2
2.	Pay him back	2
3.	Go to another store	2
4.	I'd tell him to stop. [Q] Go tell mother—wouldn't fight with him.	1
5.	Wave to him to stop or go to station master and tell him	2
6.	Wood can break down easier, and wood is not strong	1
7.	'Cause they could do harm, and they could steal things	1
8.	Most important, women could get more children, and children only had short life—should have more.	1
9.	Because have deposit in bank—it's easier	1
10.	Beggar keeps to self, and charity gives to poor people.	1
11.	To see if they're good at it.	1
12.	'Cause it's light, it's good to sew for clothes	2
13.	Because hard for president to do everything for each state.	0
14.	Sometimes a promise can be very important, like guy didn't come to go out to eat, and he comes late or doesn't come, or get all dressed to go to ball game and be disappointed.	1
	Total	18

Arithmetic

		Score
1–3.		3
4.	2	1
5.	6	1
6.	14	1
7.	7	1
8.	21¢	1
9.	14	1
10.	18	1
11.	9	1
12.	10¢	1
13.	54 [*Says 24, then recognizes error, corrects very quickly. Reads very quickly with comprehension*]	1
14.	40¢	1
15.	55¢	1
16.	$3	0
	Total	15

Similarities

		Score
1–4.		4
5.	Both fruit	2
6.	Both animals	2
7.	Both liquid—drinks—liquor	2
8.	Both musical instruments	2
9.	Both burn	1
10.	Both measures	2
11.	Metal	2
12.	Both natural resources	2
13.	Salt water—together	0
14.	Both mean freedom	1
15.	Opposite	0
16.	Both numbers	0
	Total	20

Digit Span

F 7 + B 7   Total Score   14

Vocabulary

		Score
1.	A thing you ride on—two-wheeled vehicle with pedal	2
2.	A handle with a blade on it for to cut something	2
3.	Something wear on head	2
4.	A note like, that you write to somebody	2
5.	Umbrella—like a circle, little curved down and stops rain from going on your head	2
6.	Soft thing—when put pressure down, comes up	2
7.	Long metal thing—sharp end—hammer into wall to keep something up.	2
8.	An animal from horse family with long ears and very good at climbing	2
9.	Skin and hair from an animal—use for girls when go out.	2
10.	Precious stone which mostly is clear	2
11.	When you want to join a club—enroll in club	2
12.	Design on card	2
13.	Handle with long sharp blade—used in ancient times instead of guns	2
14.	Somebody that always—something wrong	1
15.	He isn't scared	2
16.	Silly things	2
17.	A brave person that does something—save a person or city	2
18.	Bet money	2

19. Kind of liquid which any loud sound
    could blow up—could blow up whole city   2
20. Thing doctors or scientists use—see
    things naked eye cannot see   2
21. On a roof [*confused with shingles*]   0
22. Kind of a story—that ain't true—like a
    mayth. [*means a myth*] a legend   2
23. Don't know   0
24. No   0
25. Part of a song—few lines   2
26. No   0
27. Like a fire cracker—I'm not sure   0
28. No   0
29. No   0
30. No   0
31. Girl that is ballet thing   0
32. No   0
33. No   0

                                    Total   43

Picture Completion

                                                Score
1. Thing here—piece here   1
2. Leg   1
3. Ear   1
4. Mouth   1
5. Whiskers   1
6. Hinge   1
7. Nail   1
8. Spade   1
9. Nail that holds together   1
10. Person in jacket—I mean buttonholes   1
11. Fin from other side   0
12. Cut on top   1
13. Leg   0
14. Thing on leg there   1
15. Nothin'—oh, yeah—creases in forehead   0
16. Mercury in round piece   1
17. Button, not sure   0
18. I don't see anything.   0
19. The double hoof here.   1
20. Nothing except no smoke from
    chimney. Oh, yeah, the shadow by tree.   1

                                    Total   15

Picture Arrangement

	Time	*Order*	*Score*
A–D.			8
[*Fight*]		XYZ	
1.	21″	FIRE	4
2.	11″	THUG	5
3.	8″	QRST	6
4.	29″	EFGH [*corrected from EGFH*]	4

5.	21″	EPRCY	0
6.	33″	FSIHER	4
7.	50″	MTSEAR [*examines carefully*]	2
		Total	33

Block Design

	Time		Score
A–C.			6
1.	10″		7
2.	9″		7
3.	19″		6
4.	13″		6
5.	31″		7
6.	52″		7
7.	114″		4
		Total	50

Object Assembly

	Time		Score
M	13″		6
H	29″		7
F	49″		7
A	29″		8
		Total	28

Coding B	Total Score	47

[*Note: Whenever stopwatch used,* R *had to "beat the clock."*]

Bender–Gestalt

[R draws each design easily and without comment.]

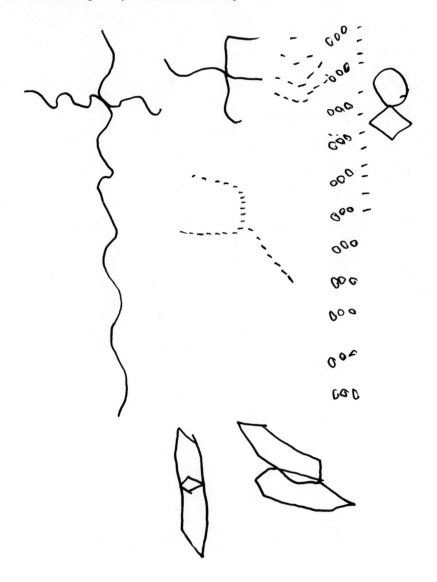

Figure Drawing

Profile or regular? [*draws profile*]

[*At this point of the figure drawings, mother opened door and came in. E asked mother to wait in waiting room. She seemed to understand. A few minutes later she opened the door and asked when lunch would be and how long he would be. She had a friend who would take them to lunch. Then she asked if she should wait or go down. E asked her to wait. R's whole aspect changed—smiling, receptive, and responsive as he does drawings.*]

Rorschach

I.   4″   1. A frog with messed-up wings—big eyes coming out like this. [*moves his hands up menacingly*] Looks like ready to kill somebody—looking like this. He also has a skeleton—like could see his insides right through his skin. Also a tail. His wings have holes in it.

I.   1. Flying to someone—coming at—flying towards his prey.

II.   7″ V 1. I see a crab face with horns—very skinny horns sticking up—no body, and legs that are attached only by very red tissue—and wings, also a tail—eyes, nose, no mouth—with invisible body.

II.   1. This is the crab—like last one. [*from card X*] This is his whole body with wings, an invisible body.

III. 17″ V 1. A skeleton with half a head and butterfly inside, and blood coming out over here. [*upper reds*] Blood stains, also fingers cut off and toes cut off—only a thumb and pinky left on both—on hands—just thumb on toe. Blood stains right here. And there's butterfly in the middle of skeleton. Also, half a head, half a skeleton.

III. 1. [*Half a head?*] Rest of head would be up here.

[*Butterfly?*] Wings —just inside there— looks like he's eating part of his body. Ate his body so only skeleton left. [*Blood?*] Because of color.

IV.   8″   1. A very small—a head—I see an animal sitting down—head, legs, and feet forward, arms. No, I don't want that one. Here, arms, legs, and sitting on two skulls together. Also, his feet are

IV.   1. One skull on top of other—no, I'll make it just big, fat, thick bone he's sitting on. [*Animal?*] Monster—just a monster. Dog's feet—dog feet—dog's—uh—shape of dogs' heads for feet.

dogs' heads—that's his feet, dogs' heads. See—very small heads—arms have one finger pointing out—and then dogs' heads attached to his body here.

V.	5"V	1.	A butterfly with wings, that's all. Wings out and has ears sticking up with little horns on top of ears and no head—no head— that's all.	V.	1.	[*Butterfly?*] Flying
VI.	4"	1.	I see a bottom of a tiger, but one thing, he's all empty with skin hanging down— no, split open bottom view—split open, nothing left but skin, cut-open skin, except don't see top of it, only bottom of it. [*asks for piece of paper and puts it above that, implying he could see the top of the skin if he did that, but then says*] No, can't see it—can't see top. [*Indicates that top of skin would be other side of card, but he can't see it.*] See top—the inside of the skin, claws hanging out; no, no, never mind that.	VI.	1.	[*Inside of skin?*] I see head; head looks like bottom of head— not top of head—so looks like folded this way—curled up a little so it is.
VII.	3"V	1.	I see a broken pelvis—mean not pelvis as is, [*indicates on self*] but pelvis flattened out instead of going around—is flat out.	VII.	1.	[*Pelvis?*] Back of pelvis—bones.
		2.	Flatten it out. [*lower center di*] Middle— opening on the crack in there. Opening— it cracks open.		2.	[*Crack?*] Extension of bones. [*vaguely indicated*] Hip. [*then he indicates on his own thigh on down.*]

VIII.   6"V   1.   Crab without a head. Also his bones and without skin, just skeleton. That's all you see. Tail there—that's all.

VIII.   1.   I see plates—like flat pieces of bone—just I see ribs there. [*very vague location until focused on rib area, then could use structure*]

IX.   13"V   1.   I see three pairs of wings and bird's body and two eyes—and bird's body without head and wings—bird's body with head and wings —two pairs of wings.

IX.   1.   Wings curled up and here's [*center*] the body—rounded so, curled up. Wings—one bird is standing on wings without head and other bird under it holding wings up. Also, bird here with wings and everything [*denies color*].

X.   6"V   1.   I get it—look—head—two eyes, nose, mouth, big ears [*refers twice to ears as wings, then corrects*], head itself is invisible, only see eyes, nose, mouth, and hair coming out from here [*indicates his eyebrows*] like this. It's a moustache coming up from lip over eyes, insides that are holding his head—vocal cords.

X.   1.   Eyes looking straight up and he's smiling. A wind is blowing up his moustache.

2.   Crab fossils on side.
3.   Spiders crawling around.
4.   Two blood stains.

3.   Spiders crawling in his ears.
4.   Color makes look like blood stain. Face is of monster crab. [*laughing—not sure if he is joking*] and spiders.

Testing of Limits:

[*Insists cards have been presented upside down. Mutters and returns them to upside down position.*]
    [*People?*] No—none—nothing.
    [*Animals?*] No—nothing.
    [*Much physical movement. Enormous effort to control anger.*]
    Oh, yeah, do see people. [*picks Card VII*] Angels trying to kiss each other with wings on heads—sitting on stones—trying to kiss each other—flat stones right side up.
    [*Shows E something that is the right color and shape for what it is.*]
    [*Chooses VI*] Tiger faces. No, right shape, but not right color.
    [*Chooses III*] Butterfly, no, right shape, but not right color.
    That's all.

TAT

1. I don't know what this is. I don't know story. I don't know what it is. He's looking at a train—I mean something—I don't know what he did, because I don't know what that is. Doesn't look like a train, ain't no tracks, so how could it be a train? [*R is angry.*] Just looking—I don't know what it is. If I knew what it is, I'd tell you, but I can't say another thing.

3 BM. He's crying. So what? Somebody crying—playing with his train and it broke. Now he's crying. [*Later?*] Mother breaks [*sic!*] him a new train. He breaks it again, and cries again. [*E asks what happens several times, and he does not respond.*] [*How come he keeps breaking it?*] Accidentally. [*Often break his things?*] Yeah. No. [*Mother feel about it?*] She says she won't break it any more. [*Mother broke it?*] Boy said he won't break it any more.

5. Lady burglar coming in. She wants to see her flowerpot, lamp, and books. Gonna bring it all home to her hideout. Sells it. [*Get away?*] Yeah, but not for long. Policeman after her. They put out in newspaper not to touch things she took, so could keep the fingerprints. Find out fingerprints—found out who it is, and go there and take her. [*Angry through this, but talks, although he walks around. Talks toward the window and wall. Can hardly hear him. Then to blackboard. If E asks him to repeat, angry, yet immediately positive to E after.*]

8 BM. Operating on a person. Boy tripping over something, and in background see them operating on some boy, and he gets better.

16. Nothing. [*laughs*] No, nothing.

12 M. Man's looking at his son in the hospital to see how he is—getting better, like from that. [*Card 8 BM*] Feels fine.

18 BM. [*Turns card over, then gives to E to see*] One day people are on an island—had nothing to eat, so doctor there cut off each guy's left arm for food, and when they got back by ship, they finally got back, but the doctor didn't cut off his own arm, so one of the guys said that you should bring your left arm to his house—to my house, because it's not fair.

   Then he came with a box with a right arm in it and a black cape over his left arm, so man would think he had his left arm, but he really had both arms—gave a right arm from somebody else, and three days later they found out and killed him. Oh, know something? Those people were in the *Arm*-y—U.S. [*points to own arm as he says it*] Good one?

10. Father is kissing son when he came home from hospital. [*Hospital?*] Got operated on—he fell. [*refers back to 8 BM*] I fell last night. Look. [*shows E he broke his tooth*]

13 B. Boy sitting down and eating an apple in his cabin during the summer.

Concluding Statement

The foregoing chapters have demonstrated the wealth of information that a child of any age can provide the diagnostician who listens. We have shown that the child clinician who listens and questions carefully can learn a great deal about the inner experiences of children. Our 3-year-olds told us as much about their inner life, abilities, and interrelationships as the almost 12-year-olds.

It is our primary thesis that the child diagnostician must be knowledgeable about developmental landmarks and expectations to appreciate the test data provided by the child. With awareness of the ever-changing nature of childhood, the child becomes comprehensible in response to any stimulus. In the same way, any stimulus can provide an array of information about the child, even though its primary identification is as an "intelligence test" or a "projective technique." We have applied our knowledge of children's developing cognition, dynamics, defenses, and affect in order to arrive at a diagnostic understanding of the whole child. To make recommendations for intervention, it is essential to arrive at a clear understanding of a given child for his given age. Through our years of experience the validity of this approach has been established by following children through the recommended interventions, or, unfortunately, when children have returned to us where the recommendations were not carried out.

We regret the investment in and preoccupation with a given diagnostic fad that periodically sweeps the nation. Fads invariably treat behavioral symptoms without consideration for their origin—the continuing search for the "magic pill." This is a disservice to the individual, as it is applied indiscriminately as if it offered the explanation.

We hope that our particular approach will provide the reader a way of understanding the complexity of each individual child so that more successful interventions can be made to enhance the child's growth to healthy adulthood.

References

American Psychiatric Association. (1968). *Diagnostic and statistical manual of mental disorders* (2nd ed.). Washington, D.C.

American Psychiatric Association. (1980). *Diagnostic and statistical manual of mental disorders* (3rd ed.). Washington, D.C.

Ames, L.B., Learned, J., Metraux, R.W., & Walker, R.N. (1974). *Child Rorschach responses: Developmental trends from two to ten years.* Rev. Ed. New York: Bruner/Mazel.

Ames, L.B., Metraux, R., & Walker, R.N. (1952). *Child Rorschach responses: Developmental trends from 2-10.* New York: Hoeber–Harper.

Beck, S.J. (1949). *Rorschach's test.* New York: Grune & Stratton.

Bellak, L., & Bellak, S. (1949). *Children's apperception test.* New York: CPS.

Bender, L. (1938). *A visual motor gestalt test and its clinical use.* (Research Monograph No. 3). New York: American Orthopsychiatric Association.

Bender, L. (1946). *Instructions for the use of visual motor gestalt test.* American Orthopsychiatric Association.

Beres, D. (1956). Ego deviation and the concept of schizophrenia. *Psychoanalytic study of the child. XI.* New York: International Universities Press.

Bowne, D. (1936). Rorschach test norms of young children. *Child Development 7.*

Erikson, E.H. (1950). *Childhood and society.* New York: W.W. Norton.

Escalona, S.K. (1948). Predictive value of psychological tests in infancy: Report on clinical findings. *American Psychologist 3.*

Escalona, S.K. (1950). Use of infant tests for predictive purposes. *Bulletin Menninger Clinic 14.*

Escalona, S.K., & Heider, G. (1950). *Prediction and outcome.* New York: Basic Books.

Escalona, S.K., & Moriarty, A. (1961). Prediction of school age intelligence from infant tests. *Child Development 32.*

Exner, J.E. (1974). *The Rorschach: A comprehensive system.* New York: Wiley-Interscience.

Fraiberg, S. (1959). *The magic years.* New York: Charles Scribner's Sons.

Freud, A. (1934). *The ego and mechanisms of defense.* New York: International Universities Press.

Freud, A. (1965). *Normality and pathology in childhood: Assessments of development.* New York: International Universities Press.

Freud, S. (1961). The ego and the id. In J. Strachey (ed. and trans.), *The standard edition of the complete psychological works of Sigmund Freud* (vol. 19). London: Hogarth Press. (Original work published in 1923).

Geleerd, E.R. (1958). Borderline states in childhood and adolescence. *Psychoanalytic study of the child. Vol. XIII.* New York: International Universities Press.

Gesell, A., & Amatruda, C.S. (1947). *Developmental diagnosis.* New York: Harper and Brothers.

Goldman, J., Stein, C.L., & Guerry, S. (1983). *Psychological methods of child assessment.* New York: Brunner/Mazel.

Goodenough, F. (1926). *Measurement of intelligence by drawings.* Yonkers-on-Hudson, N.Y.: World Book Co.

Group for the Advancement of Psychiatry. (1966). *Psychopathological disorders in childhood: Theoretical considerations and a proposed classification.* Vol. VI. (Report No. 62). New York: Mental Health Materials Center.

Halpern, F. (1953). *A clinical approach to children's Rorschachs.* New York: Grune & Stratton.

Hartmann, H. (1958). *Ego psychology and the problem of adaptation.* New York: International Universities Press.

Hartmann, H. (1964). *Essays on ego psychology.* New York: International Universities Press.

Hartmann, H., Kris, E., & Loewenstein, R.M. (1946). Comments on the formation of psychic structure. *Psychoanalytic study of the child. Vol. II.* New York: International Universities Press.

Hertz, M.R. (1941). Evaluation of the Rorschach: Rorschach method and its application to normal childhood and adolescence. *Character and Personality 10.*

Hertz, M.R., & Margulies, H. (1943). Developmental changes as reflected in the Rorschach test responses. *Journal of Genetic Psychology 62.*

Hundley, J.M. (1971). *The small outsider.* New York: St. Martin's Press.

Jacobson, E. (1964). *The self and the object world.* New York: International Universities Press.

Kanner, L. (1966). *Child psychiatry* (3rd ed.). Springfield, Ill.: Charles C. Thomas, Publisher.

Kessler, J.W. (1966). *Psychopathology of childhood.* Englewood Cliffs, N.J.: Prentice–Hall.

Klopfer, B., Ainsworth, M.D., Klopfer, W., & Holt, R.R. (1954). *Developments in the Rorschach technique. Vols. I and II.* New York: World Book Co.

Koppitz, E.M. (1963). *Bender gestalt test for young children.* New York: Grune & Stratton.

Koppitz, E.M. (1968). *Psychological evaluation of children's human figure drawings.* New York: Grune & Stratton.

Koppitz, E.M. (1975). The Bender Gestalt Test for Young Children. Vol. II. New York: Grune & Stratton.

Ledwith, N.H. (1959). *Rorschach responses of elementary school children.* Ann Arbor, Mich.: University of Pittsburgh Press.

Machover, K. (1949). *Personality projection on the drawing of the human figure.* Springfield, Ill.: Charles C. Thomas, Publishers.

Mahler, M.S. (1952). On child psychosis and schizophrenia: Autistic and symbiotic infantile psychoses. *Psychoanalytic study of the child. Vol. VII.* New York: International Universities Press.

Malone, C.A. (1966). Safety first: Comments on the influence of external danger in the lives of children of disorganized families. *American Journal of Orthopsychiatry 36:3.*

Murphy, L., and Associates (1962). *The widening world of childhood.* New York: Basic Books.

Murray, H.A. (1943). *Thematic apperception test.* Cambridge, Mass.: Harvard University Press.

Palmer, J.O. (1970). *Psychological assessment of children.* New York: John Wiley & Sons.

Phillips, L., & Smith, J.G. (1953). *Rorschach interpretation: Advanced technique.* New York: Grune & Stratton.

Piaget, J. (1928). *Judgement and reasoning in the child.* New York: Harcourt, Brace.

Piaget, J. (1952). *The origin of intelligence in children.* New York: International Universities Press.

Piaget, J. (1954). *The construction of reality in the child.* New York: Basic Books.

Piaget, J. (1967). Six psychological studies. New York: Random House.

Piotrowski, Z.A. (1957). *Perceptanalysis.* New York: Macmillan.

Rank, B. (1949). Adaptation of the psychoanalytic techniques for treatment of young children with atypical development. *American Journal of Orthopsychiatry 19.*

Rapaport, D. (1951). *Organization and pathology of thought.* New York: Columbia University Press.

Rapaport, D., Gill, M.G., & Schafer, R. (1968). *Diagnostic psychological testing.* New York: International Universities Press.

Rorschach, H. (1921). *Psychodiagnostics plates.* Bern, Switzerland: Hans Huber. (Distributed New York: Grune & Stratton).

Rosenfeld, S.K., & Sprince, M.P. (1963). An attempt to formulate the meaning of the concept "borderline." *Psychoanalytic study of the child. Vol. XVIII.* New York: International Universities Press.

Schachtel, A.H. (1956). The Rorschach test with young children. *American Journal of Orthopsychiatry 26.*

Slater, B.R., & Thomas, J.M. (1983). *Psychodiagnostic evaluation of children.* New York: Teacher's College Press.

Spitz, R.A. (1950). Anxiety in infancy. *International Journal of Psychoanalysis 31.*

Spitz, R.A., Emde, R.N., & Metcalf, D.R. (1970). Further prototypes of ego formation. *Psychoanalytic study of the child. Vol. 25.* New York: International Universities Press.

Terman, L.M., & Merrill, M.A. (1937). *Measuring intelligence.* Boston: Houghton Mifflin Co.

Terman, L.M., & Merrill, M.A. (1973). *Stanford–Binet intelligence scale: Manual for the third revision, Form L–M.* Boston: Houghton Mifflin Co.

Wechsler, D. (1949). *Wechsler intelligence scale for children (WISC).* New York: Psychological Corp.

Wechsler, D. (1967). *Wechsler pre-school and primary scale of intelligence (WPPSI).* New York: Psychological Corp.

Wechsler, D. (1974). *Wechsler intelligence scale for children-revised (WISC-R).* New York: Psychological Corp.

Index

Academic achievement test, 11
Adaptation, ego and, ix, xi
Adult psychiatry, 1
Affective expression: of normal children, 8; of 3- to 5-year-olds, 18, 23, 29, 36, 41; of 5- to 7-year-olds, 46, 51, 64–65, 76–77, 90; of 7- to 9-year-olds, 102, 156, 157; of 9- to 12- year-olds, 178, 182, 183, 200–201, 215, 233
Ainsworth, M.D., x, 13, 14
Amatruda, C.S., x
American Psychiatric Association, 1
Ames, L.B., x, 13
Anxiety disorders, 7
Attention deficit disorder, 7
Autism: examples of, 39–43, 157; infantile, 4
Avoidance, 46, 102

Battery testing, 11–15
Beck, S.J., 14
Behavior disorders. *See* Neuroses, childhood
Bellar, L., x
Bellar, S., x
Bender, L., x, 13
Bender-Gestalt test (B-G): as part of classic battery, 11, 13; vs. other tests, 13, 18, 47; for 3- to 5-year-olds, 18; for 5- to 7-year-olds, 47; for 7- to 9-year-olds, 103; for 9- to 12-year-olds, 178
Beres, D., ix–x
Bilingual child, 13

Borderline children, 2, 6–7; psychological portraits of, 33–39, 137–152, 211–229
Brain syndrome, 8

Character formation, 102
Children's Apperception Test (CAT), 13, 14
Cognitive functioning: of 3- to 5-year-olds, 17; of 5- to 7-year-olds, 45; of 7- to 9-year-olds, 101; of 9- to 12-year-olds, 177
Competitiveness, 17, 45, 102
Compulsive behavior, 46, 102
Concrete operational stage, 101, 102, 177
Confidants, parents as, 177–178
Contamination, 19
Coping patterns: flexibility of, 1, 3, 8; parents' influence on, 17, 18
Culture, intelligence tests and, 13

Dark, fear of, 46
Defenses, 18, 46, 102, 178; of borderline children, 2, 6–7; flexibility of, 1, 3; of neurotic children, 2, 3; of 3- to 5-year-olds, 18; of 5- to 7-year-olds, 46; of 7- to 9-year-olds, 102; of 9-to 12-year-olds, 178
Denial, 46, 102
Developmental expectations: of 3- to 5-year-olds, 17–18; of 5- to 7-year-olds, 45–47; of 7- to 9-year-olds, 101–102; of 9- to 12-year-olds, 177–178

About the Authors

L illian Schwartz received her Ph.D. in clinical psychology from Adelphi University, where she had a teaching fellowship from 1950 to 1952. For the next seven years she worked as a school psychologist in the New York City public schools, then she joined the Jewish Board of Guardians, where she became the assistant chief psychologist. For sixteen years she was an assistant professor in the Department of Psychiatry, Division of Child Psychiatry, at the Albert Einstein College of Medicine, where her responsibilities included the supervision of trainees and clinic staff members in psychiatry, psychology, and social work in child/adolescent evaluation and treatment. Since 1963 she has supervised and taught seminars in the diagnostic testing of children and adolescents at both JBG and AECOM. Since the fall of 1983 she has been in private practice in New York City.

Carol J. Eagle received her Ph.D. in clinical psychology from New York University in 1964, where she had been a National Institute of Mental Health predoctoral fellow in the Research Center for Mental Health. For seven years she was a clinical psychologist at the Jewish Board of Guardians. For the next three years she was assistant director of the Children's Mental Health Services of the Lincoln Hospital Community Mental Health Center, after which she became the director of the Evaluation Unit of the Department of Psychiatry, Lincoln Hospital. In 1972 she was appointed Head of the Division of Child Psychiatry at the Montefiore Medical Center. Since 1983 she has been Head of Child and Adolescent Psychology at the Montefiore/Albert Einstein College of Medicine, where she is also an associate professor in the Department of Psychiatry. For the past twenty years she has taught normal and pathological child development to students in medicine, psychiatry, psychology, and social work. She has published several papers on children's mental health.